RAPTURE of the CHURCH

Bound for Heaven, BUT . . .

MICHAEL E. PFEIL

RAPTURE of the CHURCH

Bound for Heaven, BUT . . .

MICHAEL E. PFEIL

WestBow
PRESS
A DIVISION OF THOMAS NELSON

WestBow Press books may be ordered through booksellers or by contacting:
WestBow Press
A Division of Thomas Nelson
1663 Liberty Drive
Bloomington, IN 47403
www.westbowpress.com
1-(866) 928-1240

Because of the dynamic nature of the Internet, any web addresses or links contained in this book may have changed since publication and may no longer be valid. The views expressed in this work are solely those of the author and do not necessarily reflect the views of the publisher, and the publisher hereby disclaims any responsibility for them.

Any people depicted in stock imagery provided by Thinkstock are models, and such images are being used for illustrative purposes only.
Certain stock imagery © Thinkstock.

Permission to Use Credits:

Except as noted, Scripture taken from the NEW AMERICAN STANDARD BIBLE®. Copyright © 1960, 1962, 1963, 1968, 1971, 1972, 1973, 1975, 1977, 1995 by The Lockman Foundation. Used by permission.

Reprinted by permission. The Prewrath Rapture of the Church, Marvin J. Rosenthal. Copyright © 1990, Thomas Nelson Inc. Nashville, Tennessee. All rights reserved.

Reprinted by permission. The MacArthur Study Bible, John MacArthur, Copyright © 2006, Thomas Nelson Inc. Nashville, Tennessee. All rights reserved.

Quotes taken from The Rapture Question by John F. Walvoord. Copyright © 1979 by The Zondervan Corporation. Copyright ©1957 by Dunham Publishing Co. Used by permission of Zondervan. www.zondervan.com.

Quotes taken from Major Bible Prophecies by John F. Walvoord. Copyright © 1991 by The Zondervan Corporation. Used by permission of Zondervan. www.zondervan.com.

Quotes taken from Coming Events in Prophecy by M. R. DeHaan. Copyright © 1962 by The Zondervan Corporation. Used by permission of Zondervan. www.zondervan.com.

Quotes from the following articles: "Abomination," "Apostasy," "Great Tribulation," "Imminence," "Rapture" and "Restrainer," taken from: The Popular Encyclopedia of Biblical Prophecy © 2004 by Tim LaHaye and Ed Hindson, Published by Harvest House Publishers, Eugene, Oregon 97402-9173, www.harvesthousepublishers.com. Used by Permission.

Personal comments on Greek word usage are added by Alan Kurschner, Eschatos Ministries, Pompton Lakes, NJ; January 2013, www.alankurschner.com.Used by Permission.

Personal comments on this book's Greek word studies are added by Dr. Gary G. Cohen, Orlando, FL; one of the translators of the NKJB; May 2008. Used by Permission.

ISBN: 978-1-4497-9981-6 (sc)
ISBN: 978-1-4497-9982-3 (hc)
ISBN: 978-1-4497-9980-9 (e)
Library of Congress Control Number: 2013918347

Printed in the United States of America.
WestBow Press rev. date: 06/04/2014

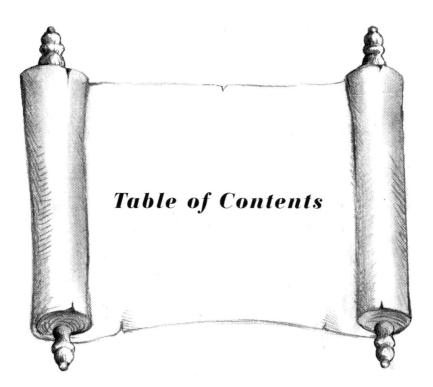

Table of Contents

This and the cover photographic work by Susan Mueller of Dyer Mountain Photography.

"Come My Beloved"

The marvelous portrayal of the rapture on the cover of this book was painted by Marjorie Nordwall, an artist with a very special gift for expressing in her art the precious compassion of our Savior.

My wife found Marjorie's painting after a great deal of searching for an appropriate image, and we both knew immediately that it was perfect for the cover. When I called Marjorie to request permission to use "Come My Beloved", she praised the Lord and explained that she had been praying for another opportunity to glorify Him with her artwork!

Marjorie's painting not only shows the multitude rising as the Bride of Christ to meet Him in the air, but it also shows that our gathering at the rapture will be a glorious individual experience for each of us.

Thank you, Marjorie! I am so privileged to have "Come My Beloved" as the cover photo for *Rapture of the Church*. It should inspire us all as we look forward to that incredible day when we are called home!

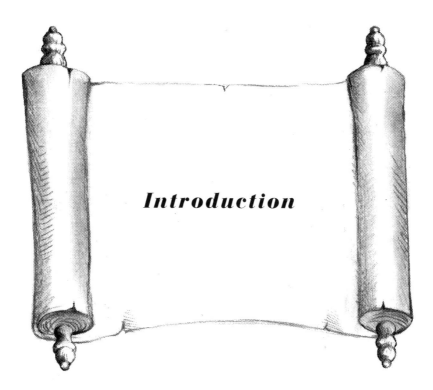

Introduction

I open this study with one very important encouragement. Different doctrinal positions on the end-time events do not have any effect on our salvation. They also *should not* have any effect on our Christian walk. I plead with you to not separate yourself from Christians who hold to a different rapture timing position. The church must be united as the day draws near. It is important for us to keep in mind that it will no longer matter when the rapture will have happened once we are together in heaven. Our focus will be on our Lord and Savior, not on when or how we ended up there!

You may be surprised by what I am about to say. I am sincere in stating that my primary purpose is not to convert people to the Pre-Wrath rapture position. Instead, the purpose of this book is much more elementary—that Christians may become familiar with the sequence of events after the peace treaty so that if we do see these end-time events happening, we will remain strong and faithful.

God has never promised that we will escape tribulation; He has promised we will escape His end-time judgments. Knowing the difference and knowing what it will be like before the Lord raptures us will keep us from being caught off guard if we end up seeing events that we thought were only for those left on earth after the rapture.

Do I want everyone to agree with me about the Pre-Wrath rapture? Of course! Am I convinced that the sequence of events presented in this book is correct? Absolutely! However, in my being conciliatory to you, the reader of this book, you may be willing to compare my evidence to your position. That will contribute to your ability to serve the Lord regardless of world events.

I began a study of the pretrib rapture more than fifteen years ago in preparation for teaching the position. As you might expect, I started with the book of Revelation. It was in the midst of studying Revelation that I realized the pretrib rapture position fails the test of Scripture. Thus began my quest to compare the pretrib rapture to the very Scriptures that were claimed to prove the position. This book is the consummation of that effort. A few years after I began this pursuit, I discovered that my own conclusions were consistent with what is called the Pre-Wrath rapture.

This book draws a clear line between the pretrib and the Pre-Wrath rapture positions. Nothing exemplifies this division more than the pretribulationist's teaching that God's end-time judgments cover the full seven-year tribulation period. The Pre-Wrath rapture teaches that significantly more than half of Daniel's seventieth week will pass *before* God begins His judgments against the Antichrist and this evil world. It is critical to remember throughout this book that, although we place the rapture after the great tribulation is cut short for the sake of the elect, we agree with the pretribulationist that Christians will be raptured by the Lord *before* His judgments begin.

The defining question that separates the pretrib from the Pre-Wrath rapture is, "Are all of the seals of Revelation 5–8 the judgments of God?" The answer is found in the fifth seal of Revelation.

⁹ And when He broke the fifth seal, I saw underneath the altar the souls of those who had been slain because of the word of God, and because of the testimony which they had maintained;

¹⁰ and they cried out with a loud voice, saying, "How long, O Lord, holy and true, wilt Thou refrain from judging and avenging our blood on those who dwell on the earth?"

¹¹ And there was given to each of them a white robe; and they were told that they should rest for a little while longer, until the number of their fellow servants and their brethren who were to be killed even as they had been, should be completed also.
(Revelation 6:9–11)

Revelation 6:9 claims that these martyrs were slain "because of the word of God and because of the testimony which they had maintained." This testimony about the fifth-seal martyrs caused me to question, "Does this sound like a transgression that would cause God to judge them? Would it even remotely be consistent with how God operates to judge those who maintain a faithful testimony of Him?" In verse 10, the martyrs ask God how long before He judges the people who had killed them. When I read this, I wondered how the martyrs could even consider asking the Lord to judge their

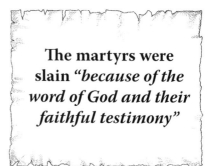

The martyrs were slain *"because of the word of God and their faithful testimony"*

killers if, as the pretribulationist claims, they were "killed by God in His fifth seal judgment." There is nothing in Revelation 6:9–11 that would cause the fifth-seal martyrs to be the recipients of God's end-time judgments!

I certainly would rather that the pretrib rapture be true, since I seek neither persecution nor martyrdom. However, the more I studied the Scriptures, the more shocked I was that I could not prove the very position I was preparing to teach! That surprise caused me to be deeply concerned for the church. For those who have been guaranteed that we would be raptured before the beginning of Daniel's seventieth week, the discouragement that would result from seeing many end-time events unfold could monumentally affect their usefulness in the last days! That discouragement would become even deeper if Christians were to see the Antichrist claim that he is God at the abomination of desolation and then see the beginning of the great tribulation (a time of unprecedented persecution of Jews and Christians). Would Christians question their salvation? Would they question the majority of things that were taught to them from the Bible? This concern should give everyone a strong reason to carefully examine the Scriptures and be prepared for what is coming.

Instead of fearing these events, if God should choose to lead any of us into Daniel's seventieth week, we should rejoice! This shocking statement comes from a heavenly perspective; we would have the wonderful privilege of being used by the Lord in His calling of the last ones written in the Book of Life.

Although the fifth seal was the turning point for me, what settled my mind conclusively on what is called the Pre-Wrath rapture position was the compilation of the events surrounding the darkening of the sun and moon. This darkening event will become a centering pillar that defines where all of the end-time events fit into the chronology. The result will provide an almost shocking proof that the pretrib rapture is impossible. In chapter 2, we will look at the darkening of the sun and moon in Matthew 24, Acts 2, and Revelation 6–7. In the Appendix, we will add Isaiah, Joel, Mark, and Luke. Near the end of both chapters, the events will be charted chronologically.

Our calling is to worship and glorify God, encourage one another in Christ, proclaim Jesus to the world, and care for those in need. We are to do this even if we see signs that we are in Daniel's seventieth week and even if we will be persecuted for being faithful. Our minds and hearts must be set on being His servants regardless of world events.

Notes

➢ This book primarily covers the events within Daniel's seventieth week that are presented when the Lord breaks the seals of the seven-sealed scroll (Revelation 5:1–8:1). You may wonder why I am only focusing on this portion of Daniel's seventieth week. There actually is a very reasonable answer. We will be gone before the first trumpet judgment begins. Therefore, I am focusing on the events we will see, since we must be prepared for them. The trumpet and bowl judgments are mentioned only when it is necessary to differentiate them from the seven-sealed scroll. Unlike the pretrib rapture—which teaches that God's end-time judgments cover all of the seal, trumpet, and bowl events—the Pre-Wrath rapture teaches that God does not begin these end-time judgments until after the seventh seal is broken. As you would expect, that also causes the relative position of the events within Daniel's seventieth week to differ from what the pretribulationist teaches. The chart after this paragraph summarizes the chronological order of the events presented in this book.

	THE MAIN EVENTS OF DANIEL'S SEVENTIETH WEEK
1	The seven year peace treaty
2	The first seal is broken: The rise of the Antichrist
3	The second seal is broken: worldwide war
4	The third seal is broken: worldwide famine
5	The abomination of desolation
6	The great tribulation begins
7	The fourth seal is broken: unsaved are killed
8	The fifth seal is broken: Christ's elect are martyred
9	The great tribulation is cut short for the elect
10	The sixth seal is broken (covering items 11–16)
11	The sun and moon darken
12	The sign of the Son of Man appears in the sky
13	The Son of Man comes on clouds visible to all
14	Angels are sent to gather the elect
15	144,000 sons of Israel are sealed
16	A great uncountable multitude appear in Heaven These are the elect gathered at the rapture
17	The seventh seal is broken: silence in Heaven
18	**THE DAY OF THE LORD BEGINS**
19	The seven trumpet judgments
20	The seven bowl judgments
21	The Millennial Kingdom

➢ For the sake of those who have not had the opportunity to study prophecy, I give brief descriptions of sixteen end-time prophecy terms in the first chapter. I will also compare the pretrib and Pre-Wrath rapture interpretations of these terms.

➢ Both the pretrib and Pre-Wrath rapture positions recognize that the seven-sealed scroll contains God's end-time judgments. However, the two positions are divided regarding the interpretation of the events displayed when the seals are broken. The pretribulationist claims that when the seals are broken, the earlier stages of God's judgments are displayed. The Pre-Wrath rapture claims that, since the scroll cannot be opened until after *all* of the seals are broken, the events displayed when each seal is broken *precede* the beginning of God's judgments.

➢ In order to show respect to my brothers and sisters in Christ who teach the pretrib rapture and to avoid accidently twisting what they say, I will often use their terms in this book. However, whenever appropriate, I will explain why the terms I use are more consistent with the Scriptures. For instance, I may use the pretribulationist's terms "tribulation" and "tribulation period," even though the much more appropriate term is "Daniel's seventieth week," since the seven-year treaty is defined by the prophet Daniel.

➢ For the same reason, I will often speak of the second coming from the perspective of pretribulationists. They teach that the Lord will come to rapture His church before the tribulation period begins, yet pretribulationists claim His return with the gathered church at the end of the tribulation period is Christ's second coming. It should be noted that the pretrib and Pre-Wrath rapture positions agree that this second coming occurs at Matthew 24:29–31. However, we disagree regarding when this event happens. The Pre-Wrath rapture teaches that there is one second coming of Christ which includes His rapture of the church. After the rapture, Christ will personally oversee His end-time judgments.

➤ It is important that I explain the phrase "author and agent" that I will use in this book. When I say, "God is not the author and agent of [an event]," I use that phrase to mean that God is not personally responsible for the events. He does not cause them or cause people on earth to carry them out for Him. The phrase "author and agent" will primarily be used when the pretribulationist claims that God is responsible for events that actually are carried out by people on earth independent of God's will.

➤ Looking at the Table of Contents, you may have already discovered that this book is designed with each chapter divided into multiple subchapters. Each subchapter is a subject of its own, meaning that you can read as much or as little as you want at a time without compromising the message. Much of this book does not even have to be read in order. You can read them in whatever order you prefer with little degradation of the message. I do recommend you initially read the first and second chapters, since they set the foundation to this whole book. For the ease of your reading, I have also included all of the Scripture passages that I refer to.

There have been a multitude of authors who claim to have discovered "hidden secrets" to understanding end-times prophecy. There are no hidden secrets. We merely need to search the Scriptures as the Bereans did, with our minds, hearts, and eyes open.

> [10] The brethren immediately sent Paul and Silas away by night to Berea, and when they arrived, they went into the synagogue of the Jews.
> [11] Now these were more noble-minded than those in Thessalonica, for they received the word with great eagerness, examining the Scriptures daily to see whether these things were so.
> (Acts 17:10–11)

I pray our Savior will richly bless you as you study His holy Word and prepare for the future time of trouble. This time may be right around the corner!

Contact Information

I welcome all responses, whether in agreement or disagreement with the position presented in this book. Please contact me at:

Michael E. Pfeil
Sharp Focus Ministries, LLC
11300 Brandon Drive, Denton, TX 76207
SharpFocusMin@grandecom.net
www.SharpFocusMinistries.com
(940) 262-0473

Acts 17:11

CHAPTER 1

Biblical Terms

In this chapter, I wish to explain the basic meaning of a few key terms for those who have not had the opportunity to study end-times prophecy. Most of these terms will be discussed at length throughout this book.

The Use of "Church" in the End Times

The word *church* (Greek *ekkleesia*) can refer to a local church as well as the full body of believers in Christ (including those who are alive as well as those who have died in Christ). Some may recommend that the term *church* not be used with regard to end-times prophecy, since the only use of the term in Revelation refers to a local church or local churches (Revelation 1–3, 22:16). However, since Jesus used the word to define His followers (Matthew 16:18), please allow the usage in this book. This is advantageous, since the pretribulationists whom I quote use the term *church* to refer to all true believers in Christ. I need to respond to pretribulationists' claims in the way that is consistent with how they use *church*.

The "Futurist" Approach to Interpreting Scripture

Futurist is not a term found in the Bible; it is an interpretive umbrella that applies to those who believe that the end-time prophecies have not yet been fulfilled. The two primary futurist positions presented in this book are the pretrib rapture and Pre-Wrath rapture. Both of these positions place the beginning of God's end-time judgments *after* the rapture. The two other futurist positions (midtrib and posttrib) are only mentioned when context requires it.

The Elect

The Pre-Wrath rapture position claims that the elect within Daniel's seventieth week are true Holy Spirit indwelled Christians. This is rejected by pretribulationists. Most pretribulationists claim that, as of the beginning of Daniel's seventieth week, there will not be any believers in Christ on earth who are indwelled by the Holy Spirit. The Pre-Wrath rapture teaches that, since God's end-time judgments begin with the first trumpet judgment, true Christians can still be on earth until just before that time.

The Antichrist

The word *Antichrist* only exists in the first and second epistles of John. Futurists often use this name for the one who will sign a seven-year peace treaty with Israel and become the ruler of the world. The Bible calls this leader "the man of lawlessness," "the son of destruction," and "the beast." Since most pretribulationists I quote use the name Antichrist for the ultimate anti-Christ, I will use the name as well.

Imminency

Imminency is a uniquely pretribulationist-specific teaching that is fundamental to the defense of their timing of the rapture. According to this position, there are no prophetic end-time events that must precede the rapture.

The Pre-Wrath rapture position agrees with the pretribulationist that one cannot set a date for the rapture; however, that does not mean that no end time events can precede the Lord's coming for His church. In fact, in the Appendix, we will discover over forty events that *must* happen before the rapture! In chapter 4, the pretribulationist's concept of imminency will be examined in detail.

The Seven-Year Peace Treaty

The Pre-Wrath rapture agrees with the pretrib rapture that Daniel's seventieth week begins when the Antichrist signs the peace treaty with Israel. However, beyond that, the two positions differ greatly regarding who is the cause of the end-time events from the peace treaty to the cutting short of the great tribulation. The pretrib rapture teaches that as soon as the peace treaty is signed, God (through the Antichrist) will begin His end-time judgments.

The Pre-Wrath rapture teaches that everything through the fifth seal of Revelation shows the Antichrist and his followers acting on their own according to Satan's will, not according to God's will. The Antichrist is merely allowed to carry out his evil acts, just as was the case with Hitler in World War II. Outside of limiting the Antichrist's actions in the third and fifth seals, God will not begin to take an active role in the end-time events until after the sixth seal is broken.

The Scroll with Seven Seals

And I saw in the right hand of Him who sat on the throne a book written inside and on the back, sealed up with seven seals. (Revelation 5:1)

Book is the Greek word *biblion,* which in New Testament times was normally a scroll. There have been many interpretations regarding the structure of this scroll. The majority of pretribulationists believe that each time a seal of the seven-sealed scroll is broken, the contents of that portion of the scroll are exposed and displayed to John.

The Pre-Wrath rapture teaches that, consistent with sealed scrolls found that date to biblical times, all seals are visible on the outside. That would require all of the seals to be broken before the scroll can be unrolled and the contents revealed. Therefore, the breaking of each new seal presents events leading up to the presentation of the scroll's contents. The comparison of these two positions is presented in the chapter 11, subchapter "How Is the Scroll of Revelation Sealed?"

Daniel's Seventieth Week and the Tribulation Period

[24] "Seventy weeks have been decreed for your people and your holy city, to finish the transgression, to make an end of sin, to make atonement for iniquity, to bring in everlasting righteousness, to seal up vision and prophecy and to anoint the most holy place.
[25] "So you are to know and discern that from the issuing of a decree to restore and rebuild Jerusalem until Messiah the Prince there will be seven weeks and sixty-two weeks; it will be built again, with plaza and moat, even in times of distress.
[26] "Then after the sixty-two weeks the Messiah will be cut off and have nothing, and the people of the prince who is to come will destroy the city and the sanctuary. And its end will come with a flood; even to the end there will be war; desolations are determined.
[27] "And he will make a firm covenant with the many for one week, but in the middle of the week he will put a stop to sacrifice and grain offering; and on the wing of abominations will come one who makes desolate, even until a complete destruction, one that is decreed, is poured out on the one who makes desolate".
(Daniel 9:24–27)

There was a fulfillment of Jerusalem's destruction (including the temple) in AD 70. This destruction was by the "people of the prince who is to come" (Daniel 9:26). However, the final prince to come (Satan's Antichrist) does not come until the time of Daniel's seventieth week; yet it appears he will come out of the lands controlled by the Roman Empire as it existed at the time of AD 70. This included all of the lands surrounding the Mediterranean Sea plus at least parts of what are now England, Switzerland, Austria, Germany, Hungary, Bulgaria, Romania, Syria, Jordan, Iraq, Kuwait, and Iran. The apostle John added that the Antichrist will become the eighth ruler.

[9] "Here is the mind which has wisdom. The seven heads are seven mountains on which the woman sits,
[10] and they are seven kings; five have fallen, one is, the other has not yet come; and when he comes, he must remain a little while.

[11] "And the beast which was and is not, is himself also an eighth, and is one of the seven, and he goes to destruction.
(Revelation 17:9–11)

The eighth ruler will come out of the first seven (recognized by most biblical historians to be Egypt, Assyria, Babylon, Medo-Persia, Greece, Rome, and the Antichrist's kingdom within Daniel's seventieth week). Notice verse 11. The Antichrist is the seventh king—but then he is not. It is likely that around the time of the abomination of desolation, Satan will take over and become the eighth king. Satan would now actively rule through and empower the Antichrist. This happens when the Antichrist recovers from a mortal wound to the head.

[2] And the beast which I saw was like a leopard, and his feet were like those of a bear, and his mouth like the mouth of a lion. And the dragon gave him his power and his throne and great authority.
[3] And I saw one of his heads as if it had been slain, and his fatal wound was healed. And the whole earth was amazed and followed after the beast;
[4] and they worshiped the dragon, because he gave his authority to the beast; and they worshiped the beast, saying, "Who is like the beast, and who is able to wage war with him?"
(Revelation 13:2–4)

The sixty-nine weeks of Daniel 9 are understood to be weeks of years (or seven years each). According to both the pretrib and Pre-Wrath rapture positions, there is a gap between the end of the sixty-ninth week and the start of the seventieth week. We have been in this gap for nearly two thousand years. This gap will finally be completed when the Antichrist signs the seven-year peace treaty with Israel. The last week of years is frequently called the tribulation period by pretribulationists, but the more biblically specific term is Daniel's seventieth week.

One of the features of the peace treaty is that the Antichrist will allow Israel to rebuild its temple (or possibly the tabernacle) and resume sacrifices. Three and a half years after the peace treaty is signed, the Antichrist will put a stop to the Jewish sacrifices, break the covenant, and commit the "abomination of desolation." Immediately after the abomination of desolation, the great tribulation will begin.

The Abomination of Desolation

At the midpoint of Daniel's seventieth week, the Antichrist will commit the abomination of desolation. He will desecrate the rebuilt temple in Jerusalem and then proclaim himself to be God.

> "And he will make a firm covenant with the many for one week, but in the middle of the week he will put a stop to sacrifice and grain offering; and on the wing of abominations will come one who makes desolate, even until a complete destruction, one that is decreed, is poured out on the one who makes desolate."
> (Daniel 9:27)

> [3] Let no one in any way deceive you, for it will not come unless the apostasy comes first, and the man of lawlessness is revealed, the son of destruction,
> [4] who opposes and exalts himself above every so-called god or object of worship, so that he takes his seat in the temple of God, displaying himself as being God.
> (2 Thessalonians 2:3–4)

The Great Tribulation

> [15] "Therefore when you see the abomination of desolation which was spoken of through Daniel the prophet, standing in the holy place (let the reader understand),
> [16] then let those who are in Judea flee to the mountains;
> [17] let him who is on the housetop not go down to get the things out that are in his house;
> [18] and let him who is in the field not turn back to get his cloak.
> [19] "But woe to those who are with child and to those who nurse babes in those days!
> [20] "But pray that your flight may not be in the winter, or on a Sabbath;
> [21] for then there will be a great tribulation, such as has not occurred since the beginning of the world until now, nor ever shall.

[22] "And unless those days had been cut short, no life would have been saved; but for the sake of the elect those days shall be cut short.
(Matthew 24:15–22)

Although some call the whole of Daniel's seventieth week the great tribulation, most futurists believe that the great tribulation will begin right after the abomination of desolation. This would explain why Jesus commanded those in Judea to immediately flee.

The great tribulation will be cut short for the sake of the elect. The pretribulationist teaches that the events within the great tribulation are God's judgments, and the great tribulation is cut short at the end of the tribulation period by Christ's second coming. Proponents of the Pre-Wrath rapture agree that the great tribulation will be cut short at Christ's second coming; however, its purpose will be to rapture His church *before* He begins His end-time judgments. This will happen *after* the abomination of desolation and *before* the end of Daniel's seventieth week. The Lord has not disclosed when this will happen, which is consistent with our not being able to set a date for the rapture.

The Second Coming

The Pre-Wrath rapture position teaches that there is one future coming of Christ. The primary events are Christ's gathering of His church at the rapture and His overseeing the trumpet and bowl judgments. After these judgments have been completed, the millennial kingdom will begin. The Lord will remain on earth to reign as King of kings. Since this book will primarily focus on the events from the seven-year peace treaty to the rapture and appearance of the church in heaven, I recommend the excellent detail of the events occurring after the rapture as provided by H. L. Nigro in *Before God's Wrath: The Bible's Answer to the Timing of the Rapture*, chapter 17, "Does Jesus Come Twice?"[1] As Nigro demonstrates, the two functions (rapture and second coming) are begun together according to 2 Thessalonians 2:1, Matthew 24:29–31, and 1 Corinthians 15:21–25.[2]

[1] Now we request you, brethren, with regard to the coming of our Lord Jesus Christ, and our gathering together to Him,

7

[2] that you may not be quickly shaken from your composure or be disturbed either by a spirit or a message or a letter as if from us, to the effect that the day of the Lord has come.
[3] Let no one in any way deceive you, for it will not come unless the apostasy comes first, and the man of lawlessness is revealed, the son of destruction,
[4] who opposes and exalts himself above every so-called god or object of worship, so that he takes his seat in the temple of God, displaying himself as being God.
(2 Thessalonians 2:1–4)

[29] "But immediately after the tribulation of those days the sun will be darkened, and the moon will not give its light, and the stars will fall from the sky, and the powers of the heavens will be shaken,
[30] and then the sign of the Son of Man will appear in the sky, and then all the tribes of the earth will mourn, and they will see the Son of Man coming on the clouds of the sky with power and great glory.
[31] "And He will send forth His angels with a great trumpet and they will gather together His elect from the four winds, from one end of the sky to the other.
(Matthew 24:29–31)

[21] For since by a man came death, by a man also came the resurrection of the dead.
[22] For as in Adam all die, so also in Christ all shall be made alive.
[23] But each in his own order: Christ the first fruits, after that those who are Christ's at His coming,
[24] then comes the end, when He delivers up the kingdom to the God and Father, when He has abolished all rule and all authority and power.
[25] For He must reign until He has put all His enemies under His feet.
(1 Corinthians 15:21–25)

Marvin Rosenthal notes that this is a single-event coming. That is proven by the fact that whenever the Scriptures speak about Christ's coming, it is *always* a singular event[3] (for example: Matthew 24:3, 27, 30, 37, and 39 as well as 1 Thessalonians 2:19, 3:13, 4:15, and 5:23). Here are a couple of other examples:

Now we request you, brethren, with regard to the coming of our Lord Jesus Christ, and our gathering together to Him,
(2 Thessalonians 2:1)

And then that lawless one will be revealed whom the Lord will slay with the breath of His mouth and bring to an end by the appearance of His coming;
(2 Thessalonians 2:8)

Notice that Paul says we will be gathered together at Christ's coming (2 Thessalonians 2:1), and Christ will judge the lawless one at His coming (2 Thessalonians 2:8). Christ's coming to rapture His church is the same coming that will begin His end-time judgment of the world.

The Blessed Hope

looking for the blessed hope and the appearing of the glory of our great God and Savior, Christ Jesus,.
(Titus 2:13)

Pretribulationists teach that our blessed hope is the guarantee that the church will be raptured before the tribulation period begins. Without realizing it, this results in pretribulationists limiting the application of the blessed hope only to those alive at the time of the rapture. Here is an example from Tim LaHaye:

If Christ does not rapture His church before the Tribulation begins, much of the hope is destroyed, and thus it becomes a *blasted* hope rather than a blessed one.[4]

The Pre-Wrath rapture agrees that the church will be raptured before God's end-time judgments begin. However, in chapter 5, we will properly expand the blessed hope to the context of Titus 2:11–14 in order to include those who have already died in Christ. Once the dead in Christ are included, the interpretation of the blessed hope takes on a much broader meaning than merely the rapture of those alive at Christ's coming.

The Rapture

Christians who have already died will be raised at Christ's coming. We who are alive will then be caught up with them to meet the Lord in the air. The rapture is presented in a number of verses. Two examples are found in 1 Corinthians 15 and 1 Thessalonians 4.

[51] Behold, I tell you a mystery; we shall not all sleep, but we shall all be changed,

[52] in a moment, in the twinkling of an eye, at the last trumpet; for the trumpet will sound, and the dead will be raised imperishable, and we shall be changed.
(1 Corinthians 15:51–52)

[13] But we do not want you to be uninformed, brethren, about those who are asleep, that you may not grieve, as do the rest who have no hope.

[14] For if we believe that Jesus died and rose again, even so God will bring with Him those who have fallen asleep in Jesus.

[15] For this we say to you by the word of the Lord, that we who are alive, and remain until the coming of the Lord, shall not precede those who have fallen asleep.

[16] For the Lord Himself will descend from heaven with a shout, with the voice of the archangel, and with the trumpet of God; and the dead in Christ shall rise first.

[17] Then we who are alive and remain shall be caught up together with them in the clouds to meet the Lord in the air, and thus we shall always be with the Lord.

[18] Therefore comfort one another with these words.
(1 Thessalonians 4:13–18)

The Four Futurist Rapture Positions

Pretribulationists believe that the rapture occurs shortly before the beginning of Daniel's seventieth week; midtribulationists believe that the rapture occurs shortly before the midpoint of that seven-year period, and posttribulationists believe that the rapture occurs shortly after the end of Daniel's seventieth week.

The Pre-Wrath rapture teaches that the church will be raptured *after* the abomination of desolation, *after* the great tribulation is cut short, and *after* the sun and moon are darkened but still *before* the beginning of the day of the Lord's judgments and *before* the end of Daniel's seventieth week. The span from the cutting short of the great tribulation to the rapture is a very short time.

As taught by the Pre-Wrath rapture, the Bible does not tell us when the great tribulation is cut short for the sake of the elect (Matthew 24:22); therefore, it is impossible to set a date for the rapture. All that can be determined is that the rapture occurs somewhere within the second half of Daniel's seventieth week.

The Day of the Lord

The "day of the Lord" covers the time from when God cuts short the great tribulation until the beginning of the millennial kingdom. Some even include the millennial kingdom. The focus of this book will only be on the events leading up to the day of the Lord. We are guaranteed that "God did not appoint us to suffer wrath but to receive salvation through our Lord Jesus Christ" (1 Thessalonians 5:9).

The Millennial Kingdom

When commentators speak of "the millennial kingdom of Jesus Christ," they speak of the reign of Jesus Christ on earth for a thousand years. This time will begin a short time after the end of Daniel's seventieth week. *The Holman Bible Dictionary* provides definitions for the three most commonly held millennium positions.

> **MILLENNIUM** A term not found in Scripture but taken from Latin to express the "thousand years" mentioned six times in Revelation 20:1–7.[5]

[1] And I saw an angel coming down from heaven, having the key of the abyss and a great chain in his hand.
[2] And he laid hold of the dragon, the serpent of old, who is the devil and Satan, and bound him for a thousand years,
[3] and threw him into the abyss, and shut it and sealed it over him, so that he should not deceive the nations any longer, until the thousand years were completed; after these things he must be released for a short time.
[4] And I saw thrones, and they sat upon them, and judgment was given to them. And I saw the souls of those who had been beheaded because of the testimony of Jesus and because of the word of God, and those who had not worshiped the beast or his image, and had not received the mark upon their forehead and upon their hand; and they came to life and reigned with Christ for a thousand years.
[5] The rest of the dead did not come to life until the thousand years were completed. This is the first resurrection.

⁶ Blessed and holy is the one who has a part in the first resurrection; over these the second death has no power, but they will be priests of God and of Christ and will reign with Him for a thousand years.
⁷ And when the thousand years are completed, Satan will be released from his prison,
(Revelation 20:1–7)

Amillennialism The term suggests "no thousand years." The idea is no literal thousand year period, but a symbolic expression related to the spiritual blessedness of present Christian experience in which Satan is a defeated enemy and believers reign in life by Jesus Christ. Therefore, this view does not look for a literal, future thousand year reign of Christ on the earth during which Satan is bound.⁶

Postmillennialism The growth of the church and the power of the gospel will cause the world to get better and better until the present order blends into the millennium during which the righteous will be in charge on earth. Evil will be practically nonexistent. Christ will return at the end of the millennium at a time when Satan will reassert his power. The final victory of Christ will occur at that time with final judgment and the eternal order following.⁷

Premillennialism The idea is that of "before the millennium or thousand years." Such a view positions the return of Christ prior to a millennial period.⁸

Both the pretrib and the Pre-Wrath rapture positions hold to premillennialism; both also agree that the millennial kingdom is a literal thousand years.

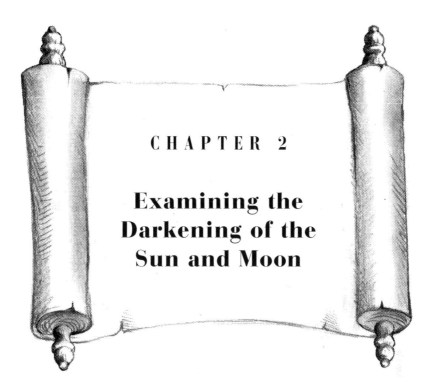

CHAPTER 2

Examining the Darkening of the Sun and Moon

Discovering that it was impossible for the fifth seal of Revelation to be the judgment of God turned me away from the pretrib rapture. However, what settled my mind conclusively on what turned out to be consistent with the Pre-Wrath rapture position was a recurring theme in the Bible. I discovered many end-time events within Daniel's seventieth week that are said to occur before, around the same time, or after the darkening of the sun and moon. In the Appendix, we will examine Isaiah, Joel, Matthew, Mark, Luke, Acts, and Revelation to compile a surprising number of events that occur within Daniel's seventieth week, yet before the day of the Lord.

In this chapter, we will examine portions of Matthew 24, Acts 2, and Revelation 6–7. Even this much smaller sampling will provide surprising proof that the pretrib rapture is impossible. At the end of this chapter, these events will be charted in chronological order from the peace treaty to the beginning of God's end-time judgments. The darkening of the sun and moon will be used as a centering pillar for determining the placement of these events.

Of course, what is presented in this chapter merely sets the study in motion. The actual proofs that the pretrib rapture cannot be supported in the Scriptures will be offered throughout this book. Let's begin our study with Matthew 24.

Matthew 24:15–22

¹⁵ "Therefore when you see the abomination of desolation which was spoken of through Daniel the prophet, standing in the holy place (let the reader understand),
¹⁶ then let those who are in Judea flee to the mountains;
¹⁷ let him who is on the housetop not go down to get the things out that are in his house;
¹⁸ and let him who is in the field not turn back to get his cloak.
¹⁹ But woe to those who are with child and to those who nurse babes in those days!
²⁰ But pray that your flight may not be in the winter, or on a Sabbath;
²¹ for then there will be a great tribulation, such as has not occurred since the beginning of the world until now, nor ever shall.
²² "And unless those days had been cut short, no life would have been saved; but for the sake of the elect those days shall be cut short.
(Matthew 24:15–22)

The abomination of desolation (Matthew 24:15) occurs at the midpoint of Daniel's seventieth week. This is prophesied by Daniel.

"And he will make a firm covenant with the many for one week, but in the middle of the week he will put a stop to sacrifice and grain offering; and on the wing of abominations will come one who makes desolate, even until a complete destruction, one that is decreed, is poured out on the one who makes desolate."
(Daniel 9:27)

The Antichrist will sign a seven-year peace treaty with Israel that allows the Israelites to build the temple and resume the sacrifices that were halted in AD 70. It is likely that, after the peace treaty, the Antichrist will make it dangerous for Jews to live anywhere other than Israel. That will lead to a massive immigration of Jews to Israel. At the midpoint of Daniel's seventieth week, the Antichrist will desecrate the temple and claim that he is God.

³ Let no one in any way deceive you, for it will not come unless
the apostasy comes first, and the man of lawlessness is revealed,
the son of destruction,
⁴ who opposes and exalts himself above every so-called god or
object of worship, so that he takes his seat in the temple of God,
displaying himself as being God.
(2 Thessalonians 2:3–4)

At this point, even Israel will be unsafe for the Jews. When the
Jews see the abomination of desolation (Matthew 24:15), they are
to immediately flee to the mountains (Matthew 24:16–20), since
the Antichrist's plan will be to slay all Jews. However, the Lord will
prepare a place for their escape.

And the woman fled into the wilderness where she had a place
prepared by God, so that there she might be nourished for one
thousand two hundred and sixty days.
(Revelation 12:6)

When they escape from the Antichrist, he will probably then
turn against those who believe in Christ. Knowing this possibility,
it will be wise for Christians who are in Israel to flee also (especially
since they know the Antichrist will soon require everyone to worship
him, his image, and take his mark to buy and sell). Led by Satan,
the pursuit of Jews and Christians will be the Antichrist's passion
throughout the great tribulation. Pretribulationists, of course, will
immediately reject this statement, since they reject any chance that
there are true Holy Spirit indwelled Christians on earth after the
peace treaty. However, we will discover that, since it is impossible to
place God's judgments at the start of Daniel's seventieth week, there
is no biblical restriction against Christians entering into this time as
long as they are still raptured before God's judgments begin. One of
the many proofs that Christians will be on earth during this time is
provided by the Lord in Matthew 24.

"Then they will deliver you to tribulation, and will kill you, and
you will be hated by all nations on account of My name.
(Matthew 24:9)

²¹ for then there will be a great tribulation, such as has not occurred
since the beginning of the world until now, nor ever shall.

²² And unless those days had been cut short, no life would have been saved; but for the sake of the elect those days shall be cut short.
(Matthew 24:21–22)

Notice that Jesus spoke about Christians ("on account of My name"). Notice also that the great tribulation is cut short for the sake of the elect. For a long time, we have been taught that the great tribulation lasts the full three-and-a-half years from the abomination of desolation to the end of Daniel's seventieth week. The next section provides one of the many rejections of that position.

Matthew 24:29–31

²⁹ "But immediately after the tribulation of those days the sun will be darkened, and the moon will not give its light, and the stars will fall from the sky, and the powers of the heavens will be shaken,
³⁰ and then the sign of the Son of Man will appear in the sky, and then all the tribes of the earth will mourn, and they will see the Son of Man coming on the clouds of the sky with power and great glory.
³¹ And He will send forth His angels with a great trumpet and they will gather together His elect from the four winds, from one end of the sky to the other.
(Matthew 24:29–31)

The pretribulationist claims that these events occur at the end of the tribulation period; however, we will discover in this chapter that the darkening of the sun and moon must happen *before* God begins His end-time judgments. If this is true, then this gathering of the elect in Matthew 24:31 would be significantly *before* the pretribulationist's second coming of Christ. A gathering of the elect from earth at this time (before the pretribulationist's second coming) can only be the rapture. This conclusion will be presented throughout this book. Based on that, the order of events provided in Matthew 24 (and Daniel 9:27) is:

➢ The abomination of desolation (Daniel 9:27 and Matthew 24:15). See item 3 of the chart at the end of the chapter.

➢ Jews (and Christians) in Judea must flee to the mountains (Matthew 24:16–20). See item 4.

➢ The great tribulation begins (Matthew 24:21). See item 5.

➢ Christ's elect are martyred (Matthew 24:21–22). See item 6.

➢ The great tribulation is cut short for the sake of Christ's elect. (Matthew 24:22, 29). See item 8.

➢ The sun and moon are darkened (Matthew 24:29). See item 11.

➢ Stars fall from the sky (Matthew 24:29). See item 12.

➢ The powers of the heavens are shaken (Matthew 24:29). See item 13.

➢ The sign of the Son of Man appears in the sky (Matthew 24:30). See item 16.

➢ All the tribes of the earth mourn (Matthew 24:30). See item 17.

➢ The Son of Man comes on clouds, visible to all the people of the world (Matthew 24:30). See item 23.

➢ The Son of Man sends forth His angels with a great trumpet to gather Christ's elect. This is the rapture (Matthew 24:31). See items 26–28.

Revelation 6:9–11

Now let's turn to the seven-sealed scroll of Revelation. Once again, the conclusions from the Pre-Wrath rapture perspective are presented here. The actual study of these events will be covered in chapters 10–13. The Pre-Wrath rapture places the first three seals of the seven-sealed scroll in the first half of Daniel's seventieth week. Although there will be many killed by the Antichrist and his people before the abomination of desolation, the deaths from the fourth seal (non-Christians) and the fifth seal (Jewish and Gentile believers in Christ) will occur within the great tribulation. The sixth seal will begin after the great tribulation is cut short for the sake of the elect. Let's start the examination of Revelation with the fifth-seal martyrs.

> [9] And when He broke the fifth seal, I saw underneath the altar the souls of those who had been slain because of the word of God, and because of the testimony which they had maintained;

¹⁰ and they cried out with a loud voice, saying, "How long, O Lord, holy and true, wilt Thou refrain from judging and avenging our blood on those who dwell on the earth?"

¹¹ And there was given to each of them a white robe; and they were told that they should rest for a little while longer, until the number of their fellow servants and their brethren who were to be killed even as they had been, should be completed also.

(Revelation 6:9–11)

Notice that the fifth-seal martyrs will be slain because of the Word of God; they cry to God to avenge their blood and are given white robes of the redeemed. These facts demonstrate that their martyrdom cannot be the judgment of God.

Revelation 6:12–17

¹² And I looked when He broke the sixth seal, and there was a great earthquake; and the sun became black as sackcloth made of hair, and the whole moon became like blood;

¹³ and the stars of the sky fell to the earth, as a fig tree casts its unripe figs when shaken by a great wind.

¹⁴ And the sky was split apart like a scroll when it is rolled up; and every mountain and island were moved out of their places.

¹⁵ And the kings of the earth and the great men and the commanders and the rich and the strong and every slave and free man, hid themselves in the caves and among the rocks of the mountains;

¹⁶ and they said to the mountains and to the rocks, "Fall on us and hide us from the presence of Him who sits on the throne, and from the wrath of the Lamb;

¹⁷ for the great day of their wrath has come; and who is able to stand?"

(Revelation 6:12–17)

The events of Revelation 6 are consistent with those of Matthew 24, since the passages are tied together at the darkening of the sun and moon. It is now clear why the "great men" of the earth are terrified! There appears to be a great worldwide earthquake (verse 12) *before* the sun and moon darken, and "every mountain and island were moved out of their places" (verse 14) *after* the sun and moon darken. As we saw in Matthew 24, at this time, the sign of the Son of Man will also appear in the sky. There will be no question that God's judgments are about to begin!

Revelation 7:1–8

[1] After this I saw four angels standing at the four corners of the earth, holding back the four winds of the earth, so that no wind should blow on the earth or on the sea or on any tree.

[2] And I saw another angel ascending from the rising of the sun, having the seal of the living God; and he cried out with a loud voice to the four angels to whom it was granted to harm the earth and the sea,

[3] saying, "Do not harm the earth or the sea or the trees, until we have sealed the bond-servants of our God on their foreheads."

[4] And I heard the number of those who were sealed, one hundred and forty-four thousand sealed from every tribe of the sons of Israel:

[5] from the tribe of Judah, twelve thousand were sealed, from the tribe of Reuben twelve thousand, from the tribe of Gad twelve thousand,

[6] from the tribe of Asher twelve thousand, from the tribe of Naphtali twelve thousand, from the tribe of Manasseh twelve thousand,

[7] from the tribe of Simeon twelve thousand, from the tribe of Levi twelve thousand, from the tribe of Issachar twelve thousand,

[8] from the tribe of Zebulun twelve thousand, from the tribe of Joseph twelve thousand, from the tribe of Benjamin, twelve thousand were sealed.
(Revelation 7:1–8)

Four angels hold back the wind, and they are instructed to not harm the earth until the 144,000 sons of Israel are sealed. Therefore, the day of the Lord has still not begun.

Revelation 7:9

After these things I looked, and behold, a great multitude, which no one could count, from every nation and all tribes and peoples and tongues, standing before the throne and before the Lamb, clothed in white robes, and palm branches were in their hands;
(Revelation 7:9)

After the 144,000 are sealed, a great uncountable multitude from every people group in the world appears in heaven. According to the Pre-Wrath rapture position, this is speaking about the great multitude having been raptured out of the great tribulation when it is cut short for the sake of the elect (Matthew 24:21–22, 29–31). The rapture, of course, includes those who have died in Christ. This conclusion will come into sharp focus in chapter 13. The events of Revelation 6:9–7:9 are presented in this order:

➢ The fifth seal is broken; Christ's elect are martyred and appear under the altar in heaven (Revelation 6:9). See item 6.

➢ The martyrs are given white robes and are told to rest a little while longer until the martyrdom is complete (Revelation 6:10-11). See item 7.

➢ The sixth seal is broken (Revelation 6:12). See item 9.

➢ A great earthquake (Revelation 6:12). See item 10.

➢ The sun turns black and the moon becomes like blood (Revelation 6:12). See item 11.

➢ The "stars" fall to the earth (Revelation 6:13). See item 12.

➢ Every mountain and island is moved out of its place (Revelation 6:14). See item 14.

➢ The sky is split apart like a scroll when it is rolled up (Revelation 6:14). See item 15.

➢ All the unsaved people of the earth are terrified, hide in caves and among the rocks of the mountains, and cry for the mountains and rocks to fall on them (Revelation 6: 15–16). See items 17–19.

➢ The people of the earth know that what is about to happen is the wrath of the Lamb (Revelation 6:16–17). See item 20.

➢ Four angels hold back the four winds of the earth (Revelation 7:1). See item 41.

➢ Another angel instructs the four angels to not harm any of the earth until the bondservants of God are sealed (Revelation 7:2–3). See item 22.

- ➤ One hundred and forty-four thousand—twelve thousand from each tribe of Israel—are sealed on their foreheads (Revelation 7:3–8). See item 24.

- ➤ The great uncountable multitude arrives in heaven, having come out of the great tribulation. They come from all nations, tribes, peoples, and tongues (Revelation 7:9). See item 28.

- ➤ This great multitude stands before the Lamb of God (Revelation 7:9). See item 29.

- ➤ The people of this great multitude are clothed in white robes and washed in the blood of the Lamb (Revelation 7:9). See item 29.

The great multitude that came out of the great tribulation certainly appears to be the raptured church, since this event happens at the same time as the darkening of the sun and moon in Matthew 24:29–31. However, that can only be possible if the day of the Lord's judgments do not begin at the peace treaty. That conclusion leads us to one of the most monumental end time passages in the entire Bible.

Acts 2:20–21

[20] 'THE SUN SHALL BE TURNED INTO DARKNESS, AND THE MOON INTO BLOOD, BEFORE THE GREAT AND GLORIOUS DAY OF THE LORD SHALL COME.
[21] 'AND IT SHALL BE, THAT EVERYONE WHO CALLS ON THE NAME OF THE LORD SHALL BE SAVED.'
(Acts 2:20–21).

This is Peter's quote of Joel 2:31–32. At Pentecost, Peter stood up and proclaimed to the people in Jerusalem that the sun would darken and the moon would turn into blood *before* the day of the Lord (Acts 2:20)! There is no possible way for the pretribulationist to refute Peter's prophecy. Notice that verse 21 shows a saving of those who call on the name of the Lord; that would be consistent with the Lord cutting short the great tribulation for the sake of

The sun darkens and the moon turns to blood *before* the day of the Lord (Acts 2:20)!

the elect. Those saved right after the sun and moon darken would be the raptured church. The events presented in Acts 2:20–21 are:

➢ The sun is turned to darkness, and the moon is turned to blood (Acts 2:20). See item 11.

➢ Whoever calls on the name of the Lord will be saved (Acts 2:21). This fits the timing of the Pre-Wrath's rapture. See items 25 and 28.

➢ The darkening of the sun and moon happens before the day of the Lord (Acts 2:20)! See items 11 and 30.

	SUN, MOON, AND STARS DARKENING, BASIC
	Event & Supporting Scriptures
1	The seven year peace treaty: *Daniel 9:27*
2	The new temple is completed: [Assumed from *Daniel 9:27; Matthew 24:15*]
3	The abomination of desolation: *Daniel 9:27; Matthew 24:15*
4	Jews (and Christians) in Judea must flee to the mountains: *Matthew 24:16–20*
5	Then the beginning of hard labor: The great tribulation *Matthew 24:21*
6	The fifth seal is broken: Christ's elect are martyred *Matthew 24:21–22; Revelation 6:9*
7	The fifth seal martyrs are told that more will die before God would judge their killers: *Revelation 6:10–11*
8	The great tribulation is cut short for the sake of Christ's elect: *Matthew 24:22, 29*
9	The sixth seal is broken: (Items 10–31 happen in very rapid succession): *Revelation 6:12*
10	A great earthquake: *Revelation 6:12*
11	The sun and stars turn black and the moon becoms like blood *before* the day of the Lord: *Matthew 24:29; Acts 2:20; Revelation 6:12*
12	"Stars" fall from the sky: *Matthew 24:29; Revelation 6:13*
13	The powers of the heavens are shaken: *Matthew 24:29*
	Chart continues on next page

	Event & Supporting Scriptures
14	Every mountain and island is moved out of its place: *Revelation 6:14*
15	The sky is split apart like a scroll when it is rolled up: *Revelation 6:14*
16	The *sign* of the Son of Man appears in the sky: *Matthew 24:30*
17	The unsaved people of earth are terrified and mourn: *Matthew 24:30; Revelation 6:15–16*
18	The wicked hide in caves and among the rocks of the mountains: *Revelation 6:15*
19	The wicked cry for the mountains and the rocks to fall on them: *Revelation 6:16*
20	The wicked know the day of the Lord is coming: *Revelation 6:16–17*
21	Four angels hold back all wind on earth *Revelation 7:1*
22	Four angels are instructed to not harm the earth until the 144,000 Jews are sealed: *Revelation 7:2–3*
23	The Son of Man comes on clouds, visible to all: *Matthew 24:30*
24	144,000 Sons of Israel, 12,000 from each tribe are sealed: *Revelation 7:3–8*
25	Whoever calls on the Name of the Lord will be saved: *Acts 2:21*
26	The Son of Man sends forth the angels to gather the elect *Matthew 24:31*
27	The great trumpet will sound: *Matthew 24:31*
28	**THE RAPTURE**: A great uncountable multitude are gathered out of the great tribulation: *Matthew 24:31; Acts 2:21; Revelation 7:9*
29	The great multitude appears in Heaven clothed in white robes washed in the blood of the Lamb: *Revelation 7:9*
30	**THE DAY OF THE LORD** begins after the sun and moon darken: *Acts 2:20*

Conclusion

The Pre-Wrath rapture agrees with the pretribulationist that shortly before the day of the Lord, the church will be raptured. However, Acts 2:20 places the darkening of the sun and moon *before* the day of the Lord. Matthew 24:29 places this darkening event *after* the great tribulation is cut short. Revelation 6:12 places it *after* the sixth seal is broken. This makes it impossible for the rapture to occur before the peace treaty! Matching the darkening of the sun, moon, and stars in Matthew 24 and Revelation 6, we discover that the elect are gathered in Matthew at the same time that the great multitude appears in heaven.

This chapter, of course, is just the beginning of the study. We will examine a wealth of pretribulationist interpretations in order to show that pretribulationism cannot stand the test of the Scriptures. For a much deeper study of the events surrounding the darkening of the sun, moon, and stars, please consider reading the Appendix. We will examine Isaiah, Joel, Matthew, Mark, Luke, Acts, and Revelation. We will then chronologically chart more than fifty events that must happen before the day of the Lord begins!

CHAPTER 3

Daniel's Seventieth Week and the Day of the Lord

It is very important to understand throughout this chapter that the Pre-Wrath rapture agrees with the pretrib rapture that we will be raptured *before* God begins His end-time judgments. We merely place that rapture at a later time than the pretribulationist does. The primary purpose of this chapter is to show that the day of the Lord will not begin right after the peace treaty.

Christians Are Protected from God's Wrath

Before God begins His day of the Lord wrath against the Antichrist and his followers, He will rescue Christians from the earth. Here are three Bible passages that guarantee we will not experience God's wrath:

> ⁹ For they themselves report about us what kind of a reception we had with you, and how you turned to God from idols to serve a living and true God,
> ¹⁰ and to wait for His Son from heaven, whom He raised from the dead, that is Jesus, who delivers us from the wrath to come.
> (1 Thessalonians 1:9–10)

⁸ But since we are of the day, let us be sober, having put on the breastplate of faith and love, and as a helmet, the hope of salvation. ⁹ For God has not destined us for wrath, but for obtaining salvation through our Lord Jesus Christ,
(1 Thessalonians 5:8–9)

Because you have kept the word of My perseverance, I also will keep you from the hour of testing, that hour which is about to come upon the whole world, to test those who dwell upon the earth.
(Revelation 3:10)

Notice that none of these verses define when God's wrath will begin. An examination of the verses related to 1 Thessalonians 1:9–10, 1 Thessalonians 5:8–9, and Revelation 3:10 will show that this is also true within their contexts. Therefore, these verses would apply to both the pretrib and Pre-Wrath rapture positions.

Confusion about "The Tribulation Period"

Although I allow the term tribulation period in this book to make sure I do not twist what pretribulationists say, it should be noted that calling the seven years of the peace treaty "the tribulation period" erroneously causes one to assume that all of the events within Daniel's seventieth week are judgments of God. Since, the term "tribulation period" is never used in the Bible to define the seven years, it would be more appropriate to call the time Daniel's seventieth week; since that name is accurate for all end-time positions.

Of course, we agree with the pretribulationist that there will be tribulation within Daniel's seventieth week. However, calling this whole seven-year period "the tribulation period" causes one to never consider the possibility that a significant portion of the tribulation within Daniel's seventieth week could be caused by the Antichrist, independent of God's action. Each event within Daniel's seventieth week must be examined (in context) to determine if it is consistent with God's end-time judgments or if it is clearly the action of Satan's Antichrist.

We also agree with the pretribulationist that the church will be raptured shortly before the day of the Lord begins. Therefore, the dividing line between the two positions is *when* God's end-time judgments will start.

Will the Church Enter into the Great Tribulation?

Nothing like the great tribulation has ever occurred in history or ever will. So terrible is it that M. R. DeHaan and John Walvoord cannot even consider the church having to endure it.

> The question is, "Will the Church of Jesus Christ pass through the coming Great Tribulation, or will she be raptured before the awful day of the Lord comes upon the earth?"[9]

> If the church is going through the Great Tribulation, it will go through the time of wrath designed not to purge the church but to deal with the Christ-rejecting world.[10]

> [21] for then there will be a great tribulation, such as has not occurred since the beginning of the world until now, nor ever shall.
> [22] 'And unless those days had been cut short, no life would have been saved; but for the sake of the elect those days shall be cut short.
> (Matthew 24:21–22)

Notice that DeHaan and Walvoord automatically assume that the great tribulation is the wrath of God—the day of the Lord. Since they believe the Lord's judgments begin right after the peace treaty, they see the great tribulation as merely being a major increase in the intensity of God's wrath. We will see that there is not one biblical reference that restricts the church from entering into Daniel's seventieth week (or even the great tribulation). In fact, the church will go through the great tribulation, and yet, still be raptured before the first trumpet judgment begins the day of the Lord.

Will Believers Be Indwelled by the Holy Spirit after the Peace Treaty?

It may surprise many readers to discover that pretribulationists generally agree there will be believers in Christ within the tribulation period. However, what you may find even more surprising is that most pretribulationists claim these "saved" people are not indwelled by the Holy Spirit! Here is an example from Walvoord:

> That the Spirit works in the Tribulation all agree. That the Spirit indwells all believers in the Tribulation is nowhere taught.[11]

The concept of one being saved in Christ after the New Testament times yet not being indwelled by the Holy Spirit cannot be found in the Bible. Pretribulationists must come to this conclusion, since the majority of pretribulationists teach that the Holy Spirit vacates the earth before the tribulation period. A new kind of believer who is not indwelled by the Holy Spirit is necessary for the pretrib rapture position to be possible. However, no such new kind of believer is defined in the Scriptures once the church had become established. Throughout this study, we will see that pretribulationists must take this and many other difficult scriptural stands in order to maintain their position. I do not claim any lack of integrity on their part; I merely say that, in aligning themselves with the pretrib rapture position, they are unable to draw any other possible conclusion from these verses.

Second Thessalonians and the Day of the Lord

For many pretribulationists, 2 Thessalonians 2 proves that the rapture will occur before the beginning of the tribulation. Here is an example from DeHaan:

> Before we close this chapter we merely call attention to Paul's overwhelming argument for the pre-tribulation Rapture, and then trust you will study the matter carefully for yourselves. It is found in II Thessalonians, chapter 2, the first twelve verses. Read it carefully and prayerfully and see how Paul settles beyond all shadow of doubt the fact that the church will not have to pass through any part of the Tribulation, but that we may confidently expect this event (the Rapture) to happen at any moment.[12]

We will examine 2 Thessalonians 2:1–12 in chapters 6–7, since it actually contributes to the defense of the Pre-Wrath rapture position. In verses 1–4, Paul settles beyond all shadow of doubt the fact that the church will not have to pass through any part of the day of the Lord. However, since there is no mention of the tribulation or Daniel's seventieth week in 2 Thessalonians 2, this passage does not prove pretribulationism.

> [1] Now we request you, brethren, with regard to the coming of our Lord Jesus Christ, and our gathering together to Him,
> [2] that you may not be quickly shaken from your composure or be disturbed either by a spirit or a message or a letter as if from us, to the effect that the day of the Lord has come.
> [3] Let no one in any way deceive you, for it will not come unless the apostasy comes first, and the man of lawlessness is revealed, the son of destruction,
> [4] who opposes and exalts himself above every so-called god or object of worship, so that he takes his seat in the temple of God, displaying himself as being God.
> (2 Thessalonians 2:1–4)

First Thessalonians and the Day of the Lord

In 1 Thessalonians 5, Paul explained the coming day of the Lord and whether Christians would experience the events related to it.

> [1] Now as to the times and the epochs, brethren, you have no need of anything to be written to you.
> [2] For you yourselves know full well that the day of the Lord will come just like a thief in the night.
> [3] While they are saying, "Peace and safety!" then destruction will come upon them suddenly like birth pangs upon a woman with child; and they shall not escape.
> [4] But you, brethren, are not in darkness, that the day should overtake you like a thief;
> [5] for you are all sons of light and sons of day. We are not of night nor of darkness;
> [6] so then let us not sleep as others do, but let us be alert and sober.
> [7] For those who sleep do their sleeping at night, and those who get drunk get drunk at night.
> [8] But since we are of the day, let us be sober, having put on the breastplate of faith and love, and as a helmet, the hope of salvation.
> [9] For God has not destined us for wrath, but for obtaining salvation through our Lord Jesus Christ,
> [10] who died for us, that whether we are awake or asleep, we may live together with Him.

[11] Therefore encourage one another, and build up one another, just as you also are doing.
(1 Thessalonians 5:1–11)

The distinction between the pretrib rapture and the Pre-Wrath rapture regarding when the day of the Lord begins is defined well by Marvin Rosenthal.

> When interpreting 1 Thessalonians 5:1–11, a most important text on the Rapture, many other sincere commentators, without intent, have likewise simply assumed that the day of the Lord encompasses the entire Tribulation Period.
>
> In verse 2 of that classic text, Paul declares, "For yourselves know perfectly that the day of the Lord so cometh as a thief in the night." In verse 4 he gives additional insight: "But ye, brethren, are not in darkness, that the day [the Day of the Lord] should overtake you as a thief." And then in verse 9 Paul gives a word of great encouragement: "For God hath not appointed us to wrath but to obtain salvation [deliverance] by our Lord Jesus Christ." From these statements an erroneous conclusion is sometimes drawn. The reasoning that leads men to that conclusion follows this path:
>
> 1. The day of the Lord will come "as a thief in the night" (v.2)—that is a correct biblical statement.
>
> 2. You (believers) "are not in darkness that the day should overtake you" (v.4)—correct again.
>
> 3. "For God has not appointed us to wrath but to obtain salvation [deliverance]" (v.9)—once again, correct.
>
> 4. Therefore, the reasoning continues, since the day of the Lord begins with the Tribulation Period, and the believer is not appointed unto wrath, the believer is raptured before the Tribulation Period begins. That conclusion, however, is incorrect.
>
> The error of such logic is that it assumes that the day of the Lord commences when the seventieth week of Daniel begins. But a careful examination of the biblical data will clearly indicate that it does not![13]

There is no reference in the Bible that shows the day of the Lord starting at the signing of the peace treaty. In fact, independent of the proofs within this book, it seems quite appropriate that the day of the Lord would commence sometime *after* the abomination of desolation in which the Antichrist desecrates the temple and sets himself up as God in the Lord's place. This is a far greater affront to the Lord than the peace treaty with Israel. This sequence of timing, of course, will be carefully examined throughout this book.

I wish to add one additional question here for you to ponder. If God's end-time judgments begin shortly after the peace treaty is signed, what crime has the Antichrist committed at this point that would cause the whole world to fall under God's final end-time judgments? The Antichrist has personally deceived Israel with the peace treaty; however, Israel has been deceived with false peace treaties throughout its history. Notice also that at the moment of this peace treaty, nothing has happened. The Antichrist has merely made peace with Israel.

Experiencing Tribulation and Persecution

> [9] For God has not destined us for wrath, but for obtaining salvation through our Lord Jesus Christ,
> [10] who died for us, that whether we are awake or asleep, we may live together with Him.
> [11] Therefore encourage one another, and build up one another, just as you also are doing.
> (1 Thessalonians 5:9–11)

Take note of the challenge to encourage one another. The Bible clearly shows that we will escape the wrath of God (verse 9); however, it does not say we will escape the wrath of Satan or any tribulation caused by the Antichrist when he vents his wrath against God's people. If we see the events of Daniel's seventieth week happening and think we are receiving the wrath of God, we *will* need encouragement! This simple issue of differentiating the wrath of the Antichrist from the wrath of God is very important.

Many pretribulationists believe that when we say God's wrath does not begin until after the great tribulation is cut short, we are saying there is no tribulation happening on earth. The source of this misunderstanding is probably our rejection of the name "the tribulation period" for Daniel's seventieth week. The Pre-Wrath rapture agrees that there is tribulation before the first trumpet judgment begins; however, Christians have experienced tribulation throughout the church age. The issue that must be answered here is whether the events before the great tribulation is cut short are caused by God or by the Antichrist independent of God.

If it is impossible for even one of the events of Matthew 24:4–26 and Revelation 6:1–11 to be part of God's end-times wrath, then the pretrib rapture position is not consistent with the Scriptures. That may seem to be an oversimplification of the issue; however, if any of the seals of Revelation cannot in any way be the judgment of God, then all of the seals up to and including that one are also not the judgments of God. This is where the fifth seal fits in. Since God would not have "judged with martyrdom" those who maintained a faithful testimony of Him, the four seals before this one cannot be the judgments of God either.

Jesus taught that Christians will be delivered to tribulation in the end times, but this tribulation is not from God. Secondly, Paul encouraged us to be conquerors in the midst of the very kind of events in Matthew 24 that both the pretrib and Pre-Wrath positions conclude are part of Daniel's seventieth week.

> [7] "For nation will rise against nation, and kingdom against kingdom, and in various places there will be famines and earthquakes.
> [8] "But all these things are merely the beginning of birth pangs.
> [9] "Then they will deliver you to tribulation, and will kill you, and you will be hated by all nations on account of My name.
> (Matthew 24:7–9)

> [35] Who shall separate us from the love of Christ? Shall tribulation, or distress, or persecution, or famine, or nakedness, or peril, or sword?
> [36] Just as it is written, "For Thy sake we are being put to death all day long; We were considered as sheep to be slaughtered."
> [37] But in all these things we overwhelmingly conquer through Him who loved us.
> (Romans 8:35–37)

Conclusion

The issue of the timing of the rapture rests on the timing of the day of the Lord. If many of the events within Daniel's seventieth week are actually caused by the Antichrist and his followers *before* the day of the Lord begins, then there is no requirement that the rapture must happen before the start of the tribulation period.

The Christian has never been exempt from tribulation; we are only exempt from experiencing God's end-time judgments. Each of the events within Daniel's seventieth week must be examined to determine if they are caused by God before we can determine if God's day of the Lord wrath has begun. Of course, even from the introduction, the fifth seal has been presented as proof that the day of the Lord does not start at the beginning of the tribulation period. It begins deep within Daniel's seventieth week, after the darkening of the sun and moon (Acts 2:20). Matthew 24:21–22, 29 places this darkening event *after* the great tribulation is cut short and Revelation 6:12 places it *after* the sixth seal is broken. Therefore, the church can still be on earth even at the time when the sixth seal is broken.

CHAPTER 4

Is the Rapture Imminent?

The pretribulationists' imminency is a concept that is critically important in their defense of the pretrib rapture position. Their definition of imminency includes these four points:

➢ The rapture can happen at any moment.

➢ There will be no signs that the rapture is about to happen.

➢ No prophetic end-time events need to precede the rapture.

➢ One cannot date the rapture.

Here are the basic definitions provided by Wayne A. Brindle and J. Dwight Pentecost:

> The term "imminence" (or imminency) as applied to the rapture of the church means that Christ may return at any moment for His church, and no biblically predicted event must necessarily precede it.[14]

> The doctrine of imminence forbids the participation of the church in any part of the seventieth week. The multitude of signs given to Israel to stir them to expectancy would then also be for the

church, and the church could not be looking for Christ until these signs had been fulfilled. The fact that no signs are given to the church, but she, rather, is commanded to watch for Christ, precludes her participation in the seventieth week.[15]

Notice that Pentecost claims "The doctrine of imminence forbids the participation of the church in any part of the seventieth week."[16] Before coming to such a conclusion, we should first determine if the Bible even teaches a doctrine of imminence. Contrary to what is claimed, we will see that the Bible shows the participation of the church in a significant portion of Daniel's seventieth week (*before* God begins His end-time judgments).

The Pre-Wrath rapture agrees with the pretribulationist that we cannot determine the day or hour of the rapture and that we will be raptured before God begins His end-time judgments. However, these truths do not mean the rapture is imminent. In this chapter, I will present many prophetic end-time events and signs that must happen *before* the rapture. If this is so, then the other three conditions of imminency cannot be true. The Pre-Wrath rapture claims that

➢ The rapture *cannot* happen at any moment.

➢ There *will* be signs that the rapture is near.

➢ Some prophetic end-time events *must* precede the rapture.

Setting the Date of the Rapture or Knowing It Is Near?

[36] "But of that day and hour no one knows, not even the angels of heaven, nor the Son, but the Father alone.
[37] "For the coming of the Son of Man will be just like the days of Noah.
[38] "For as in those days which were before the flood they were eating and drinking, they were marrying and giving in marriage, until the day that Noah entered the ark,
[39] and they did not understand until the flood came and took them all away; so shall the coming of the Son of Man be.
(Matthew 24:36–39)

It is true that "the hour or day" of the rapture cannot be known, and that statement *does* preclude the rapture from happening at an exact point that can be calculated (such as exactly at the midpoint or the end of Daniel's seventieth week). However, the fact that we cannot determine a specific date for the rapture does not force the rapture to happen before the peace treaty. Notice that in the Matthew 24:36–39 passage, the lost did not know the flood was coming until it had already begun. Even Noah did not know the day or the hour that it would begin; however, once he and his family were in the ark, he did know it was very near.

> [13] Then God said to Noah, "The end of all flesh has come before Me; for the earth is filled with violence because of them; and behold, I am about to destroy them with the earth.
> [14] Make for yourself an ark of gopher wood; you shall make the ark with rooms, and shall cover it inside and out with pitch."
> (Genesis 6:13–14)

> [1] Then the said to Noah, "Enter the ark, you and all your household; for you alone I have seen to be righteous before Me in this time.
> [2] You shall take with you of every clean animal by sevens, a male and his female; and of the animals that are not clean two, a male and his female;
> [3] also of the birds of the sky, by sevens, male and female, to keep offspring alive on the face of all the earth.
> [4] For after seven more days, I will send rain on the earth forty days and forty nights; and I will blot out from the face of the land every living thing that I have made."
> [5] And Noah did according to all that the Lord had commanded him.
> [6] Now Noah was six hundred years old when the flood of water came upon the earth.
> [7] Then Noah and his sons and his wife and his sons' wives with him entered the ark because of the water of the flood.
> [8] Of clean animals and animals that are not clean and birds and everything that creeps on the ground,
> [9] there went into the ark to Noah by twos, male and female, as God had commanded Noah.
> [10] And it came about after the seven days, that the water of the flood came upon the earth.
> (Genesis 7:1–10)

> And those that entered, male and female of all flesh, entered as God had commanded him; and the Lord closed it behind him.
> (Genesis 7:16)

Although we will not be able to know beforehand when the rapture will happen, just as Noah knew the flood was near, we will know the rapture is near, since we will see signs that God has promised would come *before* the rapture. In fact, according to Luke 21, after the "signs in sun and moon and stars" (Luke 21:25), we are called to look up, for our redemption is *near*.

> [25] "And there will be signs in sun and moon and stars, and upon the earth dismay among nations, in perplexity at the roaring of the sea and the waves,
> [26] men fainting from fear and the expectation of the things which are coming upon the world; for the powers of the heavens will be shaken.
> [27] "And then they will see the Son of Man coming in a cloud with power and great glory.
> [28] "But when these things begin to take place, straighten up and lift up your heads, because your redemption is drawing near. (Luke 21:25–28)

Must Any Events Occur Before the Day of the Lord?

The pretribulationists would be able to make the claim that the rapture is imminent only if the Bible did not present any end-time prophetic events that must happen *before* the rapture. John Walvoord claims there are none.

> In the survey of future events as predicted in the Bible, that the Rapture is never mentioned in all of the passages that relate to the Great Tribulation is most significant. Every reference to the Rapture in the New Testament is presented as an imminent event, and no preceding events are ever revealed.[17]

On the contrary, we have seen and will see that the cutting short of the great tribulation is intimately related to the signs that the rapture is very near! The pretrib and Pre-Wrath rapture positions agree that the rapture happens just before the day of the Lord begins. However, throughout this book, we will find many events within Daniel's seventieth week that occur before the rapture. One of these is the darkening of the sun and moon.

> [21] for then there will be a great tribulation, such as has not occurred since the beginning of the world until now, nor ever shall.

²² "And unless those days had been cut short, no life would have been saved; but for the sake of the elect those days shall be cut short.
(Matthew 24:21–22)

But immediately after the tribulation of those days the sun will be darkened, and the moon will not give its light, and the stars will fall from the sky, and the powers of the heavens will be shaken.
(Matthew 24:29)

'THE SUN SHALL BE TURNED INTO DARKNESS, AND THE MOON INTO BLOOD, BEFORE THE GREAT AND GLORIOUS DAY OF THE LORD SHALL COME.
(Acts 2:20)

And I looked when He broke the sixth seal, and there was a great earthquake; and the sun became black as sackcloth made of hair, and the whole moon became like blood;
(Revelation 6:12)

The sun and moon darken *before* the day of the Lord begins.

According to Acts 2, the day of the Lord begins *after* the sun and moon darken. However, according to Matthew 24 and Revelation 6, the sun and moon darken *after* the great tribulation is cut short and *after* the sixth seal is broken. Acts 2, Matthew 24, and Revelation 6 make it absolutely clear that the day of the Lord judgments must begin deep within Daniel's seventieth week! Therefore, the rapture cannot be imminent. Let's look at 1 Thessalonians 5:2–6.

² For you yourselves know full well that the day of the Lord will come just like a thief in the night.
³ While they are saying, "Peace and safety!" then destruction will come upon them suddenly like birth pangs upon a woman with child; and they shall not escape.
⁴ But you, brethren, are not in darkness, that the day should overtake you like a thief;
⁵ for you are all sons of light and sons of day. We are not of night nor of darkness;
⁶ so then let us not sleep as others do, but let us be alert and sober.
(1 Thessalonians 5:2–6)

These verses show that at the beginning of the day of the Lord, people of the world will be caught off guard and unprepared for this event. Just as we found in Matthew 24:36–39, the unbelieving ones will not see this destruction coming until it is upon them. In fact, they cannot see it coming, because they are all sons of darkness (1 Thessalonians 5:2–3). In contrast, Christians living at that time will not be caught off guard. They will be watching and ready, for they are sons of light (1 Thessalonians 5:4–6).

In responding to Marvin Rosenthal's *The Pre-Wrath Rapture of the Church*, Tim LaHaye claims a major problem with the Pre-Wrath rapture view is that it destroys imminency.

> Almost every reviewer highlights the major problem of the book: the pre-Wrath view destroys imminency, the very force that has produced so much dedication in times of persecution, worldly environment, and theological confusion.[18]

It likely will surprise you that I agree with LaHaye. The Pre-Wrath rapture does destroy the pretribulationist's imminency! Notice the subtlety of this argument: the pretrib rapture premise is that we are raptured before the peace treaty. Imminency can only be true if there are no end-time events that must occur before the rapture. Therefore, the pretribulationist's conclusion is that every position claiming that there are end-time events that happen before the rapture must be false, since that position would then destroy imminency.

The reason the Pre-Wrath rapture position destroys imminency is because imminency is a circular argument. Pretribulationists claim that the rapture must happen before the beginning of the tribulation period. That automatically requires that no end-time events precede the rapture (imminency). The pretribulationist's claim that there cannot be any events that must precede the rapture (imminency) automatically requires that the church be raptured before the beginning of the tribulation period. Imminency is merely the only possible conclusion if one already has decided that the rapture happens before Daniel's seventieth week. The pretribulationist is very comfortable with this intimate link between the pretrib rapture and imminency. However, one cannot use the pretrib rapture to prove imminency, and one cannot use imminency to prove Pretrib rapture, since they are merely two sides of the same premise. Walvoord quotes many verses that he claims prove the rapture to be imminent.

> The Rapture as presented in the Bible is always an imminent event, as indicated in references throughout the New Testament (e.g., John 14:2–3; 1 Cor. 15:51–58; 1 Thess. 4:13–18; 2 Thess. 2:1–5; Titus 2:11–14; Rev. 2:25; 3:10–11). Never in the many references to the Rapture is any event predicted as occurring before the Rapture.[19]

Of course, in Revelation 3:10–11, the Lord said that He will come quickly (suddenly). This does not prove pretribulationism; it merely means that no one can determine *when* He will come. Among all of the verses cited by Walvoord to prove imminency, the only one that specifically addresses whether any end-time prophetic events precede the rapture is 2 Thessalonians 2:1–5.

> [1] Now we request you, brethren, with regard to the coming of our Lord Jesus Christ and our gathering together to Him,
> [2] that you not be quickly shaken from your composure or be disturbed either by a spirit or a message or a letter as if from us, to the effect that the day of the Lord has come.
> [3] Let no one in any way deceive you, for it will not come unless the apostasy comes first, and the man of lawlessness is revealed, the son of destruction,
> [4] who opposes and exalts himself above every so-called god or object of worship, so that he takes his seat in the temple of God, displaying himself as being God.
> [5] Do you not remember that while I was still with you, I was telling you these things?
> (2 Thessalonians 2:1–5)

Paul's proof that the rapture has not happened is that the day of the Lord has not happened. Walvoord claims, "The rapture as presented in the Bible is always an imminent event."[20] It may surprise you that this very passage says just the opposite. It is true that we still cannot date the rapture. It is also true that the rapture happens shortly before the day of the Lord begins. However, according to 2 Thessalonians 2:3, *before* the rapture and the day of the Lord happen, the apostasy and the revealing of the Antichrist must come. According to Luke 21, as we see the developing end-time events, we will be able to conclude that the rapture is approaching.

²⁵ "And there will be signs in sun and moon and stars, and upon the earth dismay among nations, in perplexity at the roaring of the sea and the waves,

²⁶ men fainting from fear and the expectation of the things which are coming upon the world; for the powers of the heavens will be shaken.

²⁷ "And then they will see the Son of Man coming in a cloud with power and great glory.

²⁸ "But when these things begin to take place, straighten up and lift up your heads, because your redemption is drawing near." (Luke 21:25–28)

Both the "any moment" and "sign-less" attributes of imminency are rejected, since many events precede the day of the Lord (and the rapture just before it). An in-depth study of 2 Thessalonians 2 will be found in chapters 6–7.

Conclusion

By merely looking at the verses Walvoord quotes, we have shown that none of these verses can be used to prove imminency. As charted in the Appendix, there are more than forty events that precede the rapture. The rapture is not imminent; the Scriptures merely state that we cannot date the rapture. The Pre-Wrath rapture position destroys imminency—as it should, since the concept cannot be found in the Bible!

CHAPTER 5

The Blessed Hope

Pretribulationists claim that the Pre-Wrath rapture destroys the Christian's blessed hope, since we teach that the church enters into Daniel's seventieth week. There are two major problems with this claim.

The first problem is that pretribulationists project their timing of the events into the Pre-Wrath rapture and then conclude (incorrectly) that the Pre-Wrath rapture places the church within the judgments of God. We claim the church will be raptured before God begins His judgments; however, the first six seals are not God's judgments. The second problem is that the pretribulationist's interpretation of the blessed hope only applies to those who are alive at the rapture. Pretribulationists would find that to be a surprising statement; however, we will see that their interpretation of the blessed hope does not offer any hope for those who have already died in Christ!

When the blessed hope is applied to *all* Christians, we will see that the Pre-Wrath rapture does not destroy the blessed hope; in fact, the blessed hope equally applies to any position that places the rapture before God's end-time judgments. This whole chapter covers the pretribulationist's interpretation of the following verse:

> looking for the blessed hope and the appearing of the glory of our great God and Savior, Christ Jesus,
> (Titus 2:13)

Notice that Titus 2:13 is not even a complete sentence. Once we expand the quote to Titus 2:11–14, we will see that context dramatically changes the meaning of Titus 2:13.

The Blessed Hope Is Not Restricted to Those Alive at the Rapture

According to the pretribulationist, the very definition of the blessed hope is our rapture before the tribulation period starts. Here are examples from M. R. DeHaan and Tim LaHaye:

> This event, the Rapture of the church before the Tribulation, is called "that blessed hope" of the church. If the church is to go through the Tribulation as some teach, then it is neither blessed nor hopeful, but instead a fearful looking for judgment which is come upon the world.[21]

> If Christ does not rapture His church before the Tribulation begins, much of the hope is destroyed, and thus it becomes a *blasted* hope rather than a blessed one.[22]

DeHaan and Tim LaHaye conclude that any position which allows Christians to enter into the tribulation period must be false, since that conclusion would deny the pretribulationist's blessed hope. The Pre-Wrath rapture does not claim that we will enter into God's end-time judgments. We merely claim that God's judgments begin with the first trumpet judgment which begins after the great tribulation is cut short (at a time that cannot be calculated). We agree with the pretribulationist that God has guaranteed we will not experience His end-time judgments. The key to understanding this is to differentiate between tribulation in this world and the judgments of God. We are promised that we will escape God's judgments; however, the Lord also prophesied that we *will* experience tribulation.

[9] "Then they will deliver you to tribulation, and will kill you, and you will be hated by all nations on account of My name.
[10] "And at that time many will fall away and will deliver up one another and hate one another.
[11] "And many false prophets will arise, and will mislead many.
[12] "And because lawlessness is increased, most people's love will grow cold.
[13] "But the one who endures to the end, he shall be saved.
[14] "And this gospel of the kingdom shall be preached in the whole world for a witness to all the nations, and then the end shall come. (Matthew 24:9–14)

The pretribulationist agrees with the Pre-Wrath rapture that Jesus was teaching about experiencing the great tribulation that immediately follows the abomination of desolation. This tribulation and martyrdom (Matthew 24:9) would be because of Christ's name; therefore, Jesus was speaking about those who believe in Him.

Christians throughout history have been persecuted and martyred for their faith. Therefore, if God's end-time judgments do not begin until after the great tribulation is cut short, it would be reasonable to expect that there will be Christians who experience tribulation and martyrdom within the great tribulation as well.

Who Is the Blessed Hope For?

It is true that the blessed hope includes the guarantee that we will not experience God's end-times wrath. However, *that* guarantee only applies to the very few still alive as the rapture approaches. If the blessed hope is not applied equally to those alive and those who have already died in Christ, then it was a cruel deception for the New Testament believers! Notice that even Titus, the recipient of this letter from Paul, would not be a recipient of the pretribulationists concept of the blessed hope, since he has already died. Was Stephen's stoning to death (Acts 7:54–60) any less tribulation for him than what a Christian would experience within the great tribulation? None of the New Testament saints were rescued from their tribulation, since they all died before experiencing the rapture, many died as martyrs!

David Hunt claims that if imminency is lost, the blessed hope that sustained believers for centuries is also lost.[23] If the blessed hope supports imminency and is the guarantee that we will not receive persecution and martyrdom within Daniel's seventieth week, then throughout history Christians would have been denied their blessed hope! Persecution, tribulation, and martyrdom have always been the lot of faithful Christians in this evil world! The Pre-Wrath rapture agrees

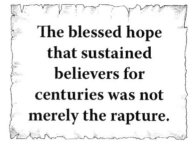

The blessed hope that sustained believers for centuries was not merely the rapture.

with the pretribulationist that we will be raptured before God's end-time judgments. However, the far greater blessing is almost completely ignored by pretribulationists, since they use Titus 2:13 out of context to prove pretribulationism. The context of Titus 2:11–14 demonstrates that the true blessed hope is for all Christians, since all Christians will experience the rapture as well as eternal life before the throne of God. Most will experience the rapture *after* death.

> [11] For the grace of God has appeared, bringing salvation to all men,
> [12] instructing us to deny ungodliness and worldly desires and to live sensibly, righteously and godly in the present age,
> [13] looking for the blessed hope and the appearing of the glory of our great God and Savior, Christ Jesus;
> [14] who gave Himself for us, that He might redeem us from every lawless deed and purify for Himself a people for His own possession, zealous for good deeds.
> (Titus 2:11–14)

Before continuing, it is necessary to answer the counter to this that surely is on the mind of every pretribulationist. The pretribulationist could respond that the blessed hope *is* for all Christians, since "the dead in Christ shall rise first and those who are alive shall be caught up together with them" (1 Thessalonians 4:16–17). However, that response would disqualify Titus 2:13 as a proof of the pretrib rapture, since Titus 2:11–14 agrees with *any* position that places the rapture before the beginning of God's end time judgments.

Of course, according to the pretribulationist, the whole "tribulation period" is the wrath of God on the Antichrist and his followers. We will see in our study of Revelation that at least part of Daniel's seventieth week is filled with the Antichrist's persecution of Christians. This persecution of the saints will happen *after* the beginning of Daniel's seventieth week yet *before* God begins His wrath. Christians within the tribulation period will receive no escape from the Antichrist's persecution. If the pretribulationist's concept of intimately linking the blessed hope and imminency is correct as Hunt claims, then Christians who become martyrs within the tribulation period will be denied the blessed hope! John Walvoord agreed that the church will experience tribulation, but he believed that the church will absolutely not experience it from within the tribulation period.

> The Scriptures reveal in many passages that the church may expect tribulation. Christ said to His disciples, "in the world ye shall have tribulation" (John 15:20). Paul and Barnabas, in exhorting the believers of Lystra, Iconium, and Antioch, warned that "through much tribulation" we must "enter into the kingdom of God" (Acts 14:22, KJV). Paul wrote the Romans, "We also rejoice in our sufferings, because we know that suffering produces perseverance" (Rom. 5:3). Similar references to endurance of tribulation are found elsewhere (Rom 8:35, 12:12; 2 Cor. 1:4, 7:4; Eph. 3:13; 2 Thess. 1:4; Rev. 1:9, 2:9–10). All these passages have to do with tribulation that is characteristic of the warfare of the saints and to be expected in any dispensation.[24]

> It is of upmost importance that every Scripture describing the participants in this future tribulation period refers to Israelites as Israelites, Gentiles as Gentiles, and the saints as saints without ever once using any of the distinctive terms that apply to believers in this present age.[25]

It is quite true that there "will be a great tribulation, such as has not occurred since the beginning of the world until now, nor ever shall" (Matthew 24:21). However, this does not require that the full seven years of the Daniel's seventieth week be God's judgment. In fact, it does not even require the great tribulation to be God's judgment. The Genesis flood provides one of the many proofs that even the great tribulation is not God's judgment. When we discuss the issue of how severe the great tribulation will be (chapter 8 subchapter "The Severity of the Great Tribulation"), we will discover that the great tribulation is the greatest distress Satan (and his Antichrist) will ever bring upon the world; however, it does not rise to the devastation of God's judgment during the Noahic flood. Of course, consistent with Satan's mode of operation, he will be specifically focused on killing every Jew and Christian. If the church enters into Daniel's seventieth week, then Christians *will* experience this time of great trouble specifically because we belong to Christ.

> [20] "Remember the word that I said to you, 'A slave is not greater than his master.' If they persecuted Me, they will also persecute you; if they kept My word, they will keep yours also.
> [21] "But all these things they will do to you for My name's sake, because they do not know the One who sent Me.
> (John 15:20–21)

John 15:20 was included in Walvoord's list above. Jesus said, "If they persecuted Me, they will also persecute you." The Lord's enemies would soon crucify our Savior! Of course, the persecution applies to the church from its founding. Could that include martyrdom for many Christians as experienced in the great tribulation?

> Then they will deliver you to tribulation, and will kill you, and you will be hated by all nations because of My name.
> (Matthew 24:9)

> [21] for then there will be a great tribulation, such as has not occurred since the beginning of the world until now, nor ever shall.
> [22] "And unless those days had been cut short, no life would have been saved; but for the sake of the elect those days shall be cut short.
> (Matthew 24:21–22)

Many pretribulationists claim that Matthew 24:9 only applies to Jews. However, non-Christian Jews are not killed because of Christ's name! Only Jews and Gentiles who become Christians are killed because of Christ's name.

Examining the Context of the Blessed Hope

> looking for the blessed hope and the appearing of the glory of our great God and Savior, Christ Jesus,
> (Titus 2:13)

We have already seen that if Titus 2:13 is only defined from the perspective of those alive at the rapture, then the blessed hope was not offered to any of the Christians who died before the rapture. Now we will examine the surrounding verses. Pretribulationists base their interpretation of the blessed hope solely on Titus 2:13. Using that approach, it is easy to see how they conclude that the blessed hope and the glorious appearing of our Lord (at the rapture) are equivalent events. Adding verses 11, 12, and 14 to Titus 2:13 dramatically changes the interpretation; therefore, the pretribulationist takes Titus 2:13 out of context.

> [11] For the grace of God has appeared, bringing salvation to all men,
> [12] instructing us to deny ungodliness and worldly desires and to live sensibly, righteously and godly in the present age,
> [13] looking for the blessed hope and the appearing of the glory of our great God and Savior, Christ Jesus;
> [14] who gave Himself for us, that He might redeem us from every lawless deed and purify for Himself a people for His own possession, zealous for good deeds.
> (Titus 2:11–14)

Within the context of Titus 2:11–14, verse 11 speaks of God's grace and our salvation. Verse 14 speaks of our redemption through Christ's sacrifice. Therefore, since verse 13 is surrounded by our redemption in Christ, it would be inconsistent with the biblical record to apply Titus 2:13 only to the rapture of living Christians. Titus 2:11 and 2:14 show that the blessed hope must include our eternal life with the Lord and our guarantee of salvation. In light of that, verse 12 answers the age-old question, "How then shall we live?" This is consistent with verses 1–10 and 15. Therefore, Titus 2:11–14 would apply to all Christians throughout history, not just those alive at the rapture.

Our blessed hope is a hope in the absolute security of our eternal life in Christ. When Christ appears at the rapture, that moment is the beginning of this eternal experience for *all* believers in Christ—those alive on earth and those who have died in Christ beforehand. Notice that the true blessed hope fits both end-time positions! That shows that the Pre-Wrath rapture position does not destroy the blessed hope, and the pretribulationist cannot claim the blessed hope proves the pretrib rapture position.

There are two other places in Titus where Paul spoke of our hope. In both cases, Paul spoke specifically about our hope of eternal life.

> [1] Paul, a bond-servant of God, and an apostle of Jesus Christ, for the faith of those chosen of God and the knowledge of the truth which is according to godliness,
> [2] in the *hope* of eternal life, which God, who cannot lie, promised long ages ago,
> [3] but at the proper time manifested, even His word, in the proclamation with which I was entrusted according to the commandment of God our Savior;
> [4] to Titus, my true child in a common faith: Grace and peace from God the Father and Christ Jesus our Savior.
> (Titus 1:1–4, emphasis added)

> [4] But when the kindness of God our Savior and His love for mankind appeared,
> [5] He saved us, not on the basis of deeds which we have done in righteousness, but according to His mercy, by the washing of regeneration and renewing by the Holy Spirit,
> [6] whom He poured out upon us richly through Jesus Christ our Savior,
> [7] that being justified by His grace we might be made heirs according to the *hope* of eternal life.
> (Titus 3:4–7, emphasis added)

First Thessalonians 4:13–18 clearly shows the relationship between the rapture and its eternal consequence for all Christians. This is the fullness of the blessed hope.

> [13] But we do not want you to be uninformed, brethren, about those who are asleep, so that you will not grieve as do the rest who have no hope.
> [14] For if we believe that Jesus died and rose again, even so God will bring with Him those who have fallen asleep in Jesus.
> [15] For this we say to you by the word of the Lord, that we who are alive and remain until the coming of the Lord, will not precede those who have fallen asleep.
> [16] For the Lord Himself will descend from heaven with a shout, with the voice of the archangel and with the trumpet of God, and the dead in Christ will rise first.

¹⁷ Then we who are alive and remain will be caught up together with them in the clouds to meet the Lord in the air, and so we shall always be with the Lord.
¹⁸ Therefore comfort one another with these words.
(1 Thessalonians 4:13–18)

Notice that Paul (and others, according to verse 15) accepted the possibility that they could still be alive at the rapture. They all died; Paul and some others died as martyrs through much tribulation. However, even in death as martyrs, they did not lose their blessed hope! Christians who are alive and those who have already died in Christ will be raptured together at Christ's appearing in glory, and we will be with Him forever. This truth rejects the claim that the blessed hope is a guarantee that the church will not enter into Daniel's seventieth week. We are all guaranteed that we will not experience God's end-time wrath. Many who are dead in Christ have already experienced tribulation from those who follow Satan; many more still will. Some of them will experience tribulation from *within* Daniel's seventieth week but *before* God begins His end-time judgments. However, every Christian is a recipient of the promise and fulfillment of the blessed hope!

Conclusion

"Our hope in being raptured alive before the tribulation period" should not be forced into Titus 2:13. Since the verses surrounding Titus 2:13 clearly teach about our eternal security in Christ, the blessed hope in verse 13 must refer to this same eternal life. The rapture at Christ's appearing is the glorious first event that will launch this eternal experience. The Titus 2:13 promise is *not* written solely for Christians who are alive at the time of the rapture; it is also written to everyone saved in Christ throughout history, just as the rapture is for everyone saved in Christ.

The Pre-Wrath rapture position successfully destroys the pretribulationist interpretation of the blessed hope! However, the Pre-Wrath rapture position fully agrees with the true application and meaning of the blessed hope.

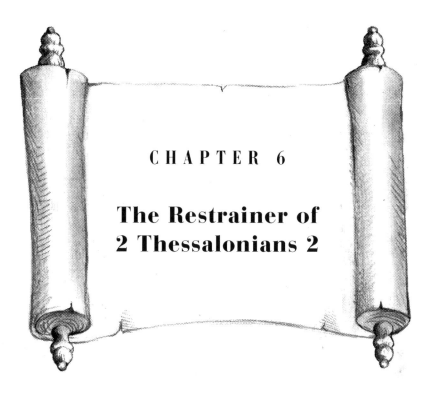

CHAPTER 6

The Restrainer of
2 Thessalonians 2

Who Is the Restrainer?

The majority of pretribulationists believe that the restrainer spoken of in 2 Thessalonians 2:6–8 is the Holy Spirit and that when He is "taken out of the way" (2 Thessalonians 2:7), He will vacate the earth, and the church will be raptured with Him. The primary purpose of this chapter is to show that when the restrainer is removed from his restraining work, that action does not require him to vacate the earth. Therefore, even if the restrainer is the Holy Spirit, the church does not need to be raptured at this time. Discovering who the restrainer is does not change this discussion. However, I will present a biblically sound alternative to the Holy Spirit for the restrainer at the end of this chapter. We will look at 2 Thessalonians 2:1–8 in significantly more detail in chapter 7.

If the Restrainer Is the Holy Spirit, What Is His Ministry?

Many pretribulationists teach that the Holy Spirit's restraining purpose is to hold back sin. John Walvoord is one who takes this position in interpreting 2 Thessalonians 2:3–8.

> If restraint of sin is taken away, it must be traced to a divine removal and the release of satanic evil.[26]

> The exegesis of the key words of the passage, while indecisive, is easily harmonized with the concept that the restraining power is that of the Holy Spirit Himself.[27]

> The passage teaches that the order of events is as follows: (1) the restrainer is now engaged in restraining sin; (2) the restrainer will be taken away at a future point in time; (3) then the man of sin can be revealed.[28]

According to this interpretation, when the Holy Spirit is taken out of the way, sin is released to have full reign. If that is what happens when the restrainer is taken out of the way, then the restrainer must not be very powerful. Wickedness is rampant in this world *today,* and it is clearly accelerating! However, Walvoord does conclude that the restrainer keeps the man of sin from being revealed until the Lord's time has come (although he still relates the restrainer's ministry to the restraint of sin).

> The ultimate decision on the reference to the restrainer goes back to the larger question of who, after all, is capable of restraining sin to such an extent that the man of sin cannot be revealed until the restraint is removed.[29]

> [3] Let no one in any way deceive you, for it will not come unless the apostasy comes first, and the man of lawlessness is revealed, the son of destruction,
> [4] who opposes and exalts himself above every so-called god or object of worship, so that he takes his seat in the temple of God, displaying himself as being God.
> [5] Do you not remember that while I was still with you, I was telling you these things?
> [6] And you know what restrains him now, so that in his time he may be revealed.

7 For the mystery of lawlessness is already at work; only he who now restrains will do so until he is taken out of the way.
8 And then that lawless one will be revealed whom the Lord will slay with the breath of His mouth and bring to an end by the appearance of His coming;
(2 Thessalonians 2:3–8)

Second Thessalonians 2 makes it clear that the restrainer does not merely hold back or restrain sin in general; he does not even hold back or restrain Satan. The restrainer's ministry is specifically holding back the revealing of the lawless one (the Antichrist). God has set a specific moment in time for when He will allow the Antichrist to be revealed. Neither humans nor Satan can alter God's timing!

Must the Restrainer Vacate the Earth?

Once pretribulationists conclude that the restrainer is the holy Spirit and that He must be removed from the earth before the peace treaty, they must conclude that the church is raptured at the same time. Read how Walvoord presents it.

> Inasmuch as the man of sin is identified with the world ruler, the "ruler who will come" of Daniel 9:26, it should be clear to students of prophecy that the restrainer must be taken away before the beginning of the last seven years of Daniel's prophecy.[30]

> If this removal of the Holy Spirit in the church takes place before the lawless one can be revealed, it points to an event that must precede the Tribulation. In a word, it is stating that the Rapture precedes the Tribulation.[31]

There is nothing in 2 Thessalonians 2:1–12 that even mentions or implies the peace treaty. Therefore, no relationship between the church and the beginning of Daniel's seventieth week can be drawn from this passage. The presupposition that "before the peace treaty the Holy Spirit must vacate the earth and the church must be raptured" is a stumbling block for pretribulationists, since many admit there are believers in Christ within Daniel's seventieth week. Even if the restrainer is the Holy Spirit, what actually happens when He is taken out of the way? If He vacates the earth, how can anyone become a Christian without the work of the Holy Spirit? Seriously ponder the consequence of this question! If one's end-time conclusion creates an irresolvable problem, then that conclusion must be reexamined! Walvoord "solves" the problem of believers after the peace treaty by saying that the Holy Spirit will not completely vacate the earth.

> Pretribulationists agree that the removal of the Holy Spirit is not complete, for the Holy Spirit is still omnipresent and still exercises some restraint, as the Book of Revelation makes plain in the protection of the 144,000. But neither Gundry nor anyone else can prove that the baptizing work of the Spirit that forms the church is ever seen in the Tribulation.

> That the Spirit works in the Tribulation all agree. That the Spirit indwells all believers in the Tribulation is nowhere taught.[32]

Walvoord correctly recognizes that, since the Holy Spirit is omnipresent, He cannot vacate the earth. However, Walvoord came to an unexpected conclusion. He claims that believers within Daniel's seventieth week *will not* be indwelled by the Holy Spirit, even though the Holy Spirit will still be here! In other words, Walvoord still claims that Holy Spirit's baptizing work has ceased. This is the only conclusion possible if one has already determined that the church must be raptured before the peace treaty. However, Walvoord has defeated his own premise. If the Holy Spirit does not vacate the earth, then there is nothing that restricts Him from indwelling believers. All that must happen is that the restrainer merely stops restraining the Antichrist so that the Antichrist can be revealed. This conclusion, of course, negates any requirement that the church must be raptured before the peace treaty. J. Dwight Pentecost also recognizes this problem, but he still ends up with the same conclusion as Walvoord that the Holy Spirit will not indwell believers within Daniel's seventieth week.

> **If the Holy Spirit does not vacate the earth, then He can still indwell believers!**

Suffice it to say here that it is concluded that the restrainer is the Holy Spirit and that He will be taken away, yet it must be recognized that the Spirit is omnipresent. He will cease His particular ministry of indwelling the body of Christ, but that does not mean He will be inoperative. Before Pentecost the Lord told Nicodemus that a man must be born again by the Spirit (John 3:5–6). If a person could experience a new birth before the Holy Spirit began to indwell the body, certainly one could after He ceases that particular ministry. It should be noted that the indwelling ministry is related to the enablement of believers in their Christian walk, not to the method or means of salvation.[33]

I beg to differ with the solutions offered by Walvoord and Pentecost. Although there were unique conditions right after the Lord's ascension, according to the Bible, one cannot be saved by the blood of Jesus Christ without being indwelled by the Holy Spirit. At least by the time Paul wrote Romans and Ephesians, the Holy Spirit's indwelling was already recognized as the guarantee of salvation.

However, you are not in the flesh but in the Spirit, if indeed the Spirit of God dwells in you. But if anyone does not have the Spirit of Christ, he does not belong to Him.
(Romans 8:9)

[13] In Him, you also, after listening to the message of truth, the gospel of your salvation—having also believed, you were sealed in Him with the Holy Spirit of promise,
[14] who is given as a pledge of our inheritance, with a view to the redemption of God's own possession, to the praise of His glory.
(Ephesians 1:13–14)

The solution Walvoord and Pentecost have offered to explain believers within Daniel's seventieth week must be rejected. Since pretribulationists agree that Holy Spirit is omnipresent; there is no basis for His indwelling ministry to stop. Therefore, pretribulationists must explain their original claim that the Holy Spirit is taken away. If the Holy Spirit is the restrainer and is removed just before the peace treaty, does He come back to indwell the first post-rapture convert? And if His presence is what restrains, would His return not resume the restraining work? In case you think that the solution to this problem is that there will be no saved on earth after the rapture, this is not a viable solution for the pretrib rapture position.

"Saved after the rapture" is the only explanation the pretribulationist has for the many clear references to believers in Christ during the tribulation period, such as the great multitude who came out of the great tribulation (Revelation 7:9–17). Only one of the following three possibilities below can be biblically true:

➤ Those who become Christians within the tribulation are not indwelled by the Holy Spirit (even if the Holy Spirit does not vacate the earth).

➤ The Holy Spirit returns to indwell the first convert after the rapture and everyone thereafter.

➤ The restrainer only releases the Antichrist to carry out Satan's evil plans. This does not require the Holy Spirit to vacate the earth.

The first option is truly unbiblical; Romans 8:9 and Ephesians 1:13–14 refute this conclusion. Some pretribulationists have attempted to resolve this problem by claiming that there are saints like believers in Christ before the cross (such as Pentecost's example of Nicodemus[34]). However, the same verses (Romans 8:9 and Ephesians 1:13–14) refute this also. Therefore, at least from the time Paul wrote these verses, it is not possible to be saved in the absence of the indwelling Holy Spirit. If there was an exception within Daniel's seventieth week, Paul would surely have said so in order to avoid people believing that salvation within Daniel's seventieth week would be impossible.

The second option begs the question: if the Holy Spirit's vacating the earth released the Antichrist, then why does His return with the first convert not cause the Antichrist to be restrained again? Option two is only possible for the pretribulationist if somehow when the Holy Spirit returns; He chooses not to restrain the Antichrist as He had done before (if the restrainer is the Holy Spirit). If the Holy Spirit can return without renewing the restraint of the Antichrist, then He would never have had to leave in the first place. He merely would have to stop restraining. Option two is self-defeating.

The third option is the only solution that is consistent with the Bible. The restrainer does not vacate the earth. Notice that this solution does not require the church to be raptured before the peace treaty. Even if the restrainer is the Holy Spirit, the pretribulationist cannot use 2 Thessalonians 2 to force the rapture before the peace treaty.

What Does "Taking Out of the Way" Mean?

> For the mystery of lawlessness is already at work; only he who now restrains will do so until he is taken out of the way.
> (2 Thessalonians 2:7)

The question has already been asked: Why must the restrainer vacate the earth? Could the restrainer (while still on the earth) just stop restraining the Antichrist so that he can be revealed? John MacArthur provides an excellent answer to this question.

> **[2 Thessalonians] 2:7 taken out of the way.** This refers not to the spatial removal (therefore it could not be the rapture of the church) but rather "a stepping aside." The idea is "out of the way," not gone (cf. Col 2:14 where our sins are taken out of the way as a barrier to God); *see note on vv. 3,4.* The restraint will be in place until the Antichrist is revealed, at the midpoint of the Tribulation, leaving him 42 months to reign (Da 7:25; Rev 13:5).[35]

Even if the Holy Spirit is the restrainer, it is not necessary for Him to vacate the earth. He would merely have to step away from His task of keeping the Antichrist from being revealed. A simple way of seeing this is to picture yourself restraining your child from running in a field. When you release her, she can freely run in the field, but you do not have to disappear (vacate the field) for her to run.

The pretribulationist Mal Couch agrees that the Holy Spirit does not have to vacate the earth. He also comes to the same conclusion as the Pre-Wrath rapture position regarding what the restraining work is.

> While it is probably correct to say the restrainer moves aside at the time of the rapture of the church so that "in his time [the Antichrist] may be revealed" (2 Thessalonians 2:6), the Holy Spirit will still continue the work on earth of bringing people to salvation. While the church is still here, He is active as the power working within the lives of believers.[36] [Comment in bracket was added by Mal Couch.]

Verse 7 says, "For the mystery of this lawlessness is already working only until the one now holding [him] down [or restraining him] shall get out of the way." The Greek word *katacho* is a compound word formed from *kata* (down) and *echo* (to have, or to hold). From this comes the thought "to hold down or to restrain." *Katecho* can have the meaning "to hold back from action, to keep under control, to deprive of physical liberty, as by shackling, or arresting a criminal." The restrainer then is preventing the Anti-christ from breaking out until his appointed time, which would be during or just before the beginning of the Tribulation.[37] [Comments in parentheses and brackets were added by Mal Couch.]

Since the Holy Spirit does not have to vacate the earth at the rapture, it is not even necessary for the restrainer to be the Holy Spirit. The restrainer merely needs to be a created being that is strong enough to keep the Antichrist from being revealed.

An Alternate Identity for the Restrainer

There are many verses that show of the Lord restraining the lost, restraining His people from wrongdoing, and restraining His own action against His people (such as Genesis 20:4–6, 1 Samuel 25:26, 1 Chronicles 21:22, Psalm 78:38, Isaiah 42:14, and 2 Peter 2:16). However, nowhere does Scripture specifically call the Holy Spirit the restrainer of the Antichrist. Therefore, we should not build our theology on the assumption that the restrainer is the Holy Spirit and that He must vacate the earth when the rapture happens.

Many pretribulationists have concluded that the restrainer must be the Holy Spirit, claiming that He is the only one strong enough to restrain Satan. Here is an example from M. R. DeHaan:

Now what person can restrain Satan? Certainly it must be someone more than a mere human; someone more powerful than the Devil himself, and this, of course involves Deity. This *He* therefore, this restraining Person, must be a Person of the Trinity, and can only refer to the person of the Holy Spirit who, as we know, is in the world today indwelling and abiding in the church and in every single believer.

This blessed person of the Holy Spirit is here now, abiding in the church forever. He is the only one able to restrain Satan's man of sin from coming upon the earth. As long as this blessed Holy Spirit is here, the Antichrist cannot be revealed.[38]

The conclusion that God is the only one who can restrain Satan does not stand the test of the Scriptures. According to Revelation 20, there is an angel who can restrain Satan.

> [1] And I saw an angel coming down from heaven, having the key of the abyss and a great chain in his hand.
> [2] And he laid hold of the dragon, the serpent of old, who is the devil and Satan, and bound him for a thousand years,
> [3] and threw him into the abyss, and shut it and sealed it over him, so that he should not deceive the nations any longer, until the thousand years were completed; after these things he must be released for a short time.
> (Revelation 20:1–3)

Whoever this angel is, not only can he restrain Satan, but he can also bind him completely for one thousand years! We know that the restrainer presented in 2 Thessalonians 2:3 only restrains the Antichrist enough to keep him from being revealed until God's set time. That does not even keep the Antichrist from doing evil. Since the angel of Revelation 20 can fully restrain Satan for one thousand years, the restrainer of the Antichrist does not have to be the Holy Spirit.

If the restrainer is not the Holy Spirit, who else can he be? Michael the archangel appears to be a reasonable alternative. Let's look at Daniel 12:1–2.

> [1] "Now at that time Michael, the great prince who stands guard over the sons of your people, will arise. And there will be a time of distress such as never occurred since there was a nation until that time; and at that time your people, everyone who is found written in the book, will be rescued.
> [2] "And many of those who sleep in the dust of the ground will awake, these to everlasting life, but the others to disgrace and everlasting contempt.
> (Daniel 12:1–2)

Notice that "everyone who is found written in the book, will be rescued" and that "those who sleep in the dust of the ground will awake, these to everlasting life." This rescue and resurrection at the time of great distress is consistent with the Pre-Wrath rapture position.

> [21] for then there will be a great tribulation, such as has not occurred since the beginning of the world until now, nor ever shall.
> [22] "And unless those days had been cut short, no life would have been saved; but for the sake of the elect those days shall be cut short.
> (Matthew 24:21–22)

> [29] "But immediately after the tribulation of those days the sun will be darkened, and the moon will not give its light, and the stars will fall from the sky, and the powers of the heavens will be shaken,
> [30] and then the sign of the Son of Man will appear in the sky, and then all the tribes of the earth will mourn, and they will see the Son of Man coming on the clouds of the sky with power and great glory.
> [31] "And He will send forth His angels with A GREAT TRUMPET and THEY WILL GATHER TOGETHER His elect from the four winds, from one end of the sky to the other.
> (Matthew 24:29–31)

Although Daniel 12:1 does not necessarily prove that the restrainer is Michael the archangel, Daniel 12:1 is consistent with that conclusion. Michael stands guard (restrains), he will arise (the restrainer is taken out of the way), and the greatest time of distress ever will come (which would at least include the great tribulation). Next, let's look at Revelation 12.

> [7] And there was war in heaven, Michael and his angels waging war with the dragon. And the dragon and his angels waged war,
> [8] and they were not strong enough, and there was no longer a place found for them in heaven.
> [9] And the great dragon was thrown down, the serpent of old who is called the devil and Satan, who deceives the whole world; he was thrown down to the earth, and his angels were thrown down with him.
> (Revelation 12:7–9)

This passage identifies the archangel Michael as the one who leads the battle against Satan—and wins! Michael's strength against

Satan surely qualifies him to be a candidate for the restrainer of 2 Thessalonians 2.

> [6] And you know what restrains him now, so that in his time he may be revealed.
> [7] For the mystery of lawlessness is already at work; only he who now restrains will do so until he is taken out of the way.
> [8] And then that lawless one will be revealed whom the Lord will slay with the breath of His mouth and bring to an end by the appearance of His coming;
> (2 Thessalonians 2:6–8)

Conclusion

The pretribulationist is left with two irresolvable problems. Since it is quite reasonable that Michael the archangel could be the restrainer, the pretribulationist cannot force the Holy Spirit into 2 Thessalonians 2 and then use that conclusion to prove that the church must be raptured before the Antichrist can be revealed. Secondly, even if the restrainer is the Holy Spirit, the church does not have to leave the earth, since the Holy Spirit does not vacate the earth when the Antichrist is revealed; he merely would stop restraining him.

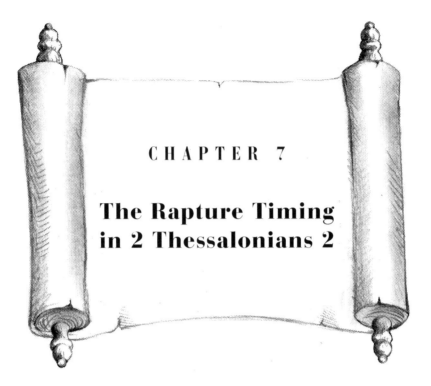

CHAPTER 7

The Rapture Timing in 2 Thessalonians 2

The Order of the Events

Having heard for such a long time that 2 Thessalonians 2 proves the pretrib rapture, you will surely be surprised to find out that the order of events presented in this letter makes that conclusion impossible!

> ¹ Now we request you, brethren, with regard to the coming of our Lord Jesus Christ, and our gathering together to Him,
> ² that you may not be quickly shaken from your composure or be disturbed either by a spirit or a message or a letter as if from us, to the effect that the day of the Lord has come.
> ³ Let no one in any way deceive you, for it will not come unless the apostasy comes first, and the man of lawlessness is revealed, the son of destruction,
> ⁴ who opposes and exalts himself above every so-called god or object of worship, so that he takes his seat in the temple of God, displaying himself as being God.
> ⁵ Do you not remember that while I was still with you, I was telling you these things?
> (2 Thessalonians 2:1–5)

Notice how tightly the rapture and the day of the Lord are linked! Paul tied them so closely together that he said, "... with regard to the coming of our Lord Jesus Christ, and our gathering together to Him, that you may not be quickly shaken from your composure ... to the effect that the day of the Lord has come" (2 Thessalonians 2:1–2). Paul comforted them with proof that, since the day of the Lord had not come, the rapture had not come. He could not say this if there were even a few hours separating the two!

This passage also gives us two other events that must happen *before* the day of the Lord begins. In *The Rapture Question*, John Walvoord claims that 2 Thessalonians 2 proves the Antichrist (the lawless one) cannot be revealed until the rapture.

> Paul taught in 2 Thessalonians 2 the important fact that the man of sin, or the lawless one, cannot be revealed as such until the Rapture, that is, the removal of the church indwelt by the Holy Spirit.[39]

Second Thessalonians 2:3 says, "For it [the day of the Lord that comes shortly after the rapture according to 2 Thessalonians 2:1] will not come unless the apostasy comes *first* and the man of lawlessness is revealed" (emphasis added). The apostasy and the revealing of the Antichrist actually *precede* the day of the Lord! John MacArthur agrees that the day of the Lord cannot come until this apostasy happens.

> **[2 Thessalonians] 2:3, 4 the apostasy.** The Day of the Lord cannot occur until a deliberate abandonment of a formerly professed position, allegiance, or commitment occurs (the term was used to refer to military, political, or religious rebellion). Some have suggested, on questionable linguistic evidence, that this refers to "departure" in a sense of the Rapture. Context, however points to a religious defection, which is further described in v. 4. The language indicates a specific event, not general apostasy which exists now and always will. Rather, Paul has in mind *the* apostasy. This is an event which is clearly and specifically identifiable and unique, the consummate act of rebellion, an event of final magnitude. The key to identifying the event is to identify the main person, which Paul does, calling him the "man of lawlessness."[40]

This "apostasy" is the abomination of desolation that takes place at the midpoint of the Tribulation, spoken of in Da 9:27; 11:31 and Mt 24:15 (*see notes there*). This man is not Satan, although Satan is the force behind him (v. 9) and he has motives like the desires of the devil (cf. Is 14:13, 14). Paul is referring to the very act of ultimate apostasy which reveals the final Antichrist and sets the course for the events that usher in the Day of the Lord.[41]

MacArthur agrees with the Pre-Wrath rapture that the Antichrist is revealed at the abomination of desolation and that the event which reveals the Antichrist "sets the course for the events that usher in the day of the Lord."[42] These events will be examined later in this chapter.

MacArthur has concluded that the apostasy is the abomination of desolation. His conclusion is understandable; however, there are also two other possibilities (apostasy within the church and Israel's apostasy). These two are exposed as a result of the abomination of desolation. Therefore, it is likely that the apostasy is the worldwide rejection of God which is expressed in three parts:

➢ The Antichrist openly rejects God, proclaiming himself to be God when he commits the abomination of desolation.

➢ Israel's rejection of God happens at the peace treaty when Israel trusts the Antichrist for peace instead of God. Their apostasy is revealed at the abomination of desolation.

➢ False Christians' rejection of God is also exposed after the abomination of desolation when the Antichrist persecutes the church.

Both the pretrib and Pre-Wrath rapture positions place the rapture immediately before the day of the Lord begins. Therefore, since the apostasy and the revealing of the Antichrist precede the day of the Lord, they must precede the rapture as well! Pretribulationists Mal Couch and Ed Hindson also recognize that the rapture will occur *after* the apostasy.

In 2 Thessalonians 2:3, Paul calls it the *apostasia*, translated "the apostasy" (NASB), "the rebellion (NIV), or "the falling away" (KJV). He says that "some shall depart from the faith" in 1 Timothy 4:1 (KJV).

Paul's language suggests that the great departure will probably reach its fulfillment sometime just before the rapture of the church (2 Thessalonians 2:2, 7–9; 2 Timothy 3:1). Paul also wrote that a form of this apostasy was already evident in his generation. These "departures" would continue throughout the ages of the church and climax in the last days (2 Thessalonians 2:7).[43]

Notice that Couch and Hindson agree that the apostasy is a departure from the faith. However, according to the order presented in 2 Thessalonians 2:1–4, if the pretrib rapture position is correct (the rapture before the peace treaty), then the only order that the pretribulationist can draw from 2 Thessalonians 2:1–4 would be that the apostasy happens, then the man of lawlessness is revealed *before* the rapture. That would destroy imminency!

What Is the Revealing of the Antichrist?

Since the three potential apostasies are all related to the revealing of the Antichrist, we will examine this revealing event first. It is explained within 2 Thessalonians 2. It is far greater than merely discovering the Antichrist's identity.

> [1] Now we request you, brethren, with regard to the coming of our Lord Jesus Christ, and our gathering together to Him,
> [2] that you may not be quickly shaken from your composure or be disturbed either by a spirit or a message or a letter as if from us, to the effect that the day of the Lord has come.
> [3] Let no one in any way deceive you, for it will not come unless the apostasy comes first, and the man of lawlessness is revealed, the son of destruction,
> [4] who opposes and exalts himself above every so-called god or object of worship, so that he takes his seat in the temple of God, displaying himself as being God.
> (2 Thessalonians 2:1–4)

It is the abomination of desolation that truly exposes the Antichrist, since he will take the seat in the temple and display himself as God. Having believed at the beginning of Daniel's seventieth week that it has finally achieved peace, Israel will be horrified when the Antichrist commits the abomination of desolation (cancelling the peace treaty). The terror in the land of Israel will be beyond anything its people can even comprehend (Isaiah 28:19). If the abomination of desolation is the revealing of the Antichrist, then according to the order presented in 2 Thessalonians 2, the abomination of desolation must happen *before* our rapture! Couch and Hindson also recognize that Paul claims the abomination of desolation will reveal the Antichrist.

> In 2 Thessalonians 2:1–12, Paul describes the work of Satan and the Antichrist at the mid-point of the seven-year Tribulation, "In accord with the activity of Satan, with all power and signs and false wonders" (verse 9), the "man of lawlessness" will reveal his true colors and take "his seat in the temple of God, displaying himself as being God" (verses 3–4).[44]

Of course, most pretribulationists read 2 Thessalonians 2 and reject this conclusion, claiming that the revealing will occur at the peace treaty. An example of this is presented by Walvoord as he defends the pretrib rapture against the midtrib rapture.

> The man of sin, however, will be clearly identified when he makes a seven-year covenant with Israel, if not before, and this requires the Rapture to occur at least seven years before the Second Coming rather than three and a half years before, as the midtribulationists hold.[45]

It should be noted that this response has a serious timing problem. According to 2 Thessalonians 2:1–4, the apostasy and the revealing of the Antichrist happen *before* we will be gathered to Him! Even if the revealing of the Antichrist could be the peace treaty, that places the rapture *within* Daniel's seventieth week, just the opposite of what the pretribulationist teaches. Later in *Major Bible Prophecies,* Walvoord recognizes that the peace treaty may not be a clear revealing of the Antichrist.

> As far as events are concerned, they do not really find detailed fulfillment until the Great Tribulation comes and the man of sin is revealed. Though he is revealed when the seven-year covenant is made with Israel, it may not be clear that he is the one described in Scripture as the coming world ruler until he breaks his covenant with Israel and begins the Great Tribulation (2 Thess. 2:3–4).[46]

Here Walvoord recognizes that the "clear" revealing of the Antichrist is when he breaks the seven-year covenant with Israel and begins the great tribulation (three-and-a-half years *after* the peace treaty, according to Daniel). Are there two revealing events—one shadowed (the peace treaty) and the other clear (the abomination of desolation)? It is much more natural to expect that the revealing of the Antichrist would be clear to all who need to know at the very first moment God wants him to be revealed. Otherwise, the Antichrist is not actually revealed, is he? That should encourage us to recognize the abomination of desolation as the revealing of the Antichrist. It should be noted that in all of 2 Thessalonians 2, the peace treaty is not even mentioned.

Even when the seven-year covenant with Israel is signed, a multitude of pretribulationist Christians will question whether they are actually witnessing the ultimate peace treaty of the Antichrist, since they have not yet been raptured. We cannot know for sure that we are witnessing the activities of the Antichrist within Daniel's seventieth week until the abomination of desolation! This would be consistent with 2 Thessalonians 2:3–4.

> [3] Let no one in any way deceive you, for it will not come unless the apostasy comes first, and the man of lawlessness is revealed, the son of destruction,
> [4] who opposes and exalts himself above every so-called god or object of worship, so that he takes his seat in the temple of God, displaying himself as being God.
> (2 Thessalonians 2:3–4)

Surely, most of Israel will have been blinded by the promise of guaranteed peace that they have never known. It is not until the covenant is broken that most Jews will recognize the Antichrist for who he is. The abomination of desolation will also be the defining event that convinces pretribulationists that they are in the end times. Grant Jeffrey and Randall Price go even farther, explaining these verses well.

> This "revealing" of the Antichrist does not occur when he is born, nor probably even when he makes a seven-year treaty with Israel (see Daniel 9:27). He will be "revealed" in his satanic nature when he seats himself in the rebuilt Temple in Jerusalem, claiming to be God and demanding worship as God. It is this act which reveals his satanic character as Antichrist and confirms that he has been totally possessed by Satan.[47]

Paul wrote to the Thessalonian church to admonish Christians who had abandoned the normal affairs of life. They believed the imminent coming of Christ that Paul had previously espoused (1 Thessalonians 4:13–18) was already set in motion (2 Thessalonians 2:2). Paul explained that before the "appearance" of the Messiah, the Antichrist must first appear (verses 3–9). The signal event that will manifest the Antichrist, whom this text refers to as "the man of lawlessness," "the son of destruction" (verse 3b), and "that lawless one" (verse 8), is his usurpation of God's place in the Temple (verse 4; see also Exodus 25:8). This act will reveal not only the Antichrist but also "the lie" (the deification of the Antichrist, Revelation 13:4–6, 15) that will mark his followers (Revelation 13:16–18) and confirm them in the eschatological judgment that will occur at the coming of the Lord (2 Thessalonians 2:8–12).[48]

Although they claim to be pretribulationists, Coach, Hindson, and now Jeffrey and Price do not realize that they have agreed with the Pre-Wrath rapture position! Let's look at the 2 Thessalonians passage once again, comparing it to Daniel 9:27 and Matthew 24:15.

[1] Now we request you, brethren, with regard to the coming of our Lord Jesus Christ, and our gathering together to Him,
[2] that you may not be quickly shaken from your composure or be disturbed either by a spirit or a message or a letter as if from us, to the effect that the day of the Lord has come.
[3] Let no one in any way deceive you, for it will not come unless the apostasy comes first, and the man of lawlessness is revealed, the son of destruction,
[4] who opposes and exalts himself above every so-called god or object of worship, so that he takes his seat in the temple of God, displaying himself as being God.
(2 Thessalonians 2:1–4)

"And he will make a firm covenant with the many for one week, but in the middle of the week he will put a stop to sacrifice and grain offering; and on the wing of abominations will come one who makes desolate, even until a complete destruction, one that is decreed, is poured out on the one who makes desolate."
(Daniel 9:27)

"Therefore when you see the abomination of desolation which was spoken of through Daniel the prophet, standing in the holy place (let the reader understand),
(Matthew 24:15)

Many Christians *will* see the Antichrist revealed through the abomination of desolation. We will also see the temple (or tabernacle) rebuilt *before* he is revealed. If the abomination of desolation is the revealing that must happen before the day of the Lord, then the events (at least through the first half of Daniel's seventieth week and the abomination of desolation at the midpoint) would be prophetic events that happen *before* the rapture. Therefore, the rapture would not be imminent! Revelation 13 sheds additional light on when the Antichrist is revealed.

> [1] And he stood on the sand of the seashore. And I saw a beast coming up out of the sea, having ten horns and seven heads, and on his horns were ten diadems, and on his heads were blasphemous names.
> [2] And the beast which I saw was like a leopard, and his feet were like those of a bear, and his mouth like the mouth of a lion. And the dragon gave him his power and his throne and great authority.
> [3] And I saw one of his heads as if it had been slain, and his fatal wound was healed. And the whole earth was amazed and followed after the beast;
> [4] and they worshiped the dragon, because he gave his authority to the beast; and they worshiped the beast, saying, "Who is like the beast, and who is able to wage war with him?"
> [5] And there was given to him a mouth speaking arrogant words and blasphemies; and authority to act for forty-two months was given to him.
> (Revelation 13:1–5)

The Antichrist is given authority to act for forty-two months. The pretribulationist agrees that these events occur *after* the abomination of desolation. Most pretribulationists also believe that the Antichrist receives the mortal wound to his head (Revelation 13:3) and is taken over by Satan near the time of the abomination of desolation. It is likely that the vast majority of the world will not realize this world ruler is the prophesied Antichrist until this defining moment.

The Apostasy

The position of the Pre-Wrath rapture is that the apostasy *(apostasia)* of 2 Thessalonians 2:3 is an absolutely unique event that will never have happened before in all of history. If it were merely a greater apostasy than had ever happened before, there would be no way to recognize it as proof that the time for the rapture and the day of the Lord has come. The rest of this chapter will cover what the apostasy is.

> [1] Now we request you, brethren, with regard to the coming of our Lord Jesus Christ, and our gathering together to Him,
> [2] that you may not be quickly shaken from your composure or be disturbed either by a spirit or a message or a letter as if from us, to the effect that the day of the Lord has come.
> [3] Let no one in any way deceive you, for it will not come unless the apostasy comes first, and the man of lawlessness is revealed, the son of destruction,
> (2 Thessalonians 2:1–3)

Many pretribulationists have appealed to the verb *aphisteemi* in order to define the noun *apostasia,* since according to the *Theological Dictionary of the New Testament* (hereafter called *TDNT*), one of the definitions of *aphisteemi* is "to remove spatially."[49] In doing so, they claim that this *apostasia* must refer to the rapture.[50] Robert H. Gundry (a posttribulationist) argued that the noun can take on a special meaning (different than the verb) and criticized the act of bypassing *apostasia* for the verb *aphisteemi.*[51] I agree with Gundry's criticism of the pretribulationist's appeal to *aphisteemi,* since *aphisteemi* is not used in 2 Thessalonians 2:3. The *TDNT* definition for *apostasia* shows that the position taken in this book is appropriate.

> ἀποστασία. In 2 Th. 2:3 ἀποστασία is used in the absol. sense as an event of the last days alongside or prior to (?) the appearance of the ἄνθρωπος τῆς ἀνομίας. Here a Jewish tradition is adopted which speaks of the complete apostasy from God and His Torah shortly before the appearance of the Messiah. This is applied to the apostasy of Christians from their faith to error and unrighteousness (v. 11 f.) in the last days (Mt. 24:11 f.). Again we have the situation of Lk. 8:13.[52] (Emphasis added.)

Notice that the *TDNT* applies this apostasy to the church; however, the *TDNT's* foundation to that application is "Here a Jewish tradition is adopted which speaks of the complete apostasy from God and His Torah shortly before the appearance of the Messiah."[53] These two conditions are consistent with the Pre-Wrath position.

Alan Kurschner notes that even pretribulationist scholar Paul D. Feinberg recognizes there is not a single instance of interpreting *apostasia* as a "physical departure" in Koine Greek writings from the second century BC through the first century AD.[54]

There are three unique end-time events in biblical prophecy that could be this apostasy. Consistent with the *TDNT's* definition, it could be speaking about the church or about Israel. If the Antichrist claims to worship God around the time of the peace treaty, that could also be included in the apostasy. Expositors are divided over which of these three choices is the fulfillment. That division is very understandable, since these three apostasies happen at different times relative to Daniel's seventieth week. Although the word apostasy is not in Matthew 24, the apostasy within the church is the theme of Matthew 24:9–10. This apostasy will be *after* the abomination of desolation. The apostasy of Israel is the theme of 2 Thessalonians 2:1–3. This apostasy will happen *before* the abomination of desolation. The apostasy of the Antichrist would be revealed at the abomination of desolation. Yet, I contend that the apostasy of the church and the apostasy of Israel will be made known as a result of the abomination of desolation. If so, then the apostasy of the Antichrist is also related to the other two. Therefore, studying all three fulfillments would be appropriate.

The Antichrist's Apostasy

It is possible that the Antichrist will claim to worship God in order to deceive Israel into trusting him for peace and safety. This would be consummated at the peace treaty and his apostasy would be exposed at the abomination of desolation.

Apostasy in the Church

The apostasy of the church applies to the separation of those who merely claim to be saved in Christ from those who are true Jewish and Gentile Christians. We would expect this separation when the church experiences severe persecution and martyrdom from the Antichrist beginning right after the abomination of desolation (Matthew 24:21–22). Surely this persecution will cause the charlatans to flee the church for their own safety. In fact, we would expect that many would prove they are not part of the church by turning against true Christians. This very conclusion is presented in Matthew 24.

> [9] "Then they will deliver you to tribulation, and will kill you, and you will be hated by all nations on account of My name.
> [10] "And at that time many will fall away and will deliver up one another and hate one another.
> (Matthew 24:9–10)

Notice that these charlatans will have already existed in the church *before* the revealing of the Antichrist. However, their presence is not discovered until *after* the great tribulation begins. Therefore, it is the abomination of desolation and the Antichrist's pursuit of true Christians that expose these charlatans.

Israel's Apostasy

> [1] Now we request you, brethren, with regard to the coming of our Lord Jesus Christ, and our gathering together to Him,
> [2] that you may not be quickly shaken from your composure or be disturbed either by a spirit or a message or a letter as if from us, to the effect that the day of the Lord has come.
> [3] Let no one in any way deceive you, for it will not come unless the apostasy comes first, and the man of lawlessness is revealed, the son of destruction,
> (2 Thessalonians 2:1–3)

The apostasy and the revealing of the Antichrist are connected. These two events must happen *before* the rapture and the day of the Lord. In fact, according to verse 3, the apostasy comes first, and *then* the revealing of the Antichrist happens. Therefore, the apostasy of Israel must also have already existed before the abomination of desolation. The consequence of this apostasy, when applied to Israel, is found in 2 Thessalonians 2:8–12.

> [8] And then that lawless one will be revealed whom the Lord will slay with the breath of His mouth and bring to an end by the appearance of His coming;
> [9] that is, the one whose coming is in accord with the activity of Satan, with all power and signs and false wonders,
> [10] and with all the deception of wickedness for those who perish, because they did not receive the love of the truth so as to be saved.

[11] And for this reason God will send upon them a deluding influence so that they might believe what is false,

[12] in order that they all may be judged who did not believe the truth, but took pleasure in wickedness.

(2 Thessalonians 2:8–12)

There is one event in the end times during which Israel specifically turns away "from God and His Torah"[55] as the end times approach. Israel's own blindness to God's plan will leave its people defenseless and unprepared for the activities of Satan. Therefore, they will trust in the Antichrist for their safety instead of trusting God. In signing the peace treaty, the leaders of Israel will think that they have secured that protection. As 2 Thessalonians 2:11 explains, "God will send upon them a deluding influence so that they might believe what is false" (the Antichrist's promise of peace). Notice the reason for God sending the delusion! Israel rejected the truth and instead trusted Satan's man (verse 10). Had they trusted God and accepted His salvation, they would never have fallen for Satan's scheme.

It is possible that once the peace treaty is signed, the Antichrist will make it illegal (or at least far too dangerous) for a Jew to live anywhere else in the world. Therefore, Jews will only find safety by dwelling in Israel. Once the immigration to Israel is complete, the Antichrist will have effectively created a huge concentration camp! Appropriately, Isaiah calls this peace treaty the "covenant with death."

[15] Because you have said, "We have made a covenant with death, and with Sheol we have made a pact. The overwhelming scourge will not reach us when it passes by, for we have made falsehood our refuge and we have concealed ourselves with deception."

[16] Therefore thus says the Lord God, "Behold, I am laying in Zion a stone, a tested stone, a costly cornerstone for the foundation, firmly placed. He who believes in it will not be disturbed.

[17] "And I will make justice the measuring line, and righteousness the level; then hail shall sweep away the refuge of lies, and the waters shall overflow the secret place.

[18] "And your covenant with death shall be canceled, and your pact with Sheol shall not stand; when the overwhelming scourge passes through, then you become its trampling place.

[19] "As often as it passes through, it will seize you. For morning after morning it will pass through, anytime during the day or night. And it will be sheer terror to understand what it means."

(Isaiah 28:15–19)

Notice that belief in the cornerstone (Christ) will keep that one from being disturbed (Isaiah 28:16). This ties the Jews and Christians together, since it is only believers in the cornerstone who will not be disturbed. Although the apostasy of 2 Thessalonians 2 is focused on Israel's covenant with death, Christians will urge them to immediately flee when the Antichrist commits the abomination of desolation.

It is significant that, although the apostasy begins when Israel signs the seven-year treaty with the Antichrist, its people will not realize what they have done until the abomination of desolation. Therefore, it is the abomination of desolation that also exposes the Jewish apostasy. All three of the apostasies we have studied are directly related to the abomination of desolation.

➢ The Antichrist will specifically protect the Jews in Israel (possibly even claiming to worship their God). This will lead to the Jews immigrating to Israel. After the immigration is complete, the Antichrist will commit the abomination of desolation, proving to be Satan's man and proving that he does not worship God.

➢ Although the covenant with death (Isaiah 28:15–19) is signed at the beginning of Daniel's seventieth week, the Jews will not realize what they have done and why they must flee until the Antichrist commits the abomination of desolation. This sequence of the peace treaty (Israel's apostasy) then the abomination of desolation (the revealing of the Antichrist) is consistent with 2 Thessalonians 2:3.

> Let no one in any way deceive you, for it will not come unless the apostasy comes first, and the man of lawlessness is revealed, the son of destruction,
> (2 Thessalonians 2:3)

➢ The Antichrist will surely turn against all true Christians, since they will refuse to worship him or take his mark. Although charlatans will be within the church at the peace treaty, the Antichrist's persecution of the church after the abomination of desolation will cause charlatans within the church to fall away from and betray true believers.

[9] "Then they will deliver you to tribulation, and will kill you, and you will be hated by all nations on account of My name.

[10] "And at that time many will fall away and will deliver up one another and hate one another.
(Matthew 24:9–10)

Conclusion

Paul places the rapture just *before* the day of the Lord and *after* the revealing of the Antichrist. That timing, of course, places the rapture sometime after the abomination of desolation. Even using the pretribulationist's timing, 2 Thessalonians 2 still places the rapture within the tribulation period! How far beyond the abomination of desolation the rapture happens will come into sharp focus as we continue. I will not predict a date for the rapture, since the Bible is clear that setting the date is impossible. I will merely show through the Bible where the rapture fits in the chronological sequence of end-time events.

CHAPTER 8

Matthew 24:1–28
Birth Pangs and
Hard Labor

As we enter into this study of Matthew, please keep in mind that both the pretrib and Pre-Wrath rapture positions teach that we will be raptured before God begins His end-time judgments. As shown in this chapter, the Pre-Wrath rapture claims that God will not begin His judgments until *after* He cuts short the great tribulation for the sake of the elect; therefore, the rapture does not have to happen before the peace treaty.

Is Matthew 24 Written to Israel or the Church?

Within Daniel's seventieth week, there will be saved Jews and Gentiles as well as lost Jews and Gentiles. This section discusses who Christ addressed in Matthew 24:1–28. Matthew 23:37–39 is often quoted in an attempt to prove that the prophecies of Matthew 24 are only related to the nation of Israel.

> [37] "O Jerusalem, Jerusalem, who kills the prophets and stones those who are sent to her! How often I wanted to gather your children together, the way a hen gathers her chicks under her wings, and you were unwilling.

³⁸ "Behold, your house is being left to you desolate!
³⁹ "For I say to you, from now on you shall not see Me until you say, 'Blessed is He who comes in the name of the Lord!'"
(Matthew 23:37–39)

It is true that in Matthew 23:37–39, Jesus spoke to the unbelieving Jews of Israel, not the church. Jesus wanted to gather the children of Israel, but Israel's leaders would not let Him. However, in Matthew 24:1, we see a turning point.

¹ And Jesus came out from the temple and was going away when His disciples came up to point out the temple buildings to Him.
² And He answered and said to them, "Do you not see all these things? Truly I say to you, not one stone here shall be left upon another, which will not be torn down."
³ And as He was sitting on the Mount of Olives, the disciples came to Him privately, saying, "Tell us, when will these things be, and what will be the sign of Your coming, and of the end of the age?"
⁴ And Jesus answered and said to them,
(Matthew 24:1–4a)

Since Jesus was speaking to His disciples in Matthew 24, the church cannot be excluded as a possible fulfillment of the prophecy that follows. If the church enters into Daniel's seventieth week before the rapture, then Matthew 24:1 is the dividing line between the unfaithful people of Israel who have rejected Him and the faithful Jewish and Gentile believers in Christ.

The pretribulationist claims that there are no Bible passages that show the church within the tribulation period. Here is an example from John Walvoord in which he claims that the saints in the tribulation period are not equivalent to the saints of today.

The Scriptures teach plainly, however, that in sharp contrast to the general tribulation, which all may expect, there is in prospect a future period of unprecedented tribulation that will overshadow and be distinct from all previous times of trouble. This future time of trouble, according to Scripture, will concern three classes of people: (1) the nation of Israel, (2) the pagan Gentile world,

(3) the saints or elect who will live in that time of trouble. It is of utmost significance that every Scripture describing the participants in this future tribulation period refers to Israelites as Israelites, Gentiles as Gentiles, and the saints as saints without ever once using any of the distinctive terms that apply to believers in this present age.[56]

Yes, saints are called saints in Matthew 24. However, we will see that these saints within the great tribulation are Christians in the same sense as "Christian" is defined in this present age of the church.

The Disciples' Question

And as He was sitting on the Mount of Olives, the disciples came to Him privately, saying, "Tell us, when will these things be, and what will be the sign of Your coming, and of the end of the age?" (Matthew 24:3)

Before answering the disciples' question, Jesus explained the events that will happen before the sign of Christ's coming and the end of the age. We will discuss the Lord's answer to the disciples' question in the next chapter.

Birth Pangs and Hard Labor

The Pre-Wrath rapture teaches that God will begin His end-time judgments significantly beyond the abomination of desolation. Pretribulationists would not agree, of course, since they claim that the events of Matthew 24:4–8 are the active judgments of God in the first half of the tribulation period. Let's examine these verses.

4 And Jesus answered and said to them, "See to it that no one misleads you.
5 "For many will come in My name, saying, 'I am the Christ,' and will mislead many.
6 "And you will be hearing of wars and rumors of wars; see that you are not frightened, for those things must take place, but that is not yet the end.
7 "For nation will rise against nation, and kingdom against kingdom, and in various places there will be famines and earthquakes.

[8] "But all these things are merely the beginning of birth pangs."
(Matthew 24:4–8)

Notice that wars, rumors of wars, famines, and earthquakes are merely the beginning of birth pangs (Matthew 24:7–8). Using the metaphor of childbirth, birth pangs and hard labor must come before the end. The chart below demonstrates how they fit into the Pre-Wrath rapture timing.

BIRTH PANGS AND HARD LABOR		
Scripture	*Event*	*Timing*
Matthew 24:4-8	Birth Pangs	The first half of Daniel's seventieth week
Matthew 24:9-14	Hard Labor	The abomination of desolation and the great tribulation
Matthew 24:29-31	Delivery	The rapture and the time for God's judgments have arrived

The pretribulationist assigns all of these events to God. However, the events from the peace treaty through the great tribulation are also consistent with the actions of Satan and evil men, independent of God. These events should not be exclusively assigned to God unless it is impossible for Satan to lead men into these actions.

Matthew 24:9–14: Hard Labor

Continuing the birth metaphor, just as the birth pang events of Matthew 24:4–8 will precede the delivery (rapture), so will the hard labor events of Matthew 24:9–14. However, in this case, the intensity dramatically increases.

[9] "Then they will deliver you to tribulation, and will kill you, and you will be hated by all nations on account of My name.
[10] "And at that time many will fall away and will deliver up one another and hate one another.
[11] "And many false prophets will arise, and will mislead many.
[12] "And because lawlessness is increased, most people's love will grow cold.

¹³ "But the one who endures to the end, he shall be saved.
¹⁴ "And this gospel of the kingdom shall be preached in the whole world for a witness to all the nations, and then the end shall come. (Matthew 24:9–14)

Matthew 24:9–14 is a summary of the events from the abomination of desolation to the end of the great tribulation (Matthew 24:15–28). The great tribulation is cut short by God to rapture the church in preparation for His end-time judgments. The claims of this paragraph will be demonstrated throughout this chapter.

According to Matthew 24:9, who will be delivered to tribulation, killed, and hated by all nations? Only those who are saved by Christ can receive this persecution "on account of My name." This cannot refer to unbelieving Israel! Am I claiming that Daniel's seventieth week has nothing to do with Israel? No; of course not. I am merely saying that Matthew 24:9 proves there are also Jewish and Gentile Christians, a living part of the church, within the great tribulation. It is for their sake that the Lord will cut short the great tribulation.

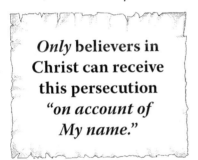

Only **believers in Christ can receive this persecution** *"on account of My name."*

Yes, there *will* be great tribulation even for the church (many Christians will even suffer martyrdom according to Revelation 6:9–11). However, that tribulation is not God's judgment. Peter explained that Christians will share in the sufferings of our Savior.

¹² Beloved, do not be surprised at the fiery ordeal among you, which comes upon you for your testing, as though some strange thing were happening to you;
¹³ but to the degree that you share the sufferings of Christ, keep on rejoicing; so that also at the revelation of His glory, you may rejoice with exultation.
(1 Peter 4:12–13)

Hard Labor Begins:
The Abomination of Desolation … Flee!

Since the abomination of desolation triggers the great tribulation, the abomination of desolation would be the transition from birth pangs to hard labor. This is where the apostasy of Israel (signing the peace treaty) and the apostasy within the church are linked. When the Jews see the abomination of desolation they will realize they have signed the covenant with death. At that point, faithful Christians will urge them to flee and assist them in their escape.

When many Jews escape, the Antichrist will also turn against Christians. Therefore, Christians in Judea must flee as well. Of course, the Antichrist will continue to pursue Christians throughout the world. This will cause the apostasy within the church. False Christians will separate themselves from true Christians in order to avoid persecution and martyrdom within the great tribulation.

> [9] "Then they will deliver you to tribulation, and will kill you, and you will be hated by all nations on account of My name.
> [10] "And at that time many will fall away and will deliver up one another and hate one another.
> (Matthew 24:9–10)

> [15] "Therefore when you see the abomination of desolation which was spoken of through Daniel the prophet, standing in the holy place (let the reader understand),
> [16] then let those who are in Judea flee to the mountains;
> [17] let him who is on the housetop not go down to get the things out that are in his house;
> [18] and let him who is in the field not turn back to get his cloak.
> [19] "But woe to those who are with child and to those who nurse babes in those days!
> [20] "But pray that your flight may not be in the winter, or on a Sabbath;
> [21] for then there will be a great tribulation, such as has not occurred since the beginning of the world until now, nor ever shall.
> (Matthew 24:15–21)

Notice the urgency. Those who are in Judea are commanded to flee as soon as they see the abomination of desolation. So critical is the urgency that they are told to bring nothing! Daniel 9:27 pinpoints the timing of the abomination of desolation.

> "And he will make a firm covenant with the many for one week, but in the middle of the week he will put a stop to sacrifice and grain offering; and on the wing of abominations will come one who makes desolate, even until a complete destruction, one that is decreed, is poured out on the one who makes desolate."
> (Daniel 9:27)

The Antichrist commits this abomination of desolation exactly half of the way through Daniel's seventieth week. Randall Price provides an excellent definition of the abomination of desolation.

> The abomination, however, is the Antichrist's act of enthroning himself in the place of deity to "display himself" (Greek, *apodeiknunta*) as God (literally, "that he is God"). This blasphemous act fulfills Daniel's prediction that the Antichrist "will exalt and magnify himself above every god and will speak monstrous things against the God of gods" (Daniel 11:36).[57]

The traditional pretribulationist holds that Matthew 24 is only focused on the people of Israel. However, Christ spoke to those who believe in Him.

> [15] "Therefore when you see the abomination of desolation which was spoken of through Daniel the prophet, standing in the holy place (let the reader understand),
> [16] then let those who are in Judea flee to the mountains;
> (Matthew 24:15–16)

Notice the separation of people: "When *you* see the abomination of desolation ... then let those who are in Judea flee." Surely the Jews will be horrified when they witness the abomination of desolation. However, non-Christian Jews would not know about the command to immediately flee, since it is unlikely they will have read the New Testament. It is only because Jewish and Gentile Christians will warn unbelieving Jews about what is coming that any of them will be prepared to flee the moment the Antichrist commits the abomination of desolation. The urgency proves that leaving *immediately* is their only hope for escape.

According to Matthew 24:15, Christians will see the abomination of desolation. This places believers in Christ at least half of the way through the tribulation period. Therefore, the rapture has not yet happened. The pretribulationist counter to this is that these believers are Jewish and Gentile converts to Christ after the rapture. Of course, there will be converts to Christ after the peace treaty. However, the pretribulationist is not able to adequately explain how they can be true Christian elect but not be part of the church. The Pre-Wrath rapture position does not have this difficulty, since the Holy Spirit does not need to end His indwelling work regardless of when the rapture happens.

Some pretribulationists have recently challenged the Pre-Wrath rapture's position with Matthew 24:20 ("But pray that your flight may not be in the winter or on a Sabbath"). Their claim is that this verse can only apply to Jews, since the church is not required to keep the Sabbath. As we have just seen, Christians will warn the Jews to flee and know that immediate escape is a mandatory action. A careful examination of the circumstances will show that Matthew 24:20 can indeed apply to Jewish and Gentile Christians.

➤ It must be remembered that this command to flee only applies to those who are in Judea. Therefore, the question regarding the application of Matthew 24:20 to the church only needs to be answered for the Christian within Israel at this time.

➤ As we discussed in chapter 7, it is possible that before the abomination of desolation, Israel will become the only safe haven for Jews, effectively creating a huge concentration camp. It would be expected that God would lead many Christians to minister to Jews in Israel, just as many in Europe were led to minister to Jews during World War II.

➤ Anyone who has been in Israel knows how difficult it is to travel on the Sabbath, even as a non-Jew. Many acts (such as driving a motor vehicle or operating an elevator) are considered to be a violation of Sabbath law from sundown Friday to sundown Saturday.

➢ Jewish believers in Christ within Israel will likely still obey the Sabbath laws for the sake of the unsaved Jew. They will also encourage their Gentile brothers to obey the Sabbath laws while they are among these unsaved Jews. This is especially true for anyone called to proclaim the gospel in Israel. Jews would never listen to anyone who enters their land and disobeys their religious laws. This is not merely my opinion; it is consistent with Paul's way.

> [19] For though I am free from all men, I have made myself a slave to all, that I might win the more.
> [20] And to the Jews I became as a Jew, that I might win Jews; to those who are under the Law, as under the Law, though not being myself under the Law, that I might win those who are under the Law;
> (1 Corinthians 9:19–20)

➢ It is likely that many Jews in Israel will turn to Christ as a result of Christians who show them the prophecies about their peace treaty with the Antichrist. Christians in Israel will surely help the Jews escape after the abomination of desolation. This escape will be far more difficult on the Sabbath.

➢ It will likely be Christians who will be used by God to prepare the place for their escape.

> "And the woman fled into the wilderness where she had a place prepared by God, so that there she might be nourished for one thousand two hundred and sixty days."
> (Revelation 12:6)

Since the Antichrist will also turn against all Christians (Matthew 24:9), Christians in Israel must flee as well. Of course, after the abomination of desolation, Christians and Jews will be pursued and persecuted throughout the world.

The Severity of the Great Tribulation

> [21] for then there will be a great tribulation, such as has not occurred since the beginning of the world until now, nor ever shall.
> [22] "And unless those days had been cut short, no life would have been saved; but for the sake of the elect those days shall be cut short.
> (Matthew 24:21–22)

Matthew 24:21–22 explains why Jesus commanded the people in Judea to flee. The great tribulation apparently begins immediately after the abomination of desolation. In the next section, we will examine what "cutting short the great tribulation for the sake of the elect" means. Here, we will address the severity of the great tribulation.

Rather than automatically assuming that the great tribulation is God's judgment, we must objectively look at the evidence to determine if this event is greater than any previous judgment the Lord has brought upon the world. If there is any judgment of God that is more severe than the great tribulation, then the testimony of Matthew 24:21 makes it impossible for the great tribulation to be part of God's end-time judgments. This is where the Noahic flood contributes to the understanding of the great tribulation. When God sent the flood upon the world, every single person died except for Noah's family of eight who entered the ark. Is the great tribulation a greater devastation than the flood? Revelation 7:9–14 states that a great uncountable multitude came *out of* the great tribulation. We will discover in chapter 13 that this great multitude is the raptured church; therefore, the great multitude came out alive!

Even without counting the great multitude, a very large number of non-believers are left on earth *after* the great tribulation is cut short (the pretribulationist agrees). Therefore, far more people who deserve God's judgment survive the great tribulation than the eight who survived the Noahic flood. How then can this be an event "such as has not occurred since the beginning of the world until now, nor ever shall" (verse 21)? This is a very difficult question to answer if the great tribulation is the judgment of God on the world, as the Noahic flood was. However, if the great tribulation represents the Antichrist's independent actions against the world, Jews, and Christians as taught by the Pre-Wrath rapture, there is no conflict, since this would still be *before* the day of the Lord begins. Therefore, it will be a greater tribulation than Satan and his followers have ever before brought upon the world, certainly greater than World War I and World War II. Renald E. Showers rejects the Pre-Wrath claim that the great tribulation is not God's judgment.

> Christ's statement in Matthew 24:21 indicated that the Great Tribulation will be the unparalleled time of trouble in all of world history. Because God's wrath is far greater than man's

wrath, if the Great Tribulation ends before God's wrath begins, then it will not involve the greatest outpouring of wrath in all of world history. If the Great Tribulation does not involve both God's wrath and man's wrath, then it cannot be the unparalleled time of trouble.[58]

Showers automatically assumes that, since Jesus said it would be "a great tribulation, such as has not occurred since the beginning of the world until now" (Matthew 24:21), it must be caused by God, since God's wrath is far stronger than wrath of Satan and his Antichrist. It is noteworthy that the Lord does not say this is "a great [judgment or wrath] such as has not occurred since the beginning of the world." Jesus told us that this will be the greatest tribulation of all time. Of course, part of the reason the pretribulationists see the great tribulation as more severe than the Pre-Wrath rapture does is because they place both the trumpet and bowl judgments within this time. The Pre-Wrath rapture claims the great tribulation is cut short for the elect *before* the trumpet and bowl judgments begin. This is based on the darkening of the sun and moon after the great tribulation is cut short (Matthew 24:29) but before the seventh seal (Revelation 6:12).

If the great tribulation is God's judgment, all of the unsaved would have to die, or it would not even begin to equal the flood, since none of the lost survived the flood. However, the great tribulation allows a very large number of the lost on earth to survive. Therefore, Jesus must have spoken about demonic and human actions, not God's judgments! Of course, we have to be very careful with the circumstantial evidence gained by merely counting the number of people killed. There must be actual evidence that this is not God's judgment—that it must be Satan's great tribulation. Therefore, let's look at the passage again, since it provides the evidence we need.

> [21] for then there will be a great tribulation, such as has not occurred since the beginning of the world until now, nor ever shall.
> [22] "And unless those days had been cut short, no life would have been saved; but for the sake of the elect those days shall be cut short.
> (Matthew 24:21–22)

Notice that instead of carrying out the greatest act of judgment against the world, God will *limit* the effect of the great tribulation!

Some pretribulationists recognize that God limits the effect of the great tribulation. The solution they offer is that Matthew 24:22 means it would be greater than the flood if God was not going to cut it short. This is not consistent with what the verses say. Jesus stated that this "will be a great tribulation, such as has not occurred since the beginning of the world until now, nor ever shall." The Lord stated this, knowing that He would cut short the great tribulation. The fact that God shortens and limits the effect of the great tribulation for the sake of the elect rejects any conclusion that claims the great tribulation is God's end-times judgment.

The Great Tribulation Is Cut Short

The pretrib and Pre-Wrath rapture positions accept the events of Matthew 24:15–22 as chronological from the abomination of desolation (Matthew 24:15) to the command to flee (Matthew 24:16–20) and then through the great tribulation until it is cut short (Matthew 24:21–22). It is also agreed that the great tribulation begins immediately after the abomination of desolation.

The pretribulationist teaches that the great tribulation lasts three-and-a-half years from the abomination of desolation to the end of Daniel's seventieth week, and the event that causes the shortening of the great tribulation is Christ's second coming. Here are examples of this thought from John Walvoord and Arnold Fruchtenbaum. In the second quote below, Fruchtenbaum specifically responds to the Pre-Wrath rapture position.

> The entire period of three and one-half years is so awful that Christ Himself predicted that if it were not terminated by His second coming, the whole human race would be destroyed (Matt. 24:22).[59]

> God will bring the period of persecution to a stop. What is being "shortened" is the persecution period, so as to allow the Jews to survive. But how long is this period of Jewish persecution to last? Is it only 21 months? Is it only one quarter: the third quarter of the last seven years? On the contrary, the period of persecution of the Jews, which is the context of Matthew 24:15–22 and Mark 13:14–20, is exactly three-and-one-half years, the second half of the seven years. This is twice stated in Daniel (9:27; 12:5–7), and it is Daniel who gave the beginning point of the persecution

as being the abomination of desolation. It is this very point that Jesus picked up (Matt. 24:15; Mark 13:14) and gave as a sign for the Jews to flee the land. The book of Revelation also gives the timing of Jewish persecution as being three-and-one-half years (12:6, 13–14), even specifying that it will be exactly 1260 days.[60]

By the way, Fruchtenbaum's claim that we teach the great tribulation is cut short in the third quarter of the last seven years is merely a common pretribulationist misunderstanding of the Pre-Wrath rapture. Pretribulationists draw this false conclusion from the many charts of Daniel's seventieth week found in Marvin Rosenthal's *The Pre-Wrath Rapture of the Church*. The Pre-Wrath rapture position agrees with the pretrib rapture that we cannot calculate when the rapture will happen. The pretribulationist's misunderstanding is demonstrated, explained, and resolved in chapter 12 subchapter "Is the Fifth Seal the Judgment of God?" I include an image of the chart found on page 112 of Rosenthal's book in that section.

The pretribulationist claims that if there are any Christians on earth within the great tribulation, they must have turned to Christ after the peace treaty, since the church has already been raptured. Part of the confusion is caused by the pretribulationist's assumption that the great tribulation covers the full second half of the tribulation period. This will be discussed later in this chapter.

It is noteworthy that if the great tribulation is God's judgment, He will not cut it short. Once God begins His end-time judgments, He will bring them to completion. In Matthew 24:22, God intervenes to limit the length and effect of the great tribulation. Do not take lightly Christ's prophecy. The fact that the great tribulation is cut short by God stands as a testimony that the great tribulation is not God's judgment! God will do just the opposite of what the pretribulationist claims. He will intervene to terminate the plans of the Antichrist against the Lord's chosen people. Showers claims that God determined beforehand to cut the great tribulation short at three-and-a-half years rather than let it last indefinitely.

> In light of what has been seen, one can conclude that in eternity past God shortened the Great Tribulation in the sense that He decreed or determined to cut it off at a specific time rather than let it continue indefinitely. He sovereignly fixed a specific time

for the Great Tribulation to end—when it had run its course for three and one-half years, or for forty-two months or 1260 days. That fixed time cannot be changed.[61]

Of course, it is true that God has determined beforehand when to cut short the great tribulation. That does not in any way prove that God cuts it short after lasting three-and-a-half years. Showers has merely given the pretribulationist interpretation of when God cuts it short. If the great tribulation is cut short to rapture His elect, as the Pre-Wrath rapture claims, then the date that it is cut short cannot be calculated. It is important to note that the Pre-Wrath rapture agrees that Christ's second coming happens at Matthew 24:30; however, we will see in the next chapter that Matthew 24:30 is not the end of Daniel's seventieth week!

Daniel's Time of Distress and the Great Tribulation

At this point, you may think that I ignore Daniel's prophecy. Daniel 12 is often used by pretribulationists to claim that the great tribulation is only for Jews who are alive at that time. They also depend on this passage to prove that the great tribulation lasts three-and-a-half years. Did Daniel actually make these claims? Surprisingly, no! Daniel 12:1–7 is fully consistent with the Pre-Wrath rapture.

> [1] "Now at that time Michael, the great prince who stands guard over the sons of your people, will arise. And there will be a time of distress such as never occurred since there was a nation until that time; and at that time your people, everyone who is found written in the book, will be rescued.
> [2] "And many of those who sleep in the dust of the ground will awake, these to everlasting life, but the others to disgrace and everlasting contempt.
> [3] "And those who have insight will shine brightly like the brightness of the expanse of heaven, and those who lead the many to righteousness, like the stars forever and ever.
> [4] "But as for you, Daniel, conceal these words and seal up the book until the end of time; many will go back and forth, and knowledge will increase."
> [5] Then I, Daniel, looked and behold, two others were standing, one on this bank of the river, and the other on that bank of the river.

⁶ And one said to the man dressed in linen, who was above the waters of the river, "How long will it be until the end of these wonders?"

⁷ And I heard the man dressed in linen, who was above the waters of the river, as he raised his right hand and his left toward heaven, and swore by Him who lives forever that it would be for a time, times, and half a time; and as soon as they finish shattering the power of the holy people, all these events will be completed. (Daniel 12:1–7)

The pretribulationist appears to have missed a separation of the people into two groups. Notice that "at that time [the time of distress] your people, everyone who is found written in the book, will be rescued" (Daniel 12:1). The people rescued are composed of believers, since their names are "written in the book" (see Revelation 3:5 and 21:27). Included in this group of people written in the book are those who have died and who will awake unto everlasting life (Daniel 12:2). These resurrected believers are separated from those who receive everlasting contempt.

It is during this time of distress, that there is a rescue. The end of the great tribulation (the rescue of Daniel 12:1 and Matthew 24:21–22, 29–31) and the "end of these wonders" (Daniel 12:7) are not the same! The confusion is caused by the chapter break at Daniel 12:1. Chapter 12 looks back over the events of Daniel 11:36–45. Since Daniel 12:1 begins with "Now at that time," we must examine what Daniel referred to.

³⁶ "Then the king will do as he pleases, and he will exalt and magnify himself above every god, and will speak monstrous things against the God of gods; and he will prosper until the indignation is finished, for that which is decreed will be done.

³⁷ "And he will show no regard for the gods of his fathers or for the desire of women, nor will he show regard for any other god; for he will magnify himself above them all.

³⁸ "But instead he will honor a god of fortresses, a god whom his fathers did not know; he will honor him with gold, silver, costly stones, and treasures.

³⁹ "And he will take action against the strongest of fortresses with the help of a foreign god; he will give great honor to those who acknowledge him, and he will cause them to rule over the many, and will parcel out land for a price.

⁴⁰ "And at the end time the king of the South will collide with him, and the king of the North will storm against him with chariots, with horsemen, and with many ships; and he will enter countries, overflow them, and pass through.

⁴¹ "He will also enter the Beautiful Land, and many countries will fall; but these will be rescued out of his hand: Edom, Moab and the foremost of the sons of Ammon.

⁴² "Then he will stretch out his hand against other countries, and the land of Egypt will not escape.

⁴³ "But he will gain control over the hidden treasures of gold and silver, and over all the precious things of Egypt; and Libyans and Ethiopians will follow at his heels.

⁴⁴ "But rumors from the East and from the North will disturb him, and he will go forth with great wrath to destroy and annihilate many.

⁴⁵ 'And he will pitch the tents of his royal pavilion between the seas and the beautiful Holy Mountain; yet he will come to his end, and no one will help him.

(Daniel 11:36–45)

The pretribulationist agrees that these are the Antichrist's campaigns from the abomination of desolation (Daniel 11:36) until he meets his end (Daniel 11:45). It is "these wonders" (Daniel 12:6) during the time of distress that last three-and-a-half years. In the midst of these wonders, there is a rescue of those written in the book.

> "Now at that time Michael, the great prince who stands guard over the sons of your people, will arise. And there will be a time of distress such as never occurred since there was a nation until that time; and at that time your people, everyone who is found written in the book, will be rescued.
> (Daniel 12:1)

The Daniel 12:1 rescue is not for all of the Jews; it is only for those who are written in the book. You may wonder why only Jewish believers are mentioned in this passage. The Bible will frequently focus on one group from within the larger group of all who saved and destined for Heaven. Daniel 12:1–3 only looks at the elect from among the Jews. Revelation 6:9–11 looks at His elect who are martyred within the great tribulation. In Revelation 7:4–8 we see the 144,000 elect from the twelve tribes of Israel who receive a protective seal to remain on earth after the rapture. Finally, in

Revelation 7:9–17 we are shown the elect who are the great multitude raptured out of the great tribulation.

According to Daniel 12:4, Daniel was told more than he was allowed to write. It is likely that the inclusion of the church in this rescue was sealed up.

> But as for you, Daniel, conceal these words and seal up the book until the end of time; many will go back and forth, and knowledge will increase."
> (Daniel 12:4)

The rescue of Daniel 12:1–2 is consistent with the rapture after the great tribulation is cut short. It is also fully consistent with the great rapture passage in 1 Thessalonians.

> [13] But we do not want you to be uninformed, brethren, about those who are asleep, so that you will not grieve as do the rest who have no hope.
> [14] For if we believe that Jesus died and rose again, even so God will bring with Him those who have fallen asleep in Jesus.
> [15] For this we say to you by the word of the Lord, that we who are alive and remain until the coming of the Lord, will not precede those who have fallen asleep.
> [16] For the Lord Himself will descend from heaven with a shout, with the voice of the archangel and with the trumpet of God, and the dead in Christ will rise first.
> [17] Then we who are alive and remain will be caught up together with them in the clouds to meet the Lord in the air, and so we shall always be with the Lord.
> [18] Therefore comfort one another with these words.
> (1 Thessalonians 4:13–18)

It is true that when we look at the full "seventy weeks" of Daniel 9, the primary focus of the passage is on Israel and Jerusalem. However, as Daniel 12:1–2 shows, that does not mean that the church must be raptured before the start of the seventieth week or that the church cannot still be within a major part of Daniel's seventieth week. It merely means that Daniel understood more than he was allowed to write.

The pretribulationist will claim that this rescue and resurrection only applies to Jews and happens at the Lord's second coming at the end of the tribulation period. Contrary to what the pretribulationist claims, the rapture within Daniel's seventieth week is the only explanation for the rescue of the living who are written in the book at the same time as the resurrection of their brothers and sisters who have died (Daniel 12:1–2). What would cause me to be so sure of this? We must not base our theology on one passage; we must also examine complimentary Bible passages.

Simply returning to the testimony of Matthew 24, Acts 2, and Revelation 6 will show that Matthew 24:29–31 cannot be what the pretribulationist calls Christ's second coming. In Matthew 24:29, the sun and moon darken *after* the great tribulation is cut short. In Revelation 6:12, the sun and moon darken *before* the seventh seal is broken. In Acts 2:20, the sun and moon darken *before* the day of the Lord begins. Most pretribulationists agree that the sixth and seventh seals are broken *before* the trumpet and bowl judgments. Matthew 24:29–31, of course, shows events *after* the end of the great tribulation. If Christ's appearance is the pretribulationist second coming, then they are left explaining how this happens *before* the first trumpet judgment! This fits the Pre-Wrath's rapture (and the gathering of Daniel 12:1–2), not the pretribulationist's second coming.

You may now want to ask, *If the great tribulation does not last three-and-a-half years, why are the three-and-a-half years so important to Daniel?* Satan's reign on earth through the Antichrist lasts three-and-a-half years. During that time, he will attempt to kill all Jews before the Messiah King takes His throne on earth in the millennial kingdom. These Jews have not yet recognized Jesus as their Messiah. Of course, this also explains why God cuts short the great tribulation for the sake of the elect Christians. Up to that mement, Satan will also use the Antichrist to pursue all Christians.

It is noteworthy that in Daniel 12:6, the prophet asked, "How long will it be until the end of these wonders?" Referring back to Daniel 11:36–12:3, "these wonders" would include:

➢ Daniel 11:36–37—the abomination of desolation and the start of the last 3½ years of Daniel's seventieth week.

➢ Daniel 12:1—a 3½ year time of distress begins *after* the abomination of desolation.

➢ Daniel 12:1—*before* the end of the full three-and-a-half years, the elect written in the book are rescued (this is the rapture of those alive on earth).

➢ Daniel 12:2—a raising to life everlasting for the elect who have died, including those who died within Daniel's seventieth week.

➢ Daniel 12:2—after the rescue and resurrection happens for those written in the book, judgment comes for those not written in the book.

➢ Daniel 12:3—rewards in heaven for those rescued.

➢ Daniel 11:38–45—continuation of the last three-and-a-half years of Daniel's seventieth week.

➢ Daniel 12:6–7—the completion of these wonders will be three-and-a-half years after the abomination of desolation.

This sequence is consistent with the Pre-Wrath rapture position. This deliverance is *after* the great tribulation is cut short, *before* the completion of the three-and-a-half years of great distress, and *before* the end of Daniel's seventieth week. Nowhere in the Bible does it claim that the great tribulation is stopped by Christ's coming at the end of the tribulation period. This merely happens to be the only conclusion pretribulationists can come to, since they have already decided that the rapture happens before the peace treaty. However, as we have shown repeatedly, the sequence of events from Matthew 24, Acts 2, and Revelation 6 shows that *after* the great tribulation is cut short, God will bring the church home to safety in heaven (the rapture) *before* He begins His wrath. Therefore, God cuts short the great tribulation for the elect at a time no one expects. Stanley D. Toussaint also tries to deny that "cut short" means anything other than the full three-and-a-half years.

> Here one must think theologically. If according to Acts 17:26, God has marked out the times for the nations, His sovereignty would include the length of time of the Great Tribulation. Another passage says the very day of entering God's rest has been determined (Heb. 4:7). Certainly, the shortening of the days is fixed. Who is to deny that the three-and-half years have already been amputated from what they may have been?

Certainly the world and Israel deserve more than seven years of tribulation! This shortening to seven years is an evidence of God's grace.[62]

It is true that God has set the date for cutting short the great tribulation, but God does not always tell us when He will do something. He does say how long the Antichrist's reign of terror will be after the abomination of desolation (three-and-a-half years, Daniel 11:36–45, 12:6–7), and Daniel's seventieth week has always been understood by futurists to be a literal seven years (Daniel 9:27). In that context, "cutting short the great tribulation after three-and-a-half years" is meaningless. There would be nothing to cut short, since the full three-and-a-half years are already defined as the end of Daniel's seventieth week. However, if the great tribulation is cut short for the rapture of believers before the Lord begins His judgments; it would be at a time neither we nor the Antichrist can know. This would be *before* the end of Daniel's seventieth week.

Who Are God's Elect?

"And unless those days had been cut short, no life would have been saved; but for the sake of the elect those days shall be cut short.
(Matthew 24:22)

The Greek word for God's "elect" in verse 22 *(eklektos)* refers specifically to Christians in Romans 8:33, Colossians 3:12, Titus 1:1, 1 Peter 1:1, 2 John 1:1, and 2 John 1:13. Therefore, it is appropriate to consider the possibility that the elect in Matthew 24:22 are true Christians. Understanding who the elect are in Matthew 24:22 is necessary for a proper interpretation of this verse. Jesus explained the great tribulation to the disciples in Matthew 24:9.

"Then they will deliver you to tribulation, and will kill you, and you will be hated by all nations on account of My name.
(Matthew 24:9)

It would be unreasonable to assume that those killed on account of Christ's name (Matthew 24:9) have nothing to do with the elect of the great tribulation (Matthew 24:22). There will be Christians who die within the great tribulation, and there will be Christians who will be rescued out of the great tribulation. John MacArthur agrees that the elect of Matthew 24:22 here are redeemed.

> **[Matthew] 24:22 those days had been cut short.** If the afflictions of this time were to continue, "no life would have been saved," i.e., no one would survive. But "for the sake of the elect" (so that redeemed people do not suffer more than they can bear) the time is "cut short"—i.e., held short of total destruction.[63]

In the quote below, Walvoord does not deny that there will be believers in Christ in the tribulation period (correctly referring to them as saints). However, he claims they are not the same as members of the church today.

> All agree that saints will be found in the Tribulation. Pretribulationism necessarily requires a distinction between these saints and the saints of the present age forming the church.[64]

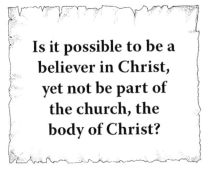

Is it possible to be a believer in Christ, yet not be part of the church, the body of Christ?

Notice that Walvoord admits his pretribulationist position requires this distinction. Since he is already convinced that the rapture will happen before the peace treaty, it is impossible for Walvoord to even consider the possibility that the church will enter into Daniel's seventieth week. Therefore, he must conclude that these saints are believers in Christ who are not part of the church! It is so difficult for Walvoord to see the church in the great tribulation that in his attempt to hold on to the pretrib rapture position, he comes to a surprising conclusion.

> It is significant that none of the truths discussed as distinctive of the church are found in the description of saints in the Tribulation. Never are tribulation saints referred to as a church or as the body of Christ or as indwelt by Christ or as subject to translation or as the bride. As the church is a distinct body with special promises and privileges, it may be expected that God will fulfill His program for the church by translating the church out of the earth before resuming His program for dealing with Israel and with the Gentiles in the period of the Tribulation.[65]

Notice that Walvoord claims the elect of Matthew 24:22 are not subject to translation (the rapture).[66] In the next chapter, we will discover that they are indeed subject to translation!

Apparently, Walvoord believes that since the church is not specifically mentioned as being within the tribulation, the church must not be on earth at this time. It is inappropriate to apply an argument from silence to the elect of Matthew 24:22. Using that same kind of argument, we would have to conclude that according to Revelation 19:7 and the surrounding verses (the marriage of the Lamb), the church cannot be present at this ceremony, since the church *(ekkleesia)* is not mentioned as being there either. If it is appropriate for Walvoord to apply the argument from silence to Matthew 24, then he must also apply the argument to Revelation 19, forcing a conclusion that the church is absent from the wedding ceremony! Of course, no one claims this.

In addition to claiming that the elect are not part of the church, Walvoord claims that the elect of Matthew 24 are not even indwelled by Christ; in spite of the fact that Walvoord correctly calls the elect of Matthew 24:22 "saints!" Matthew 24:9 says that the people in the great tribulation will be killed because of Christ's name. Where is the evidence that these whom Walvoord agrees are believers in Christ are not indwelled by Christ?

However, the pretribulationist's principal claim related to the tribulation period is that at the peace treaty, the Holy Spirit is taken out of the way. Therefore; he must make his argument based on the issue of the indwelling Holy Spirit, since he claims the Holy Spirit is taken out of the way, and His indwelling work is terminated. I will respond based on that issue.

Pretribulationists claim that the church does not enter into Daniel's seventieth week. That arbitrarily forces them to conclude that these "saints" within the tribulation period cannot be indwelled by the Holy Spirit. Walvoord admits that, "Pretribulationism necessarily requires a distinction between these saints and the saints of the present age."[67] Nowhere does the Bible allow the possibility of Christians on earth today or in the future who are not indwelled by the Holy Spirit. This is not an argument from silence, since by the time Paul wrote Romans and Ephesians, the Holy Spirit's indwelling was already recognized as the guarantee of salvation.

> However, you are not in the flesh but in the Spirit, if indeed the Spirit of God dwells in you. But if anyone does not have the Spirit of Christ, he does not belong to Him.
> (Romans 8:9)

> [13] In Him, you also, after listening to the message of truth, the gospel of your salvation—having also believed, you were sealed in Him with the Holy Spirit of promise,
> [14] who is given as a pledge of our inheritance, with a view to the redemption of God's own possession, to the praise of His glory.
> (Ephesians 1:13–14)

There is also no passage in the Bible claiming that the Holy Spirit's indwelling ministry ceases. This is merely the only conclusion the pretribulationist can come to.

Where Does Matthew 24:23–28 Fit in the Chronology?

> "And unless those days had been cut short, no life would have been saved; but for the sake of the elect those days shall be cut short.
> (Matthew 24:22)

> "But immediately after the tribulation of those days the sun will be darkened, and the moon will not give its light, and the stars will fall from the sky, and the powers of the heavens will be shaken,
> (Matthew 24:29)

Matthew 24:29 happens *immediately* after the great tribulation is cut short. The question that must now be answered is this: where in this timing do the verses *between* Matthew 24:22 and 24:29 fit?

> [23] "Then if anyone says to you, 'Behold, here is the Christ,' or 'There He is,' do not believe him.
> [24] "For false Christs and false prophets will arise and will show great signs and wonders, so as to mislead, if possible, even the elect.
> [25] "Behold, I have told you in advance.

²⁶ "If therefore they say to you, 'Behold, He is in the wilderness,' do not go forth, or, 'Behold, He is in the inner rooms,' do not believe them.
(Matthew 24:23–26)

The answer is actually quite simple. Since Matthew 24:29 happens immediately after the great tribulation is cut short, the natural understanding would be that in Matthew 24:23–26, Jesus exhorted the disciples (and through the disciples, all Christians) not to be deceived by false Christs *during* the time of the great tribulation.

You may think, *Placing Matthew 24:23–26 within the great tribulation is an arbitrary assumption for the benefit of the Pre-Wrath rapture position.* Not only is this not arbitrary, it is absolutely necessary for the pretribulationist to take this position as well! If Matthew 24:23–26 instead explains events that occur *after* the pretribulationist's second coming, then Christians would have to worry about false Christs trying to deceive them *after* the end of Daniel's seventieth week! Since no pretribulationist comes to this conclusion, pretribulationists must agree that Matthew 24:23–26 looks back to the great tribulation.

This is where Matthew 24:27–28 fits in. Once the Lord warns His children about Satan's deceit, He introduces the proof that His coming will not have happened yet. Matthew 24:27–28 also proves that everyone will see the Lord's coming. His coming will proclaim deliverance to His elect and judgment to the lost:

²⁷ "For just as the lightning comes from the east, and flashes even to the west, so shall the coming of the Son of Man be.
²⁸ "Wherever the corpse is, there the vultures will gather.
²⁹ "But immediately after the tribulation of those days the sun will be darkened, and the moon will not give its light, and the stars will fall from the sky, and the powers of the heavens will be shaken,
³⁰ and then the sign of the Son of Man will appear in the sky, and then all the tribes of the earth will mourn, and they will see the Son of Man coming on the clouds of the sky with power and great glory.
³¹ "And He will send forth His angels with A GREAT TRUMPET and THEY WILL GATHER TOGETHER His elect from the four winds, from one end of the sky to the other.
(Matthew 24:27–31)

Now we can see the link between Matthew 24:23–26 and these cosmic disturbances. While believers are within the great tribulation, false Christs will arise, claiming to be our Savior. These false Christs will be able to perform such great signs and wonders that they will appear to be true miracles from the Lord. We will know that the deceivers of Matthew 24:23–26 are not the Christ, because we have not yet witnessed the darkening of the sun and moon or seen the sign of the Son of Man appear in the sky. We can ignore all false Christs, because the real Christ will not come until *after* these events happen. Notice that this conclusion is true regardless of whether Matthew 24:29–31 is the rapture or the pretribulationist's second coming!

Conclusion

"But immediately after the tribulation of those days the sun will be darkened, and the moon will not give its light, and the stars will fall from the sky, and the powers of the heavens will be shaken,
(Matthew 24:29)

'THE SUN SHALL BE TURNED INTO DARKNESS, AND THE MOON INTO BLOOD, BEFORE THE GREAT AND GLORIOUS DAY OF THE LORD SHALL COME.
(Acts 2:20)

And I looked when He broke the sixth seal, and there was a great earthquake; and the sun became black as sackcloth made of hair, and the whole moon became like blood.
(Revelation 6:12)

Combining the events in Matthew 24:29, Acts 2:20, and Revelation 6:12 shows that the cutting short of the great tribulation happens *after* the sixth seal is broken and *before* the day of the Lord begins. Clearly, the great tribulation is *not* cut short by the pretribulationist second coming, since pretribulationists do not place their second coming before the first trumpet judgment (which comes after the seventh seal is broken).

Secondly, the great tribulation is cut short for the sake of the elect (Matthew 24:22). The elect gathered in Matthew 24:31 must be the same Christians as Matthew 24:22, since Matthew 24:29 ties them together.

"And unless those days had been cut short, no life would have been saved; but for the sake of the elect those days shall be cut short.
(Matthew 24:22)

"But immediately after the tribulation of those days the sun will be darkened, and the moon will not give its light, and the stars will fall from the sky, and the powers of the heavens will be shaken,
(Matthew 24:29)

"And He will send forth His angels with A GREAT TRUMPET and THEY WILL GATHER TOGETHER His elect from the four winds, from one end of the sky to the other.
(Matthew 24:31)

In the next chapter, the events beginning at Matthew 24:29 will come into sharp focus.

CHAPTER 9

Matthew 24:29–25:46
The Rapture

The Disciples' Question

The pretrib and Pre-Wrath rapture positions are sharply divided over the events of Matthew 24:29–31. The pretribulationist claims these verses present the Lord's second coming seven years after the rapture. The Pre-Wrath rapture claims this is actually the rapture at His second coming *before* the first trumpet judgment. In order to examine Matthew 24:29–31 in context, we need to return to the disciples' question at the beginning of the chapter.

> [1] And Jesus came out from the temple and was going away when His disciples came up to point out the temple buildings to Him.
> [2] And He answered and said to them, "Do you not see all these things? Truly I say to you, not one stone here shall be left upon another, which will not be torn down."
> [3] And as He was sitting on the Mount of Olives, the disciples came to Him privately, saying, "Tell us, when will these things be, and what will be the sign of Your coming, and of the end of the age?" (Matthew 24:1-3)

In the three related gospel passages (Matthew 24, Mark 13, and Luke 21), Jesus did not tell the disciples when the destruction of the temple would happen. This is likely because the destruction of the temple (in AD 70) is not related to the rest of the question which the Lord will answer. Before addressing the sign of Christ's coming and of the end of the age, it would be advantageous to revisit the prophetic events leading up to the fulfillment of this prophecy.

➢ Wars and rumors of wars (Matthew 24:6–7).

➢ Famine (Matthew 24:7).

➢ Earthquakes in various places (Matthew 24:7).

➢ The new temple is built (assumed from Matthew 24:15).

➢ The abomination of desolation (Matthew 24:15).

➢ Jews (and Christians) in Judea are commanded to flee to the mountains (Matthew 24:16–20).

➢ The great tribulation begins (Matthew 24:21).

➢ False Christs and false prophets arise, performing great signs and wonders (Matthew 24:5, 11, 23–26).

➢ Christ's elect are hated by all the nations (Matthew 24:9).

➢ Great apostasy arises from within the church (Matthew 24:10).

➢ Christ's elect are betrayed (Matthew 24:10).

➢ Christ's elect are martyred (Matthew 24:9, 21–22).

➢ Those who endure to the end are saved (Matthew 24:13).

➢ The gospel is preached to the whole world and then the end comes (Matthew 24:14).

➢ The great tribulation is cut short for the sake of Christ's elect (Matthew 24:22).

The above list covers the main events from the beginning of Daniel's seventieth week through the cutting short of the great tribulation. The Lord is now ready to answer the disciples' second question.

The Disciples' Question and the Sign of His Coming

Notice that the disciples asked for a sign (singular) of Christ's coming and of the end of the age. They appear to understand that there is a direct relationship between the two events. We will see that the two aspects of this sign are so tightly linked that one cannot be separated from the other. When Christ comes, it will be the end of the age.

Matthew 24:30 provides the answer to the first half of the disciples' request for a sign. There will absolutely be no question what is happening when the sign of the Son of Man appears.

> And as He was sitting on the Mount of Olives, the disciples came to Him privately, saying, "Tell us, when will these things be, and what will be the *sign* of Your coming, and of the end of the age?" (Matthew 24:3, emphasis added)

> and then the sign of the Son of Man will appear in the sky, and then all the tribes of the earth will mourn, and they will see the Son of Man coming on the clouds of the sky with power and great glory.
> (Matthew 24:30)

The Disciples' Question and the Sign of the End of the Age

Just as the sign of Christ's coming is an absolutely unique event that has never happened before, so is the sign of the end of the age.

> [29] "But immediately after the tribulation of those days the sun will be darkened, and the moon will not give its light, and the stars will fall from the sky, and the powers of the heavens will be shaken,
> [30] and then the sign of the Son of Man will appear in the sky, and then all the tribes of the earth will mourn, and they will see the Son of Man coming on the clouds of the sky with power and great glory.
> [31] "And He will send forth His angels with a great trumpet and they will gather together His elect from the four winds, from one end of the sky to the other.
> (Matthew 24:29–31)

Immediately after the great tribulation is cut short, the sun and moon darken, and the sign of the Son of Man appears. Notice that, as we would expect from Matthew 24:3, this is not two signs, since the two events are directly linked. The sun and moon darken in order for the whole world to see the sign of the Son of Man appear in the sky!

It would be very difficult to apply "the end of the age" (Matthew 24:3) to the end of the pretribulationist's tribulation period, since the sun and mood darken *before* the seventh seal is broken (Revelation 6:12). It is also hard to claim "the end of the age" is the end of the pretribulationists' church age, since *their* church age ends before the tribulation period begins. However, the Pre-Wrath rapture's church age fits this sequence, since it ends when the great tribulation is cut short for the rapture. Immediately after the great tribulation is cut short, the sun and moon darken (the sign of the end of the age), and the sign of the Son of Man appears in the sky (the sign of Christ's coming). After the sign of His coming and the end of the age, we will see the Son of Man come on clouds, and He will then send forth His angels to gather His elect.

The Rapture or the Pretribulationist's Second Coming?

In this chapter, I will frequently compare the rapture to the second coming in order to show that many of the verses claimed to teach about the pretribulationist's second coming actually present the rapture. Since pretribulationists separate the rapture from the second coming, their separation has resulted in inadvertently hiding the truth of what the Scriptures teach. As we examine these passages, keep in mind that the Pre-Wrath rapture teaches that there is one second coming in which the rapture is the first event *after* Christ's appearing. He then remains to oversee the trumpet and bowl judgments.

According to the pretribulationist, after the rapture, Christ will return to heaven with His church and will not return again to earth until He gathers His armies at the end of the tribulation period. Of course, the pretribulationist claims that only His return seven years after the peace treaty would be "the second coming of Christ."

Many specifically claim that this would not be two comings, since the Lord does not touch ground at the rapture. However, there are two separate and distinct comings to earth according to the pretrib rapture, they merely have different functions. The events have a separate time relative to Daniel's seventieth week, a separate purpose, a separate final destination, and a separate result. In both the pretribulationist's rapture and second coming, Christ leaves heaven and comes to earth. Claiming that the rapture does not count as their second coming does not match the Scriptures. First Thessalonians 4:15–17 and 2 Thessalonians 2:1 state that the rapture happens at the coming of the Lord.

> [15] For this we say to you by the word of the Lord, that we who are alive and remain until the coming of the Lord, will not precede those who have fallen asleep.
> [16] For the Lord Himself will descend from heaven with a shout, with the voice of the archangel and with the trumpet of God, and the dead in Christ will rise first.
> [17] Then we who are alive and remain will be caught up together with them in the clouds to meet the Lord in the air, and so we shall always be with the Lord.
> (1 Thessalonians 4:15–17)

> Now we request you, brethren, with regard to the coming of our Lord Jesus Christ, and our gathering together to Him,
> (2 Thessalonians 2:1)

Either pretribulationists must agree with the Pre-Wrath rapture that the Lord's coming occurs at the rapture, or they must agree that they teach two comings. The pretribulationists cannot claim that their rapture does not count as His coming.

Some pretribulationists may claim that the Pre-Wrath rapture position also has two comings. This claim stems from the fact that the Lord takes the church to heaven before He begins His day of the Lord judgments. When the Pre-Wrath rapture is compared to the pretrib rapture, it becomes clear that the two conditions are not even remotely equivalent. With the Pre-Wrath rapture, Christ takes the raptured church to heaven for the wedding ceremony and wedding feast. Then He personally oversees the trumpet and bowl judgments. This is very much like a general in the army gathering innocent civilians from a warzone, escorting them to safety, and then immediately thereafter returning to the warzone to lead the battle against the enemy. His protecting the innocent is part of his duties as the general in the midst of war. Let's look at Matthew 24:29–31 again.

> [29] "But immediately after the tribulation of those days the sun will be darkened, and the moon will not give its light, and the stars will fall from the sky, and the powers of the heavens will be shaken,
> [30] and then the sign of the Son of Man will appear in the sky, and then all the tribes of the earth will mourn, and they will see the Son of Man coming on the clouds of the sky with power and great glory.
> [31] "And He will send forth His angels with a great trumpet and they will gather together His elect from the four winds, from one end of the sky to the other.
> (Matthew 24:29–31)

Most pretribulationist's claim the language does not allow it to be interpreted as the rapture, since all of the events occur in the sky, not on earth. Therefore, they claim that it teaches about Christ coming at the end of the tribulation period with the raptured church. There are many reasons to reject the conclusion.

➢ When one examines Matthew 24:31 as if from the eyes of the Christian being raptured, it is understandable why most will not be focused on the earth, since our eyes will be drawn to the sky:

❖ We will see the sun and moon darken (Matthew 24:29).

❖ We will see the sign of the Son of Man appear in the sky (Matthew 24:30).

❖ We will see the Son of Man coming on the clouds with power and great glory (Matthew 24:30).

❖ We will see Christ's angels sent forth with a great trumpet to gather His elect (Matthew 24:31).

❖ We will see the dead in Christ rise up from their graves (1 Thessalonians 4:16).

❖ We will rise with them to meet the Lord in the air (Matthew 24:31).

❖ As we rise up to meet the Lord in the air from the four winds, it would appear to us to be from one end of the sky to the other, since the sky will be filled with raptured saints!

> Every other instance of this Greek word for wind *(anemoon)* in the New Testament specifically refers to wind in the atmosphere; therefore, this gathering from the four winds is a gathering of the elect from earth. The pretribulationist's second coming does not gather Christians from earth to meet Christ in the air.

> We will cover the companion verses Mark 13:24–27 and Luke 21:25–28 in a few pages. They clearly show that the saints are gathered from earth. If this is the pretribulationist's second coming, it would require those who became believers in Christ within the tribulation period to be gathered from earth and then immediately returned to earth without going to heaven.

> Finally, the timing of the events in Matthew 24 and Revelation 6 makes it absolutely impossible for this to be the pretribulationist's second coming. The gathering of the elect in Matthew 24:31 is right after the darkening of the sun and the moon. In Revelation, this darkening event is placed *before* the first trumpet judgment. If Matthew 24:31 is the pretribulationists' second coming, then their second coming of Christ would have to happen shortly *before* the first trumpet judgment!

The pretribulationist believes that the rapture is invisible to the unbelieving world. That is the reason the pretribulationist cannot see

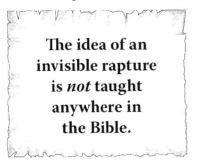

The idea of an invisible rapture is *not* taught anywhere in the Bible.

Matthew 24:29–31 as the rapture. The idea of an invisible rapture is not taught anywhere in the Bible; the Bible merely teaches that the events from the cutting short of the great tribulation to the gathering of the elect covers a very short amount of time. Everyone will see these events. In fact, seeing the Lord rapture His church will be another visible sign to the world that God is preparing to judge them. Revelation 1:7 says that every eye will see Christ come.

> Behold, He is coming with the clouds, and every eye will see Him, even those who pierced Him; and all the tribes of the earth will mourn over Him. Even so. Amen.
> (Revelation 1:7)

In Matthew 24:29–30, the darkening of the sun and moon and the sign of the Son of Man cause the tribes of the earth to mourn. This is consistent with Revelation 1:7 and it also matches the sixth seal.

> [29] "But immediately after the tribulation of those days the sun will be darkened, and the moon will not give its light, and the stars will fall from the sky, and the powers of the heavens will be shaken,
> [30] and then the sign of the Son of Man will appear in the sky, and then all the tribes of the earth will mourn, and they will see the Son of Man coming on the clouds of the sky with power and great glory.
> (Matthew 24:29–30)

> [12] And I looked when He broke the sixth seal, and there was a great earthquake; and the sun became black as sackcloth made of hair, and the whole moon became like blood;
> [13] and the stars of the sky fell to the earth, as a fig tree casts its unripe figs when shaken by a great wind.
> [14] And the sky was split apart like a scroll when it is rolled up; and every mountain and island were moved out of their places.
> [15] And the kings of the earth and the great men and the commanders and the rich and the strong and every slave and free man, hid themselves in the caves and among the rocks of the mountains;
> [16] and they said to the mountains and to the rocks, "Fall on us and hide us from the presence of Him who sits on the throne, and from the wrath of the Lamb;
> [17] for the great day of their wrath has come; and who is able to stand?"
> (Revelation 6:12–17)

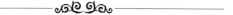

Now let's look at the parallel passages in Mark 13 and Luke 21. These passages contribute much to the conclusion that Matthew 24:31 is the rapture, not the pretribulationist's second coming of Christ.

> [24] "But in those days, after that tribulation, the sun will be darkened, and the moon will not give its light,
> [25] and the stars will be falling from heaven, and the powers that are in the heavens will be shaken.

26 "And then they will see the Son of Man coming in clouds with great power and glory.
27 "And then He will send forth the angels, and will gather together His elect from the four winds, from the farthest end of the earth, to the farthest end of heaven.
(Mark 13:24–27)

Take note of the phrase "He ... will gather together His elect *from* the four winds, *from* the farthest end of the earth, *to* the farthest end of heaven" (Mark 13:27, emphasis added). That has nothing to do with the pretribulationist's second coming. It also does not match John Walvoord's interpretation of this verse.

Mark indicated that the gathering of the elect will not simply be from earth but also from heaven, "*from* the ends of the earth *to* the ends of the heavens" (Mark 13:27).[68] (Emphasis added.)

Even as Walvoord quoted the verse ("*from* the ends of the earth *to* the ends of the heavens" [emphasis added]), it is clear that Mark 13:27 does not say the elect will be gathered from heaven, as Walvoord interprets the passage. The order does not even match. Pretribulationist's believe that, at Christ's coming, He first gathers His elect from heaven and transports these believers to earth and then remains on earth for the millennial kingdom. Mark 13:24–27 cannot be interpreted as the pretribulationist's second coming; however, it is an excellent depiction of the rapture.

25 "And there will be signs in sun and moon and stars, and upon the earth dismay among nations, in perplexity at the roaring of the sea and the waves,
26 men fainting from fear and the expectation of the things which are coming upon the world; for the powers of the heavens will be shaken.
27 "And then they will see the Son of Man coming in a cloud with power and great glory.
28 "But when these things begin to take place, straighten up and lift up your heads, because your redemption is drawing near.
(Luke 21:25–28)

Notice that these events are specifically related to redemption, since Luke 21:28 tells us to "straighten up and lift up your heads, because your redemption is drawing near." Once again, this cannot be speaking about the pretribulationist's second coming, since it occurs before the seventh seal, not after the trumpet and bowl judgments. This passage speaks about the rapture. At the pretribulationist's second coming, any new Christians on earth will see Christ come to earth. There would be no need for them to meet Him in the air unless one believes in a second rapture! John MacArthur agrees that this is the redemption of true believers in Christ.

> [**Luke**] **21:28 lift up your heads.** The dreadful tribulations and signs that mark the last days are a cause of great expectation, joy, and triumph for the true believer. **redemption**. I.e., the final fullness of the redemption, when the redeemed are reunited with Christ forever.[69]

Finally, consistent with Matthew 24, Daniel 12 also agrees with the Pre-Wrath rapture.

> [1] "Now at that time Michael, the great prince who stands guard over the sons of your people, will arise. And there will be a *time of distress* such as never occurred since there was a nation until that time; and at that time *your people*, everyone who is *found written in the book*, will be *rescued*.
> [2] "And many of *those who sleep* in the dust of the ground will *awake, these to everlasting life*, but the others to disgrace and everlasting contempt.
> (Daniel 12:1–2, emphasis added)

Can this be anything other than the rapture? At the time of great distress, those found written in the book will be rescued, and those who have died will be raised to everlasting life!

Matthew 24:29–51: The Coming Rapture

[29] "But immediately after the tribulation of those days the sun will be darkened, and the moon will not give its light, and the stars will fall from the sky, and the powers of the heavens will be shaken,

[30] and then the sign of the Son of Man will appear in the sky, and then all the tribes of the earth will mourn, and they will see the Son of Man coming on the clouds of the sky with power and great glory.

³¹ "And He will send forth His angels with a great trumpet and they will gather together His elect from the four winds, from one end of the sky to the other.
(Matthew 24:29–31)

If Matthew 24:29–31 is the pretribulationist's second coming, it would be reasonable to expect that the verses following it would only speak of events related to a second coming at the end of Daniel's seventieth week and of the Lord's establishment of His millennial kingdom. However, if Matthew 24:29–31 is much earlier in the sequence of events (in other words, at the time of the rapture, as claimed by the Pre-Wrath rapture), we would expect the verses after Matthew 24:29–31 to progressively speak of events related to the rapture, then the wedding ceremony between Christ and His church, and then Christ's final judgment of the lost. The parables and illustrations found in Matthew 24:32–25:46 should clearly support the pretrib rapture and reject the Pre-Wrath rapture, or they should support the Pre-Wrath rapture and reject the pretrib rapture. The Pre-Wrath rapture position claims that the events of Matthew 24:29–25:46 are chronological. That conclusion will unfold as we progress through this chapter.

³² "Now learn the parable from the fig tree: when its branch has already become tender, and puts forth its leaves, you know that summer is near;
³³ even so you too, when you see all these things, recognize that He is near, right at the door.
³⁴ "Truly I say to you, this generation will not pass away until all these things take place.
³⁵ "Heaven and earth will pass away, but My words shall not pass away.
(Matthew 24:32–35)

If we only look at these verses, they could be applied to either the last moments before the rapture or the last moments before the pretribulationist's second coming. However, the next verse helps differentiate the two positions.

"But of that day and hour no one knows, not even the angels of heaven, nor the Son, but the Father alone.
(Matthew 24:36)

Matthew 24:36 is used by pretribulationists to prove that we cannot date the rapture, a conclusion I agree with. However, Matthew 24:36 says, "But, of *that* day and hour no one knows." Matthew 24:36 specifically refers to Matthew 24:32–35. Either both Matthew 24:32–35 and Matthew 24:36 refer to the rapture or both refer to the pretribulationist's second coming.

As the pretribulationist correctly states, we do not know when Christ will rapture His people, but we know that three-and-a-half years after the abomination of desolation, Daniel's seventieth week will end! Verse 36 must teach about the rapture. We are left with only one possible conclusion: since verse 36 refers to the previous passage, Matthew 24:32–35 must refer to the rapture as well. Let's continue in our study of Matthew 24. Verse 36 will be included again, since verse 37 refers to it.

> [36] "But of that day and hour no one knows, not even the angels of heaven, nor the Son, but the Father alone.
> [37] "For the coming of the Son of Man will be just like the days of Noah.
> [38] "For as in those days which were before the flood they were eating and drinking, they were marrying and giving in marriage, until the day that Noah entered the ark,
> [39] and they did not understand until the flood came and took them all away; so shall the coming of the Son of Man be.
> (Matthew 24:36–39)

Noah and his family were lifted up by the flood (protected from God's judgment) while God judged the people who remained on earth. In like manner, we will be lifted up by Christ (raptured) while He judges the remaining people on earth. The Noahic flood is consistent with the rapture. Notice that the "for" at the start of verse 37 is in response to verse 36; therefore, the coming of the Son of Man (verse 37) must be related to the rapture (verse 36), not the pretribulationist's second coming. We can calculate when the end of Daniel's seventieth week is; however, no one knows the day or hour of His coming to rapture the church.

The next passage (Matthew 24:40–41) could be applied to the separation of the sheep from the goats at the end of Daniel's seventieth week, or it could be applied to the separation of Christians from non-Christians at the rapture. Therefore, I will add Matthew 24:42–44 to help define the interpretation of Matthew 24:40–41.

> [40] "Then there shall be two men in the field; one will be taken, and one will be left.
> [41] "Two women will be grinding at the mill; one will be taken, and one will be left.
> (Matthew 24:40–41)

> [42] "Therefore be on the alert, for you do not know which day your Lord is coming.
> [43] "But be sure of this, that if the head of the house had known at what time of the night the thief was coming, he would have been on the alert and would not have allowed his house to be broken into.
> [44] "For this reason you be ready too; for the Son of Man is coming at an hour when you do not think He will.
> (Matthew 24:42–44)

Matthew 24:42–44 calls for the Christian to be alert, and once again, we are told that we do not know when the Lord is coming. We can calculate the end of Daniel's seventieth week, but we cannot date the rapture. Only the rapture fits here. Based on the chronological nature of Matthew 24, we must conclude that since Matthew 24:36–39 and Matthew 24:42–44 illustrate the rapture, Matthew 24:40–41 must also illustrate the rapture. This is substantiated by the fact that the "therefore" at the start of Matthew 24:42 links Matthew 24:40–41 to Matthew 24:42–44.

Walvoord claims that the next passage (Matthew 24:45–51) speaks of the second coming and not the rapture. He also claims that it speaks of the Israelite nation, not the church.

> [45] "Who then is the faithful and sensible slave whom his master put in charge of his household to give them their food at the proper time?
> [46] "Blessed is that slave whom his master finds so doing when he comes.
> [47] "Truly I say to you, that he will put him in charge of all his possessions.
> [48] "But if that evil slave says in his heart, 'My master is not coming for a long time,'

⁴⁹ and shall begin to beat his fellow slaves and eat and drink with drunkards;

⁵⁰ the master of that slave will come on a day when he does not expect him and at an hour which he does not know,

⁵¹ and shall cut him in pieces and assign him a place with the hypocrites; weeping shall be there and the gnashing of teeth. (Matthew 24:45–51)

This passage is properly interpreted as belonging to the Second Coming rather than to the church, though expositors in general are not always of one mind on this. The people in view are the Israelite nation. Of these, some are watching and are faithful, taking care of the household of God. They are contrasted to those who beat their fellow servants, and "eat and drink with drunkards" (v. 49). It is obvious that something more than mere carelessness is in view. The faithfulness of those watching is evidence of true faith in Christ, whereas the unfaithfulness of those who are drunken is indicative of failure to believe in the saving of the soul. While works are in view, they are indicative of vital faith or its lack. In any case, there is nothing whatsoever said about the Rapture, or translation of the faithful. It is doubtful whether there is any specific reference at all to the Rapture or translation in the entire context of Matthew 24–25.[70]

Walvoord recognizes that the faithful ones demonstrate true faith in Christ. Yet his pretribulationist position requires that the faithful believers can only be Israelites! There is absolutely no restriction in the passage or its context that requires the faithful to be Israelites; the passage can include any Jewish or Gentile Christian.

Of course, if there are Christians (saved after the rapture) on earth at the pretribulationists' second coming, they would be able to calculate when the Master would come. They would also warn the evil slaves about that day. However, in this passage, neither the evil slave nor the faithful slave knows when the master is coming! Since the end of Daniel's seventieth week can be calculated (three-and-a-half years after the abomination of desolation), Matthew 24:45–51 can only apply to the rapture.

Matthew 25:1–46: The Rapture and Beyond

If Matthew 24:32–51 demonstrates the rapture as the Pre-Wrath rapture claims, we would expect that at some point, the scene would move to the wedding ceremony. This is exactly what we find in Matthew 25.

> [1] "Then the kingdom of heaven will be comparable to ten virgins, who took their lamps and went out to meet the bridegroom.
> [2] "Five of them were foolish, and five were prudent.
> [3] "For when the foolish took their lamps, they took no oil with them,
> [4] but the prudent took oil in flasks along with their lamps.
> [5] "Now while the bridegroom was delaying, they all got drowsy and began to sleep.
> [6] "But at midnight there was a shout, 'Behold, the bridegroom! Come out to meet him.'
> [7] "Then all those virgins rose and trimmed their lamps.
> [8] "The foolish said to the prudent, 'Give us some of your oil, for our lamps are going out.'
> [9] "But the prudent answered, 'No, there will not be enough for us and you too; go instead to the dealers and buy some for yourselves.'
> [10] "And while they were going away to make the purchase, the bridegroom came, and those who were ready went in with him to the wedding feast; and the door was shut.
> [11] "Later the other virgins also came, saying, 'Lord, lord, open up for us.'
> [12] "But he answered, 'Truly I say to you, I do not know you.'
> [13] "Be on the alert then, for you do not know the day nor the hour. (Matthew 25:1–13)

In properly understanding this passage, it is very important to note that none of the Greek words for dinner, supper, or feast exist in Matthew 25:10. Many pretribulationists (depending on the English translations) claim that this passage speaks about events *after* the end of Daniel's seventieth week. Some even claim that the wedding occurs in heaven, and the wedding feast occurs on earth. Since "feast" is not found in the Greek manuscripts, Matthew 25:10 speaks about the wedding ceremony that happens in heaven *after* the rapture, not the pretribulationist's supposed wedding feast on earth after the end of Daniel's seventieth week.

The start of Matthew 25:1 ("Then") demonstrates that we are about to look beyond the events of Matthew 24:32–51. This step forward is at a very important point in the chronology! The parable of the ten virgins shows Christ taking the prudent virgins to the wedding ceremony. Notice that even the prudent virgins did not know it was time for the bridegroom to gather them until the moment he arrived; and when the virgins were called, there was no time left for the foolish virgins to prepare. Once again, the end of Daniel's seventieth week can be calculated; the rapture cannot be calculated. Let's look at the wedding ceremony and wedding feast in Revelation 19.

> [7] "Let us rejoice and be glad and give the glory to Him, for the marriage of the Lamb has come and His bride has made herself ready."
> [8] And it was given to her to clothe herself in fine linen, bright and clean; for the fine linen is the righteous acts of the saints.
> [9] And he said to me, "Write, 'Blessed are those who are invited to the marriage supper of the Lamb.'" And he said to me, "These are true words of God."
> [10] And I fell at his feet to worship him. And he said to me, "Do not do that; I am a fellow servant of yours and your brethren who hold the testimony of Jesus; worship God. For the testimony of Jesus is the spirit of prophecy."
> [11] And I saw heaven opened; and behold, a white horse, and He who sat upon it is called Faithful and True; and in righteousness He judges and wages war.
> (Revelation 19:7–11)

According to the order in Revelation 19, the wedding ceremony comes first, then the wedding feast ("marriage supper" in the NASB), and *after* that, Christ mounts a white horse to judge and wage war against the Antichrist and his followers. Therefore, even the wedding feast must happen in heaven *before* the pretribulationist's second coming, not on earth after the second coming! This eliminates any possibility that Matthew wrote about a wedding feast on earth. Secondly, the idea of the wedding feast being postponed for seven years after the pretribulationist's rapture is also not taught anywhere in the Bible.

Walvoord is one pretribulationist who understands that the parable of the ten virgins cannot present events related to his second coming. However, since he adheres to the pretrib rapture position, Walvoord is left with no choice but to exclude this passage from being a representation of the true church.

> The church is ordinarily the bride, and in a figure of a wedding feast it would be incongruous to conceive of the church as represented by maidens attending the feast. The passage itself uses none of the characteristic terms relating to the church, such as bride, body, or the expression in Christ. There is no reference whatever to translation or resurrection. The bridegroom comes to the place where the virgins are waiting in an earthly scene and remains in that earthly scene as far as the figure is concerned. These and many other observations point to excluding this passage from consideration.[71]

The wedding and wedding feast between Christ and His bride are only open to those who are already part of the church. Only those who have been prepared and kept for the Bridegroom will be gathered to Him. Therefore, the gathering of these virgins can only represent the rapture in this parable.

Walvoord's claim that "The bridegroom comes to the place where the virgins are waiting in an earthly scene and remains in that earthly scene as far as the figure is concerned"[72] is not a good representation of the passage. Matthew 25:10 does not say that the bridegroom stayed where the virgins were. The virgins went in with the bridegroom to the wedding, and then the door was shut. From this perspective, this event fits the rapture perfectly. Christ comes to earth, gathers His church in the rapture, and takes the raptured saints to a place where the lost have no access (heaven).

It is true that the parable is insufficient to develop a theology of the rapture. However, the same argument can be applied to all of the illustrations and parables in Matthew 24–25. Walvoord wants to reject this passage, because it does not use terms such as *body, translation,* or *resurrection.* The purpose of Matthew 24:32–25:36 is to illustrate what the time will be like. These verses are not intended to be exhaustive doctrinal teaching on end-time events. We turn to other verses (such as 1 Thessalonians 5:1–11) for doctrinal teaching. If Walvoord attempts to use the other parables and illustrations before this one to prove his position on the end times, he cannot exclude this one.

The pretribulationist has no choice but to claim that Matthew 25:1–13 does not apply to the verses around it. If it does apply, then Matthew 25:1–13 rejects pretribulationist's second coming! This is why the first verse of Matthew 25 is so important. After the Lord presented parables and illustrations in Matthew 24:32–25 teaching about the coming rapture, Matthew 25:1 states: "*Then* the kingdom of heaven will be comparable to ten virgins" (emphasis added). This passage is directly related to the parables and illustrations before it.

Significantly, Matthew 25:1–13 shows the prudent virgins who were ready for the bridegroom. These virgins went in with him to the wedding ceremony. Let's look at the wedding and wedding feast in Revelation again.

> ⁷ "Let us rejoice and be glad and give the glory to Him, for the marriage of the Lamb has come and His bride has made herself ready."
> ⁸ It was given to her to clothe herself in fine linen, bright and clean; for the fine linen is the righteous acts of the saints.
> ⁹ Then he said to me, "Write, 'Blessed are those who are invited to the marriage supper of the Lamb.'"
> (Revelation 19:7–9)

According to Revelation 19, the bride made herself ready for the marriage with the Lamb. This is quite consistent with the parable of the ten virgins. Since Matthew 25:1–13 can only speak of the rapture and the wedding, its location at this point in Matthew 24–25 is extremely important! Through Matthew 25:13, all of the illustrations and parables present the rapture, not the pretribulationist's second coming. The next event in Matthew 25 is the parable of the talents.

> ¹⁴ "For it is just like a man about to go on a journey, who called his own slaves and entrusted his possessions to them.
> ¹⁵ "To one he gave five talents, to another, two, and to another, one, each according to his own ability; and he went on his journey.
> ¹⁶ "Immediately the one who had received the five talents went and traded with them, and gained five more talents.
> ¹⁷ "In the same manner the one who had received the two talents gained two more.
> ¹⁸ "But he who received the one talent went away, and dug a hole in the ground and hid his master's money.

¹⁹ "Now after a long time the master of those slaves came and settled accounts with them.

²⁰ "The one who had received the five talents came up and brought five more talents, saying, 'Master, you entrusted five talents to me. See, I have gained five more talents.'

²¹ "His master said to him, 'Well done, good and faithful slave. You were faithful with a few things, I will put you in charge of many things; enter into the joy of your master.'

²² "Also the one who had received the two talents came up and said, 'Master, you entrusted two talents to me. See, I have gained two more talents.'

²³ "His master said to him, 'Well done, good and faithful slave. You were faithful with a few things, I will put you in charge of many things; enter into the joy of your master.'

²⁴ "And the one also who had received the one talent came up and said, 'Master, I knew you to be a hard man, reaping where you did not sow and gathering where you scattered no seed.

²⁵ 'And I was afraid, and went away and hid your talent in the ground. See, you have what is yours.'

²⁶ "But his master answered and said to him, 'You wicked, lazy slave, you knew that I reap where I did not sow and gather where I scattered no seed.

²⁷ 'Then you ought to have put my money in the bank, and on my arrival I would have received my money back with interest.

²⁸ 'Therefore take away the talent from him, and give it to the one who has the ten talents.'

²⁹ "For to everyone who has, more shall be given, and he will have an abundance; but from the one who does not have, even what he does have shall be taken away.

³⁰ "Throw out the worthless slave into the outer darkness; in that place there will be weeping and gnashing of teeth.
(Matthew 25:14–30)

We have already seen in 2 Thessalonians 2 that the Holy Spirit does not vacate the earth when the Antichrist is revealed, even if the restrainer is the Holy Spirit. Therefore, during the portion of Daniel's seventieth week *after* the rapture, it is reasonable to expect the possibility that many more Jews and Gentiles will come to faith in Christ and will live faithfully in His name, in spite of massive persecution. The parable of the talents explains how Christ will judge the faithful and the unfaithful on earth before the millennial kingdom begins. In the next illustration, Christ explained the separation between the faithful and the unfaithful. The faithful join Christ in the millennial kingdom, and the unfaithful are sent to eternal punishment.

> [31] "But when the Son of Man comes in His glory, and all the angels with Him, then He will sit on His glorious throne.
>
> [32] "All the nations will be gathered before Him; and He will separate them from one another, as the shepherd separates the sheep from the goats;
>
> [33] and He will put the sheep on His right, and the goats on the left.
>
> [34] "Then the King will say to those on His right, 'Come, you who are blessed of My Father, inherit the kingdom prepared for you from the foundation of the world.
>
> [35] 'For I was hungry, and you gave Me something to eat; I was thirsty, and you gave Me something to drink; I was a stranger, and you invited Me in;
>
> [36] naked, and you clothed Me; I was sick, and you visited Me; I was in prison, and you came to Me.'
>
> [37] "Then the righteous will answer Him, 'Lord, when did we see You hungry, and feed You, or thirsty, and give You something to drink?
>
> [38] 'And when did we see You a stranger, and invite You in, or naked, and clothe You?
>
> [39] 'When did we see You sick, or in prison, and come to You?"
>
> [40] "The King will answer and say to them, 'Truly I say to you, to the extent that you did it to one of these brothers of Mine, even the least of them, you did it to Me.'
>
> [41] "Then He will also say to those on His left, 'Depart from Me, accursed ones, into the eternal fire which has been prepared for the devil and his angels;
>
> [42] for I was hungry, and you gave Me nothing to eat; I was thirsty, and you gave Me nothing to drink;
>
> [43] I was a stranger, and you did not invite Me in; naked, and you did not clothe Me; sick, and in prison, and you did not visit Me.'
>
> [44] "Then they themselves also will answer, 'Lord, when did we see You hungry, or thirsty, or a stranger, or naked, or sick, or in prison, and did not take care of You?'
>
> [45] "Then He will answer them, 'Truly I say to you, to the extent that you did not do it to one of the least of these, you did not do it to Me.'

[46] "These will go away into eternal punishment, but the righteous into eternal life."
(Matthew 25:31–46)

The chronological nature of the parables and illustrations becomes clear when we examine their verse-by-verse sequence. Since they explain the events of Matthew 24:29–31, I will include those verses in the list.

➤ The great tribulation is cut short for Christ's elect (Matthew 24:29).

➤ The sun and moon are darkened (Matthew 24:29).

➤ Stars fall from the sky (Matthew 24:29).

➤ The powers of the heavens are shaken (Matthew 24:29).

➤ The sign of the Son of Man appears in the sky (Matthew 24:30).

➤ All the tribes of the earth mourn (Matthew 24:30).

➤ The Son of Man comes on clouds, visible to all the people of the world (Matthew 24:30).

➤ The Son of Man sends forth angels with a great trumpet to gather His elect. This is the rapture (Matthew 24:31).

➤ Beginning at Matthew 24:32, what follows are illustrations and parables regarding the end-time events from just before the rapture to the beginning of the millennial kingdom (Matthew 24:32–25:46).

  ❖ The parable of the fig tree signals that the time of the rapture is near (Matthew 24:32–35).

  ❖ The flood and Noah's family illustrate the rapture (Matthew 24:36–41).

  ❖ The two servants illustrate the rapture (Matthew 24:42–51).

  ❖ The parable of the ten virgins illustrates the rapture and then the wedding ceremony in heaven between Christ and His bride (Matthew 25:1–13).

❖ The parable of the talents illustrates the faithful and unfaithful on earth from the rapture to the preview of Christ's separation of the lost from the saved on earth after the end of Daniel's seventieth week (Matthew 25:14–30).

❖ The final judgment of the lost on earth is followed by the saved being ushered into the millennial kingdom (Matthew 25:31–46).

Conclusion

As we studied in this and the previous chapter, the rapture of Matthew 24:31 happens *after* the abomination of desolation (Matthew 24:15), *after* the great tribulation is cut short (Matthew 24:22), *after* the sun and moon darken (Matthew 24:29), *after* the sign of the Son of Man appears in the sky (Matthew 24:30), and *after* the Son of Man comes "on the clouds of the sky with power and great glory" (Matthew 24:30). This sequence of events is substantiated by the verses that follow Matthew 24:31. Every event presented from Matthew 24:32 through Matthew 25:13 fits the rapture and arrival in heaven much better than the pretribulationist's second coming.

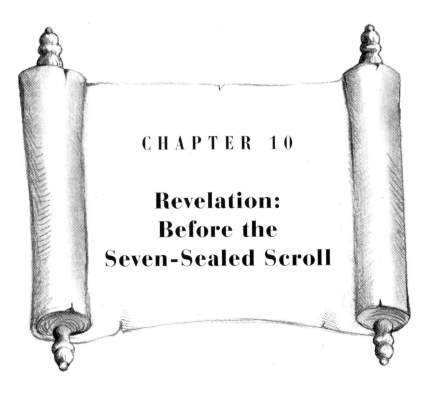

CHAPTER 10

Revelation: Before the Seven-Sealed Scroll

Studying the Revelation of Jesus Christ

With this world quickly falling into totalitarianism, we must not be caught off guard as the end times approach. Even before the peace treaty, life on earth will become so difficult that a multitude of people will cry out for a man who can unite the world in peace. As God leads us into the future, we need to be ready to glorify Him regardless of what goes on around us. That will be much easier if we allow the Lord to prepare us for the coming events.

> Blessed is he who reads and those who hear the words of the prophecy, and heed the things which are written in it; for the time is near.
> (Revelation 1:3)

The Chronological Nature of Revelation

The chronological nature of the book of Revelation is presented in the first chapter.

Write therefore the things which you have seen, and the things which are, and the things which shall take place after these things. (Revelation 1:19)

Although there are other approaches to the interpretation of Revelation (such as preterist, historicist, and idealist), the pretrib, midtrib, posttrib, and Pre-Wrath rapture positions look at the book of Revelation from the futurist perspective. The futurist insists that Revelation should be interpreted based on the following conditions:

➢ At least from the breaking of the first seal of the seven-sealed scroll (Revelation 6:1), all of the events look beyond the beginning of Daniel's seventieth week unless they are clearly events occurring previous to this time. Most futurists also teach that by the time of Revelation 4:1 the book of Revelation looks beyond today.

➢ All passages are to be interpreted as literal events unless it is unreasonable to do so.

➢ The majority of the book of Revelation is chronological in nature. Although some futurists claim that the seals, trumpets, and bowls cover the same time from different perspectives, most proponents of the pretrib and Pre-Wrath rapture positions teach that the events are strictly chronological from the seven seals to the seven trumpets to the seven bowls. The primary exceptions to this chronology from Revelation 6:1 to the end of Revelation are five future events, each lasting three-and-a-half years (Revelation 11:1–2, Revelation 11:3–10, Revelation 12:1–6, Revelation 12:13–17, and Revelation 13:1–10). It is likely that these passages cover the same time from the abomination of desolation to the end of Daniel's seventieth week.

No Mention of the Church: The Argument from Silence

Pretribulationists frequently rely on an argument from silence to prove that the rapture happens before the peace treaty. It is reasonable to use the argument from silence when the context specifically addresses the issue. However, we will see that the pretribulationist's use regarding the church is inappropriate, since the Biblical record says just the opposite of what the pretribulationist claims. We will see many events within Daniel's seventieth week that can only apply to Christians, members of the church.

The claim is that, since there is no mention of the church *(ekkleesia)* on earth during the time the seven seals are broken, the church must have already been raptured. Here is an example from John Walvoord.

> The highly significant fact stands without refutation from any post-tribulationist that the *ecclesia*, the church as the body of Christ, is never mentioned as being in the Tribulation in the major passages such as Revelation 4–8 and Matthew 24–25, and is not found in any other tribulation context. The burden of proof is not on the pretribulationists. If the church is in the Tribulation, why don't the Posttribists cite texts where ecclesia is used?[73]

I accept the challenge presented above. The burden of proof is on my shoulders to show that the church *(ekkleesia)* is on earth during Daniel's seventieth week until the church is raptured *after* the great tribulation is cut short.

The Greek word *ekkleesia* actually does not appear in Revelation from chapter 4 through chapter 21. However, it is noteworthy that the word *ekkleesia* is also not used in many of the passages that specifically define the rapture either. For instance, 1 Corinthians 15:51–58 and 1 Thessalonians 4:14–18 have no mention of *ekkleesia* either; yet the pretribulationist agrees with the Pre-Wrath rapture that they both teach about the rapture of the church.

There are many "unnamed" references to the church *after* Daniel's seventieth week has begun. For instance, at some point, the 144,000 (Revelation 7:1–8) have become Christians, since according to Revelation 14:1, they are clearly identified with Christ's name on their foreheads.

> And I looked, and behold, the Lamb was standing on Mount Zion, and with Him one hundred and forty-four thousand, having His name and the name of His Father written on their foreheads. (Revelation 14:1)

Most pretribulationists agree that the 144,000 are Jews who have become believers in Christ; even concluding that they are witnesses who proclaim the gospel. Notice that the defining statement is that they have "His name and the name of His Father written on their foreheads." It would be inconceivable to claim that the 144,000 have the name of the Son on their foreheads and yet not be saved in Christ. Nowhere are we told that the seal they received changed in its nature at a later time; therefore, it is likely that they were saved at or before Revelation 7:4.

> And I heard the number of those who were sealed, one hundred and forty-four thousand sealed from every tribe of the sons of Israel.
> (Revelation 7:4)

We should also include the fifth-seal martyrs of Revelation 6:9–11 as members of the church on earth before being slain, since they were "slain because of the word of God, and because of the testimony they had maintained" (Revelation 6:9). In heaven, they receive white robes—the robes of the redeemed. The fifth-seal martyrs will be studied in chapter 12.

Revelation 7:9–14 says there will be a great uncountable multitude that will come out of the great tribulation. Their robes were washed and made white with the blood of the Lamb. Therefore, this great multitude must be counted as part of the living church on earth *before* they arrive in heaven. The great multitude will be studied in chapter 13.

Absence of the actual word *ekkleesia* in any passage covering the events on earth during Daniel's seventieth week does not prove the church has already been raptured. If there are people on earth who are clearly believers in Christ, then the church is still on earth. Tim LaHaye and Richard Mayhue use this same argument to show that the church is in heaven.

> It is true that the Greek word for church (*ekklesia*) is not used of the church in heaven in Revelation 4–19. However, that does not mean the church is invisible. The church appears in heaven at least twice. First, the 24 elders in Revelation 4–5 symbolize the church. Second, the phrase "you saints and apostles and prophets" in Revelation 18:20 clearly refers to the church in heaven. Also,

> Revelation 19 pictures the church (the bride of Christ) in heaven prior to her triumphal return. Which rapture scenario best accounts for the church being in heaven in these texts at this time? A pretribulation rapture.[74]

I agree that the twenty-four elders at least in part represent the church (Jewish and Gentile believers in Christ). However, that does not prove that the church has already been raptured; it only proves that the church is *represented* in Heaven before the peace treaty. In fact, most pretribulationists agree that the twenty-four elders represent the church rather than being individual Christians.

I also agree with LaHaye and Mayhue that the bride of Christ will be in heaven before Revelation 18:20, since the Pre-Wrath rapture teaches that the church will be raptured between the breaking of the sixth and seventh seals. That is significantly *before* the events of Revelation 18:20.

Notice that LaHaye and Mayhue effectively claim the church is already in heaven, since individual Christians are already in heaven (Revelation 18:20). I agree with this claim also; however, the pretrib-ulationists have set their own trap. If examples of Christians in heaven after the peace treaty prove the presence of the church in heaven, then examples of Christians on earth after the peace treaty prove the presence of the church on earth! The pre-tribulationist must apply the argument equally to both earth

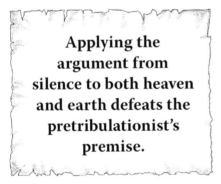

Applying the argument from silence to both heaven and earth defeats the pretribulationist's premise.

and heaven. That application, of course, defeats the pretribulation-ist's premise and shows why the argument from silence cannot be used here.

The opposite argument creates even more problems for the pretribulationist. It is true that the word church *(ekkleesia)* is not found in Matthew 24–25; however, it is not found in Revelation 4–21 either, even though many of the passages specifically focus on events in heaven! If the argument from silence proves that the church is not on earth, it also proves that the church is not in heaven. Where is the church?

──────────── ⁂ ────────────

The pretribulationist often goes far beyond merely claiming the true church does not enter into the tribulation period. Walvoord provides the following example regarding the great multitude that came out of the great tribulation.

> It is most significant that the word church is not used at all, and the saints are described simply as those who have been *saved by the blood of the Lamb* and who have come out of great trials.[75] (Emphasis added.)

Is this great multitude anything other than the church? "Saved by the blood of the Lamb"[76] is the only qualification any of us have! Walvoord also claims that the martyrs of the fifth seal are not part of the church.

> The martyrs of Revelation 6 and 7 are eloquent in their testimony; significantly there is no evidence that these martyrs are related to the church as such.[77]

> When the Lamb broke the fifth seal, I saw underneath the altar the souls of those who had been *slain because of the word of God, and because of the testimony which they had maintained;* (Revelation 6:9, emphasis added)

How can those who are "slain because of the word of God, and because of the testimony they had maintained" be denied participation in the church? I pray that I could be faithful enough in my life to have such a pure, Christ-glorifying testimony! If one merely accepts the plain biblical testimony about these martyrs and the great multitude, the pretrib rapture position crumbles.

The pretribulationist must claim that "slain because of the word of God, and because of the testimony they had maintained" (the martyrs of Revelation 6:9) and "saved by the blood of the Lamb"[78] (the great multitude of Revelation 7:9–17) are insufficient qualifications for membership in the church in order to not see these as Christians who are either slain within the great tribulation (the martyrs) or came out of the great tribulation alive (the great multitude). If they are not qualified to be part of the church, none of us are qualified!

The biblical record shows true believers in Christ on earth within the great tribulation. Therefore, there is no basis by which the pretribulationist can claim that they are not members of Christ's church. It is important to note that I do not even force the Pre-Wrath rapture conclusion into this section. I merely show that even if the pretrib rapture is true, pretribulationists cannot use the argument from silence to prove their point.

Proofs without Foundation

In the next three sections, we will look at the letters to the seven churches, John being called up to heaven, and the appearance of the twenty-four elders in heaven, since these passages supposedly prove the pretrib rapture. The pretribulationist claims that Revelation 3:10 is a promise that the church will be raptured before the tribulation period begins, that Revelation 4:1–2 represents the rapture, and that Revelation 4:4 shows the raptured church in heaven. The pretribulationist ties these passages together, since all three events appear in Revelation before the first seal of the seven-sealed scroll is broken. The purpose of the following three sections is merely to show that pretribulationists cannot use these passages to prove their timing of the rapture. I need to disprove all three of these interpretations independently, since pretribulationists use each event to support their interpretation of the other two.

Does Revelation 3:10 Prove the Pretrib Rapture?

7 "And to the angel of the church in Philadelphia write: He who is holy, who is true, who has the key of David, who opens and no one will shut, and who shuts and no one opens, says this:

8 'I know your deeds. Behold, I have put before you an open door which no one can shut, because you have a little power, and have kept My word, and have not denied My name.

9 'Behold, I will cause those of the synagogue of Satan, who say that they are Jews, and are not, but lie—behold, I will make them to come and bow down at your feet, and to know that I have loved you.

[10] Because you have kept the word of My perseverance, I also will keep you from the hour of testing, that hour which is about to come upon the whole world, to test those who dwell upon the earth. (Revelation 3:7–10)

It is likely that the seven letters to the churches of Revelation 1:4–3:22 are real letters to seven real churches existing in Asia Minor (present-day Turkey) at the time John wrote Revelation. The majority of futurists teach that the letters also have application beyond the first century, even to the time of Daniel's seventieth week. This section primarily looks at that prophetic possibility.

Pretribulationists claim that the Lord's promise to the church of Philadelphia (Revelation 3:10) proves the rapture must occur *before* the beginning of tribulation period. However, they are divided over whether the seven churches of Revelation 1:4–3:22 represent church conditions immediately before the time of the rapture, or represent progressive church conditions through the church age. Therefore, I will show how neither position proves the pretribulationist's premise. Then I will present an interpretation for these churches that is consistent with the Pre-Wrath rapture.

➢ Responses to pretribulationists who claim that the churches represent coexisting conditions just before the rapture happens:

❖ The Philadelphian church is the only one given the promise of being kept "from the hour of testing" (Revelation 3:10). If this is a promise of being raptured before the peace treaty, why are the other six "concurrently" existing churches not also promised that they will be kept from this hour of testing? Denying the same promise to the other churches can only be possible if all of the other six coexistent church types contain no Christians. The record of the churches found in Revelation 2–3 rejects that conclusion.

❖ Even the "dead" church (Sardis) has true Christians! Why would these Christians be denied the promise to be kept from the hour of testing if Revelation 3:10 represents the rapture?

> But you have a few people in Sardis who have not soiled their garments; and they will walk with Me in white; for they are worthy.
> (Revelation 3:4)

Notice that they will walk with Christ in white. The few people in Sardis who "have not soiled their garments" must be true Christians!

Conclusion: the claim that the seven churches coexist just before the tribulation period and only the Philadelphian church is raptured is rejected, since there are true Christians within the other six churches as well. The rapture would then be incomplete. Therefore, there would be true Christians who enter into Daniel's seventieth week. This is a condition that the pretribulationist claims is impossible. Therefore, claiming that the churches represent coexisting conditions just before the rapture is incompatible with pretribulationism.

➢ Responses to the pretribulationists who claim that the seven churches represent progressive conditions throughout the church age from John's writing of Revelation until the time of the pretribulationist's rapture:

❖ Although I will show below how difficult it is to claim that the seven churches represent progressive conditions throughout the church age, it should also be noted that John clearly treats these seven churches as a unit in Revelation 1:4. There is nothing from Revelation 1:1 through Revelation 3:22 that even implies a progression of church conditions.

4 John to the seven churches that are in Asia: Grace to you and peace, from Him who is and who was and who is to come; and from the seven Spirits who are before His throne; 5 and from Jesus Christ, the faithful witness, the first-born of the dead, and the ruler of the kings of the earth. To Him who loves us, and released us from our sins by His blood, (Revelation 1:4–5)

❖ We have to be very careful in applying the letters to the churches across the whole church age. That application must be consistent with history. The application of these churches to seven progressive ages is so arbitrary that expositors do not even consistently agree on the date that one church age progresses to the next.[79] Note that the vitality of one church age would not abruptly end at the start of the next church age. This makes it very difficult to define a transition point.

❖ The existence of seven progressive church ages implies that in each of the progressive stages, the stage is predominately defined by that one church's condition. This is a very hard assumption to prove. As any student of church history knows, even when the church has been its most faithful, a significant percentage of the true Christian population has been compromised in its walk. In fact, truly faithful Christians have rarely (if ever) been the majority from the time of John's writing of Revelation to the present!

❖ Of course, the pretribulationist may claim that church history merely has not reached the stage of the Philadelphian church yet. However, this potential solution creates an irresolvable problem for the pretribulationist. If the church in Philadelphia represents the church that is about to be raptured before the beginning of the tribulation period, progressive church ages would place the Laodicean church on earth *after* the peace treaty. This would be a condition in which, according to the pretrib rapture, the true church and the Holy Spirit would supposedly have already vacated the earth!

[14] "And to the angel of the church in Laodicea write: The Amen, the faithful and true Witness, the Beginning of the creation of God, says this:
[15] 'I know your deeds, that you are neither cold nor hot; I would that you were cold or hot.
[16] 'So because you are lukewarm, and neither hot nor cold, I will spit you out of My mouth.
[17] 'Because you say, "I am rich, and have become wealthy, and have need of nothing," and you do not know that you are wretched and miserable and poor and blind and naked,
[18] I advise you to buy from Me gold refined by fire, that you may become rich, and white garments, that you may clothe yourself, and that the shame of your nakedness may not be revealed; and eye salve to anoint your eyes, that you may see.
[19] 'Those whom I love, I reprove and discipline; be zealous therefore, and repent.

> ^{20} 'Behold, I stand at the door and knock; if anyone hears My voice and opens the door, I will come in to him, and will dine with him, and he with Me.
> ^{21} 'He who overcomes, I will grant to him to sit down with Me on My throne, as I also overcame and sat down with My Father on His throne.
> ^{22} 'He who has an ear, let him hear what the Spirit says to the churches.'"
> (Revelation 3:14–22)

❖ Notice that the Lord reproved the Laodicean church. Why? Because He loved them (Revelation 3:19)! He also offered blessings, encouragement, and an opportunity for repentance and true fellowship with Him. The lost cannot have true fellowship with the Savior. Who does the Lord offer this to if the true church is gone?

Combining the claim that the seven churches represent seven progressive church ages with the claim that the church in Philadelphia represents the church on earth at the time of the rapture is self-defeating. The existence of the Laodicean church would allow people to repent and turn to Christ within Daniel's seventieth week and thereby become members of the church *after* the peace treaty. If the Laodicean church has started by the time the Philadelphian church supposedly is raptured, then the Laodicean church enters into the tribulation period!

Many pretribulationists claim that the existence of the Laodicean church within the tribulation period merely identifies conditions similar to the faith Nicodemus had before Christ went to the cross. However, since they claim the Philadelphian church represents the true church raptured before the tribulation period starts and the first five churches are earlier stages of the true church, pretribulationists would then be mixing their metaphors. They would be claiming that the Laodicean church cannot be part of the true church—the body of Christ. This separating of the Laodicean church from the Philadelphian church is only appropriate if the biblical record specifically shows that the members of the Laodicean church are a different kind of believer than those of the Philadelphian church. Such a difference is not found in the passage.

It is very curious that many pretribulationists use the Revelation 3:20 passage to encourage unbelievers to surrender to Christ for salvation. They also claim that those who respond as a result of Revelation 3:20 will become true Christians, members of the church. I agree with the reasonableness of this application; however, it is noteworthy that this promise comes directly from the Lord to the Laodicean church! The pretribulationists' application of Revelation 3:20 should require them to recognize that those who respond to the gospel message within the Laodicean church are true Christians—indwelled by the Holy Spirit.

Conclusion: the existence of the Laodicean church within Daniel's seventieth week (true Christians as members of Christ's church) is radically counter to what the pretribulationist teaches is possible. That is the reason pretribulationists who believe in the progressive church ages have never been able to treat the Laodicean church the same way as they treat the Philadelphian church. The very concept of seven progressive church ages is incompatible with pretribulationism, since it places true Christians of the Laodicean church within Daniel's seventieth week. Therefore, pretribulationists must either reject their concept of seven progressive church ages or reject their concept that the church cannot be found within Daniel's seventieth week!

Both of the pretribulationist's interpretations (concurrent church types and progressive church ages) force conclusions that even the pretribulationist would not accept; therefore, the pretribulationist must reject these two interpretations.

———————————— ⚬⊚⊘⊚⚬ ————————————

Now let's look at these seven churches from the Pre-Wrath rapture perspective. It may surprise you that the basic concept of this interpretation can also be adopted by the pretrib rapture position! However, this keeps the pretribulationists from using the seven churches to prove the uniqueness of their position, since it works even more effectively for the Pre-Wrath rapture.

Marvin Rosenthal explains that the seven churches of Revelation 2:1–3:22 are chosen uniquely from among the churches existing at the time that John wrote Revelation, since they demonstrate the strengths and weaknesses of churches that will exist within Daniel's seventieth week.[80] The pretribulationist will now wonder how the Pre-Wrath rapture can claim the following conditions:

➢ Christians are still on earth during the great tribulation.

➢ Christians are persecuted throughout the great tribulation.

➢ Many Christians die as martyrs at the hand of the Antichrist within the great tribulation.

➢ Yet Christians are "kept from the hour of testing."

The answer to this question is found in Revelation 3:10. It is also consistent with Matthew 24:13.

> "But the one who endures to the end, he shall be saved. (Matthew 24:13)

> Because you have kept the word of My perseverance, I also will keep you from the hour of testing, that hour which is about to come upon the whole world, to test those who dwell upon the earth. (Revelation 3:10)

At the beginning of Daniel's seventieth week, there will be churches that exemplify the conditions existing in the loveless church (Ephesus), the persecuted church (Smyrna), the compromising church (Pergamum), the corrupt church (Thyatira), the dead church (Sardis), the faithful church (Philadelphia), and the lukewarm church (Laodicea). This sets the stage for the Antichrist who will turn his wrath against Israel and the church after the abomination of desolation. Of course, there will be persecution in the first half of Daniel's seventieth week (the time of birth pangs). However, after the abomination of desolation, there will be a dramatic increase in this persecution (becoming the time of hard labor), since the Antichrist will kill anyone who refuses to worship him and take his mark. When this happens, charlatans within the church will fall away and betray true Christians.

⁹ "Then they will deliver you to tribulation, and will kill you, and you will be hated by all nations on account of My name.
¹⁰ "And at that time many will fall away and will deliver up one another and hate one another.
(Matthew 24:9–10)

In time, because of this great tribulation, only examples consistent with the Philadelphian church will still exist, since all of the charlatans will have fled as a result of the Antichrist's persecution. Those who persevere under this persecution will experience the fulfillment of God's promise that they will be "kept from the hour of testing which is about to come upon the whole earth" (Revelation 3:10).

The pretribulationist is correct in claiming that Revelation 3:10 is a promise that the church will not experience God's day of the Lord wrath, since it is consistent with *any* position that teaches we will be raptured before God begins His end-time judgments. Therefore, the pretribulationist cannot use this verse to prove pretribulationism. However, the Pre-Wrath rapture position has a significant advantage over the pretrib rapture—we also have a straight-forward explanation for why only the faithful church is left at the time of the rapture.

John Is Called Up to Heaven Is This the Rapture?

¹ After these things I looked, and behold, a door standing open in heaven, and the first voice which I had heard, like the sound of a trumpet speaking with me, said, "Come up here, and I will show you what must take place after these things."
² Immediately I was in the Spirit; and behold, a throne was standing in heaven, and One sitting on the throne.
(Revelation 4:1–2)

Futurists generally agree that the events beginning at Revelation 4:1 look into the future. Beyond this, the two positions covered in this book diverge quickly. According to the pretrib rapture position, when John is called up to heaven, his ascent represents the rapture of the church. Therefore, the pretribulationist claims that the church is raptured before the Lord breaks the first seal of Revelation (Revelation 6:1–2). The purpose of this section is to show that John's being called up to heaven cannot be used to prove the pretrib rapture position.

It is true that Revelation 4:1 occurs right after the messages to the churches (Revelation 2–3). However, it cannot be concluded from this positioning that the rapture will happen before the beginning of the tribulation period or that the church vacates the earth at Revelation 4:1. All we can say is that John ascends to heaven after receiving the messages to the seven churches and before Christ breaks the first seal of the seven-sealed scroll. The rapture of the church should not be forced into Revelation 4:1 unless the verse and its context show that the rapture must happen at this point, prior to the breaking of the first seal. Although Revelation 4:1 sounds like the rapture, our study will show that it is a very different kind of event.

It is noteworthy that the call comes from heaven for John to come up to heaven. When the Lord raptures His church, He comes down to us, we are drawn up to meet Him in the air, and then Jesus will take us to heaven. Notice also that John says he was "in the Spirit" when he appeared before the throne of God. In this condition, it is likely that John did not even physically leave earth. We should also compare Revelation 4:1–2 with two other events in the Bible that are appropriately claimed to be images of the coming rapture.

> And Enoch walked with God; and he was not, for God took him.
> (Genesis 5:24)

> Then it came about as they were going along and talking, that behold, there appeared a chariot of fire and horses of fire which separated the two of them. And Elijah went up by a whirlwind to heaven.
> (2 Kings 2:11)

In both cases, God or His messengers came down to take the faithful one up to heaven. Genesis 5:25 and 2 Kings 2:11 are consistent with the teaching of the rapture in 1 Thessalonians 4:16–17 but the Revelation 4:1–2 passage is not.

We are told by the pretribulationist that the rapture rescues us from the tribulation period. However, *after* the supposed symbol of the rapture in Revelation 4:1, John will again experience tribulation and imprisonment on the island of Patmos! If Revelation 4:1 is the quintessential proof for the timing of the rapture, why does it not even remotely match the method or the result of 1 Thessalonians 4:16-17?

> [16] For the Lord Himself will *descend from heaven* with a shout, with the voice of the archangel, and with the trumpet of God; and the dead in Christ shall rise first.
> [17] Then we who are alive and remain shall be *caught up* together with them in the clouds *to meet the Lord in the air,* and thus we shall *always be with the Lord.*
> (1 Thessalonians 4:16–17, emphasis added)

Taking Revelation 4:1 in its natural wording avoids the obvious problem of having to allegorize John's trip to heaven to prove the rapture timing. The rapture does not fit well here, and there is no statement in the passage that this event was the rapture or an image of the rapture. The apostle John was called to heaven (in the Spirit) by a voice in heaven on a temporary trip for the purpose of special revelation. Its purpose was not to rescue him from a wicked world or protect him from experiencing tribulation. Whether the rapture occurs before Daniel's seventieth week or after the sixth seal is broken, there is no evidence in this passage that sheds any light on the rapture's timing. MacArthur agrees with this conclusion.

> **[Revelation] 4:1 Come up here.** This is not a veiled reference to the rapture of the church, but a command for John to be temporarily transported to heaven "in the spirit" (see note on 1:10) to receive revelation about the future events.[81]

Who Are the Twenty-Four Elders?

Many pretribulationists claim that the existence of the twenty-four elders in heaven right after John is called up is proof that John's call represents the rapture. Therefore, they claim, the twenty-four elders represent the already-raptured church.

> And around the throne were twenty-four thrones; and upon the thrones I saw twenty-four elders sitting, clothed in white garments, and golden crowns on their heads.
> (Revelation 4:4)

> [9] And when the living creatures give glory and honor and thanks to Him who sits on the throne, to Him who lives forever and ever,

> [10] the twenty-four elders will fall down before Him who sits on the throne, and will worship Him who lives forever and ever, and will cast their crowns before the throne, saying,
> [11] "Worthy art Thou, our Lord and our God, to receive glory and honor and power; for Thou didst create all things, and because of Thy will they existed, and were created."
> (Revelation 4:9–11)

> And when He had taken the book, the four living creatures *and* the twenty-four elders fell down before the Lamb, having each one a harp, and golden bowls full of incense, which are the prayers of the saints.
> (Revelation 5:8, emphasis added)

J. Dwight Pentecost offers the following summary of his position on the twenty-four elders' identity. It should be noted that Pentecost's reference to Israel's resurrection at the end of Daniel's seventieth week is not stated in Isaiah 26:19–21 or Daniel 12:1–2, it is merely Pentecost's pretribulationist interpretation of these passages (based on their interpretation of when Matthew 24:29–31 happens).

> Since, according to Revelation 5:8, these twenty-four are associated in a priestly act, which is never said of angels, they must be believer-priests associated with the Great High Priest. Inasmuch as Israel is not resurrected until the end of the seventieth week, nor judged or rewarded until the coming of the Lord according to Isaiah 26:19–21 and Daniel 12:1–2, these must be representatives of the saints of this present age. Since they are seen to be resurrected, in heaven, judged, rewarded, enthroned at the beginning of the seventieth week, it is concluded that the church must have been raptured before the seventieth week begins.[82]

We must be very careful in defining the ministry of angels, since the Bible only gives us a glimpse of these heavenly beings. However, the claim that "these twenty-four are associated in a priestly act, which is never said of angels" [83] is not consistent with the Word of God.

> [3] And another angel came and stood at the altar, holding a golden censer; and much incense was given to him, that he might add it to the prayers of all the saints upon the golden altar which was before the throne.

⁴ And the smoke of the incense, with the prayers of the saints,
went up before God out of the angel's hand.
(Revelation 8:3–4)

There is nothing that differentiates this angel's prayer ministry
from those of the twenty-four elders. The incense in both passages
represents prayers of the saints! In addition to that, Pentecost's own
example (Revelation 5:8) probably also rejects his claim.

And when He had taken the book, the four living creatures and
the twenty-four elders fell down before the Lamb, having each one
a harp, and golden bowls full of incense, which are the prayers of
the saints.
(Revelation 5:8)

The four living creatures engage in the same ministry as the
twenty-four elders. It is likely that the four living creatures are also
angelic beings.

That the twenty-four elders could represent the church does
not lead to the conclusion that the church must therefore have been
raptured before Daniel's seventieth week. The most we can say is
that they (at least partially) represent the church, since it does not
say the twenty-four elders are the church. It is actually very difficult
to conclude from Revelation 4:10 that the rapture has just happened.

the twenty-four elders will fall down before Him who sits on the
throne, and will worship Him who lives forever and ever, and will
cast their crowns before the throne, saying,
(Revelation 4:10)

What is the very first thing we will do when we see our Savior?
We will fall down and worship Him! It is noteworthy that Revelation
4:10 says the twenty-four elders *will* fall down, *will* worship, and *will*
cast their crowns. All of these verbs are future tense. If the twenty-
four elders represent the just-raptured church (the pretribulationist
position), why do they not immediately fall down and worship the
Lamb? Since the twenty-four elders have not yet fallen down and
worshipped God, there is nothing in this passage that forces the

twenty-four elders to be the raptured church. Of course, this does not prove the Pre-Wrath rapture; it merely shows that the rapture cannot be forced into Revelation 4.

At this point, a student of the Word may think that I have trapped myself. I have suggested that, since Revelation 4:10 is written in the future tense, the twenty-four elders are not the just-raptured church. However, I have already mentioned Revelation 5:8.

> And when He had taken the book, the four living creatures and the twenty-four elders fell down before the Lamb, having each one a harp, and golden bowls full of incense, which are the prayers of the saints.
> (Revelation 5:8)

According to Revelation 5:8, they worship the Lamb. Does this prove that the twenty-four elders now represent the just-raptured church, since this would still be before the first seal is broken? Actually, instead of my being trapped, as you might think, Revelation 5:8 shows that even at this point, the twenty-four elders cannot be the just-raptured church. We know that if they are the just-raptured church, surely the first thing they will do is worship the Lamb. What are the twenty-four elders doing at the moment they worship the Lord? They offer prayers for the saints. The problem is that if the church has been raptured just before this moment, according to the pretribulationist, there would be no saints on earth to offer prayers for! Therefore, there is nothing in Revelation 5:8 that forces the pretribulationist's rapture at this moment either!

The only possibility left for the pretribulationist is to claim that the church arrives in heaven between Revelation 4:4 and Revelation 5:8. If that is true, why does John see the twenty-four elders in Revelation 4:4? The appearance of the twenty-four elders in Revelation 4:4 shows that the twenty-four elders have already been in heaven. Therefore, neither Revelation 5:8 nor any other date between Revelation 4:4 and Revelation 5:8 can be used to prove the church has arrived in heaven. If the twenty-four elders are not the just-raptured church, what is being depicted in Revelation 5:8? It becomes clearer when we read Revelation 5:8 in context.

⁸ And when He had taken the book, the four living creatures and the twenty-four elders fell down before the Lamb, having each one a harp, and golden bowls full of incense, which are the prayers of the saints.

⁹ And they sang a new song, saying, "Worthy art Thou to take the book, and to break its seals; for Thou wast slain, and didst purchase for God with Thy blood men from every tribe and tongue and people and nation.

¹⁰ "And Thou hast made them to be a kingdom and priests to our God; and they will reign upon the earth."

¹¹ And I looked, and I heard the voice of many angels around the throne and the living creatures and the elders; and the number of them was myriads of myriads, and thousands of thousands,

¹² saying with a loud voice, "Worthy is the Lamb that was slain to receive power and riches and wisdom and might and honor and glory and blessing."

¹³ And every created thing which is in heaven and on the earth and under the earth and on the sea, and all things in them, I heard saying, "To Him who sits on the throne, and to the Lamb, be blessing and honor and glory and dominion forever and ever."

¹⁴ And the four living creatures kept saying, "Amen." And the elders fell down and worshiped.

(Revelation 5:8–14)

Among all whom John saw in heaven, only the four living creatures and the twenty-four elders are said to fall down and worship the Lamb (Revelation 5:8, 14). This next point from Revelation 5 is absolutely critical in understanding whether the twenty-four elders are the raptured church! When they sing a new song, they speak of those who were purchased by Christ's blood as "them" and "they" (in the Greek of Revelation 5:10 both are in the third person, not the first person). This is very hard to explain if the twenty-four elders are literally the already-raptured church! If they are the already-raptured church, they would say "us" and "we!"

The pretribulationist focuses on the twenty-four elders. However, as we discovered in verse 8, the four living creatures engage in a prayer ministry that is exactly the same as the twenty-four elders.

And when He had taken the book, the four living creatures and the twenty-four elders fell down before the Lamb, having each one a harp, and golden bowls full of incense, which are the prayers of the saints.
(Revelation 5:8)

Examining all the verses in Revelation that speak about the twenty-four elders (Revelation 4:4–6, 4:9–11, 5:1–14, 7:11–17, 11:16–18, 14:3 and 19:4), only in Revelation 11:16–18 are the four living creatures not mentioned. In some very special way, the twenty-four elders are linked to the four living creatures. Since the four living creatures are almost always shown with the twenty-four elders, it would be reasonable to conclude that the four living creatures are angelic beings who minister to God's elect. The most common interpretation is that the four living creatures are mighty cherubim, quite possibly the same four as the four living beings of Ezekiel 1. Finally, we need to turn to the last mention of the twenty-four elders in Revelation.

[1] After these things I heard, as it were, a loud voice of a *great multitude* in heaven, saying, "Hallelujah! Salvation and glory and power belong to our God;

[2] because His judgments are true and righteous; for He has judged the great harlot who was corrupting the earth with her immorality, and He has avenged the blood of His bond-servants on her."

[3] And a second time they said, "Hallelujah! Her smoke rises up forever and ever."

[4] And the *twenty-four elders* and the *four living creatures* fell down and worshiped God who sits on the throne saying, "Amen. Hallelujah!"

[5] And a voice came from the throne, saying, "Give praise to our God, all you His bond-servants, you who fear Him, the small and the great."

[6] And I heard, as it were, the voice of a *great multitude* and as the sound of many waters and as the sound of mighty peals of thunder, saying, "Hallelujah! For the Lord our God, the Almighty, reigns."
(Revelation 19:1–6, emphasis added)

The Pre-Wrath rapture claims that the great multitude are believers in Christ. Pretribulationists agree; however, they claim the great multitude are evangelized by the 144,000 sealed Jews after the rapture. It is noteworthy that the amazing Revelation 19 scene in heaven shows three groups: the twenty-four elders, the four living creatures, and a great multitude; yet they are still identified separately! That makes it much more likely that the twenty-four elders and the four living creatures are two sets of beings that represent the Jewish and Gentile elect before the throne of God. Consistent with that, when the great multitude arrives in heaven, they join the twenty-four elders and the four living creatures in worshipping God.

> [9] After these things I looked, and behold, a great multitude, which no one could count, from every nation and all tribes and peoples and tongues, standing before the throne and before the Lamb, clothed in white robes, and palm branches were in their hands;
> [10] and they cry out with a loud voice, saying, "Salvation to our God who sits on the throne, and to the Lamb."
> [11] And all the angels were standing around the throne and around the elders and the four living creatures; and they fell on their faces before the throne and worshiped God,
> [12] saying, "Amen, blessing and glory and wisdom and thanksgiving and honor and power and might, be to our God forever and ever. Amen."
> [13] And one of the elders answered, saying to me, "These who are clothed in the white robes, who are they, and from where have they come?"
> [14] And I said to him, "My lord, you know." And he said to me, "These are the ones who come out of the great tribulation, and they have washed their robes and made them white in the blood of the Lamb.
> (Revelation 7:9-14)

There is nothing in the Scriptures that would force the conclusion that the twenty-four elders are specifically the raptured church. It is much more likely that the twenty-four elders serve all of the elect. This elect probably even includes faithful Jews (a position many pretribulationists also take). This can be inferred by their number of twenty-four. The twenty-four elders would represent the twelve tribes of Israel and the twelve apostles, since the Lord would build His church on the foundation of the apostles and prophets (Matthew 16:18 and Ephesians 2:20). The twenty-four elders would likely be heavenly beings assigned to the faithful of Israel and the church. This conclusion is substantiated by the fact that nowhere does the Bible identify when the twenty-four elders arrive in heaven. Some may reject this conclusion, claiming that they must have arrived in heaven at Revelation 4:4, since the twenty-four elders are not mentioned until that verse. That is easily explained. Until the end of Revelation 3, all of the events occur on earth. In Revelation 4:1–2, our focus is transported to heaven.

> [1] After these things I looked, and behold, a door standing open in heaven, and the first voice which I had heard, like the sound of a trumpet speaking with me, said, "Come up here, and I will show you what must take place after these things."
> [2] Immediately I was in the Spirit; and behold, a throne was standing in heaven, and One sitting on the throne.
> [3] And He who was sitting was like a jasper stone and a sardius in appearance; and there was a rainbow around the throne, like an emerald in appearance.
> [4] And around the throne were twenty-four thrones; and upon the thrones I saw twenty-four elders sitting, clothed in white garments, and golden crowns on their heads.
> (Revelation 4:1–4)

Once again, this does not prove the Pre-Wrath rapture position. It merely shows that the pretribulationist cannot use the twenty-four elders to prove the church has already been raptured before the first seal is broken.

Conclusion

This chapter is not designed to prove the Pre-Wrath rapture position. It has only been used to show that so many of the arguments the pretribulationist uses to prove the pretrib rapture are false arguments. The primary conclusions among these are the following:

➤ The pretribulationist claims that, since the church is not mentioned between Revelation 4 and Revelation 8 as being on earth, the church must have been raptured and taken to heaven before the peace treaty (Revelation 3:14 is before the first seal is broken). One of the rejections of this argument is that the church is also not mentioned between Revelation 3:14 and Revelation

22:15 in the passages that cover heavenly scenes. If the argument from silence is appropriate here, the pretribulationist must apply it equally to both earth and heaven. Therefore, *if* the argument from silence proves the church is not on earth, it would also prove that the church is not in heaven! Where is the church? Of course, the argument from silence is self-defeating in this case. Since the pretribulationist claims that the existence of believers in heaven proves the church is in heaven, then the existence of believers on earth proves the church is on earth as well. Matthew 24:9 and Matthew 24:21–22 show believers in Christ on earth after the peace treaty:

⁹ "Then they will deliver you to tribulation, and will kill you, and you will be hated by all nations *on account of My name.*
¹⁰ "And at that time many will fall away and will deliver up one another and hate one another.
(Matthew 24:9–10, emphasis added)

²¹ for then there will be a great tribulation, such as has not occurred since the beginning of the world until now, nor ever shall.
²² And unless those days had been cut short, no life would have been saved; but for the sake of the elect those days shall be cut short.
(Matthew 24:21–22)

➤ The pretribulationist claims that when John is called to heaven, (Revelation 4:1) this is an image of the rapture. Therefore, it supposedly proves the rapture happens before the peace treaty, since the first seal of the seven-seal scroll has not been broken yet. However, John was called to heaven (in the Spirit) by a voice in heaven on a temporary trip for the purpose of special revelation. The purpose of this trip was not to rescue him from a wicked world or to protect him from experiencing tribulation, since his imprisonment on Patmos will continue after the vision has been completed. The rapture does not fit well here, and there is no statement in the passage that this event was the rapture or an image of the rapture. Taking Revelation 4:1 in its natural wording avoids the obvious problem of having to allegorize John's trip to heaven in order to prove their rapture timing.

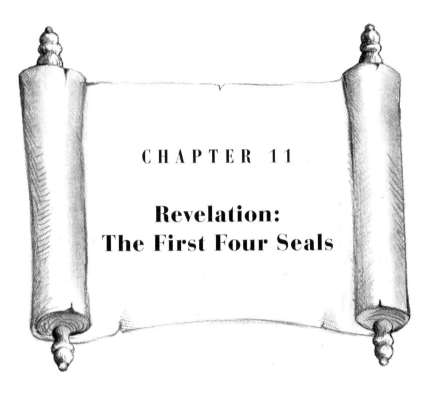

CHAPTER 11

Revelation:
The First Four Seals

Is the Pre-Wrath Rapture a Form of the Midtrib Rapture?

Before discussing the seven-sealed scroll, I wish to address a recent pretribulationist claim that the Pre-Wrath rapture is merely a form of the midtrib rapture position, since we teach that the first trumpet judgment begins right after the rapture. This one commonality between the two positions is overwhelmed by the many differences which are much more important.

➢ The midtrib rapture places the seven seals in the first half of Daniel's seventieth week; the Pre-Wrath rapture position places only the first three seals in the first half of Daniel's seventieth week.

➢ The midtrib rapture teaches that the church is raptured before the great tribulation begins. The Pre-Wrath rapture position teaches that the church is raptured after the great tribulation is cut short for the sake of the elect.

> ➤ The midtrib rapture teaches that the first trumpet judgment begins right after the abomination of desolation. The Pre-Wrath rapture position teaches that the first trumpet judgment begins after the great tribulation is cut short, after the sun and moon darken and after the rapture of the church.

> ➤ The midtrib rapture claims that the great tribulation is the judgment of God. Pre-Wrath rapture position teaches that the great tribulation is not the judgment of God.

Therefore, the only place where the two positions agree regarding the sequence of events is that we are raptured shortly before the first trumpet judgment. However, even the first trumpet judgment is far later in the timeline than is claimed by midtribulationists.

The Pre-Wrath rapture position is not in any way related to the midtrib rapture position. Once this is understood, it becomes much easier to understand why the position of the fifth seal is so important and why the pretribulationist's claim that all seven seals are of one nature must be rejected. Since only seals 1–3 are broken before the abomination of desolation, the fourth and fifth seals would be broken within the great tribulation. The first trumpet judgment is then placed *after* God cuts short the great tribulation for the sake of the elect.

The Seven-Sealed Scroll

In our study of Revelation, we will primarily focus on the seven-sealed scroll, since it is in interpreting the events related to this scroll that the pretrib and Pre-Wrath rapture positions are most clearly differentiated. Pretribulationists claim that we are shown the first stage of God's end-time judgments when the seven seals are broken. This causes him to assume that all seven seals are one unit of judgment, as are the trumpet and bowl judgments. The Pre-Wrath rapture claims that the events of the seven seals occur *before* God begins His end-time judgments and that the seals are broken into three stages rather than being one unit, as the pretribulationist claims. The three stages become clear when we match the seals of Revelation to Matthew 24.

THE SEVEN SEALS IN THREE STAGES		
Item	**Matthew 24**	**Revelation 6–8**
Birth Pangs	Before the abomination of desolation: *Matthew 24:4–8*	**Seals 1–3:** The first three horsemen: *Revelation 6:1–6*
Hard Labor	The abomination of desolation and the great tribulation: *Matthew 24:9–28*	**Seal 4:** The fourth horseman; the killing of the lost: *Revelation 6:7–8* **Seal 5:** Martyrdom of the saints: *Revelation 6:9–11*
Delivery: God's intervention before He begins His day of the Lord judgments	The great tribulation is cut short for the elect, the sun and moon are darkened, and the elect are gathered out of the great tribulation: *Matthew 24:22, 29–31*	**Seals 6–7:** The sun and moon are darkened, 144,000 Jews are sealed and a great multitude is gathered out of the great tribulation, then silence before day of the Lord judgments begin: *Revelation 6:12–8:6*

The Fourth and Fifth Seals

The fifth seal will be studied extensively in the next chapter. In this section, we will merely differentiate the fourth seal from the fifth seal. The fourth and fifth seals show people who have been killed. Some have concluded that the killings in the fourth seal are the explanation for the martyrdom of the fifth seal. However, I lean towards concluding that the fourth seal presents a different group of people who are killed within the great tribulation. As John MacArthur explains, Hades in the New Testament is always used solely as the place for the wicked awaiting their final judgment.[84] An example is found in Luke 16:23, in which the rich man went to Hades but Lazarus went to "Abraham's bosom" (a Jewish expression of heaven in New

Testament times). In Revelation 20, death and Hades can only refer to an abode for the unsaved.

> "And in Hades he lifted up his eyes, being in torment, and saw Abraham far away, and Lazarus in his bosom.
> (Luke 16:23)

> [7] And when He broke the fourth seal, I heard the voice of the fourth living creature saying, "Come."
> [8] And I looked, and behold, an ashen horse; and he who sat on it had the name *Death; and Hades* was following with him. And authority was given to them over a fourth of the earth, to kill with sword and with famine and with pestilence and by the wild beasts of the earth.
> [9] And when He broke the fifth seal, I saw underneath the altar the souls of those who had been slain because of the word of God, and because of the testimony which they had maintained;
> (Revelation 6:7–9, emphasis added)

> [13] And the sea gave up the dead which were in it, and death and Hades gave up the dead which were in them; and they were judged, every one of them according to their deeds.
> [14] And death and Hades were thrown into the lake of fire. This is the second death, the lake of fire.
> [15] And if anyone's name was not found written in the book of life, he was thrown into the lake of fire.
> (Revelation 20:13–15)

It is noteworthy that no positive testimony is given regarding those killed in the fourth seal. There is also no claim that those who die in the fourth seal are believers, nor are they said to be bound for heaven. With the breaking of the fifth seal the passage changes location. We are now shown those in heaven who have been martyred as faithful believers in Christ. The Pre-Wrath rapture teaches that the deaths of the fourth and fifth seals occur within the great tribulation. The fifth seal martyrs are killed because they refuse to worship the Antichrist or take his mark (possibly, many of the fourth seal deaths may be for refusing to worship the Antichrist as well). We will examine the fifth-seal martyrs in the next chapter.

How Is the Scroll of Revelation Sealed?

The question of how the scroll is sealed may seem to be a minor point; however, the answer to this question will show that the events displayed when the seals are broken cannot be God's judgments. The Pre-Wrath rapture agrees with the pretrib conclusion that the messages written within the scroll are the judgments of God. However, the contents within the scroll cannot be revealed until *after* all of the seals are broken. Therefore, the events that John observes when each seal is broken occur *before* God begins His end-time judgments.

The pretribulationist claims that when each seal is broken, the scroll's message underneath that seal is revealed. I can conceive of only two possible ways the scrolls can be structured in such a way that the contents under each seal can be revealed when that seal is broken.

➢ All seven seals are visible on the outside of the scroll. In order for the contents under the first broken seal to be revealed, that section of the scroll underneath the broken seal must be unrolled as a strip and displayed, and then the next seal is broken. The section under that seal is unrolled, and its message is displayed. This action is progressively done until all seals are broken and their messages have been displayed. According to this possibility, the scroll must be unrolled one strip at a time under that broken seal, since access to the rest of the scroll is still locked up by the remaining seals.

➢ The other possibility is that only one seal can be seen at a time. When the visible seal is broken, the scroll is unrolled and read until that section is completed and the next seal is exposed. Nothing more can be read until the next seal is broken. Each additional seal broken exposes that portion of the scroll's message.

Both explanations would allow the pretribulationist to claim that breaking each seal reveals the message contained within that portion of the scroll. However, they are both absolutely inconsistent with the scrolls discovered from biblical times. Similar to the first possibility above, first century scrolls would have all seven seals visible on the outside of this scroll. However, the process of reading the scroll is totally different than the above possibilities. Even what would be equivalent to the initial "page" of the scroll could not be displayed until all of the seals have been broken, since before all seals are broken, only a corner of the scroll can be turned over. Scrolls from biblical times were structured similar to the drawing below (usually without the spindle shown in this drawing):

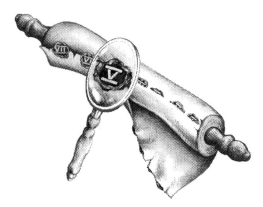

Scrolls before and after Christ's birth were frequently bound by cords, and then the cords were secured with seals. An actual example of a Samaritan seven-sealed scroll is presently housed in the Jerusalem Museum.[85] In the above drawing, I chose not to add the cords so that it would be easier to see the scroll's structure. The Scriptures are consistent with this example.

> And I saw in the right hand of Him who sat on the throne a book written inside and on the back, sealed up with seven seals. (Revelation 5:1)

It is noteworthy that if all but one of the seals were concealed inside the scroll, John would not have known how many seals there were. This is a significant point, since only rarely did the scrolls in Biblical times have as many as seven seals.[86] John would not be able to know how many seals there were unless all of the seals were on the outside, visible to him.

It is now easy to see that the sequential events displayed with the breaking of the seven seals must be events leading up to the unrolling of the scroll. In light of that, you may wonder how John knew that the scroll was "written inside and on the back." There are two reasonable explanations for this.

➤ This scroll was consistent with scrolls that had been used by the Romans during John's time on earth. The typical scroll had the message written on one side of the material (such as papyrus or parchment), and then it was rolled up to conceal the message inside. The legal recipient or subject matter would be identified on the outside. The scroll would be secured with seals. Effectively, we still do something similar whenever we send a payment for a bill in a sealed envelope. The recipient expects that there is a check inside, even if the check cannot be seen.

➤ Anyone who has seen papyrus and parchment scrolls knows that the writing on the inside can at least very faintly be seen through the material, even after it has been aged over time. In fact, this is true even with standard paper today. Therefore, John knew the scroll was "written inside and on the back," because he could see the clear writing on the back (outside), and he could faintly see the writing on the inside.

Once the seventh seal is broken, the scroll can finally be opened, and the contents of the scroll can be presented. What is presented in Revelation *after* the seventh seal is broken would be what is revealed when the scroll is unrolled. The next event after thirty minutes of silence in heaven is the first trumpet judgment.

There is another kind of scroll that was used in Old Testament and New Testament times that is consistent with the image used on this chapter's title page. In that case, if the scroll was sealed, it would be tied with cords surrounding the overall two-spindle document, binding the two rolls together with each cord. Of course, with this kind of scroll, it is also impossible to read more than a tiny portion until all of the seals and/or cords are broken. These two-roll scrolls often used spindles.

Who Can Open the Seven-Sealed Scroll?

Since the Lamb of God is the only one who can break the seals and open the scroll, Revelation 5:1–7 is often used by pretribulationists to claim that the events displayed when the seven seals are progressively broken are all caused by the Lord. Therefore, the pretribulationist claims, the entire tribulation period is the outpouring of God's wrath. I agree that Jesus is the only one who can break the seals and open the scroll, but it does not automatically follow that He personally causes all of the events presented when the seals are broken. We must also examine the events displayed as the seals are broken to determine if the seal events are God's judgments. Seriously contemplate this comment I have just presented! The fact that only God can reveal the future does not automatically make Him the cause of the future events revealed.

If all of the events displayed when the seals are broken are only consistent with the activities of God and cannot be the independent actions of Satan and humans, then it would be reasonable to assign them to Christ's authorship. However, if breaking any of the seals displays an event that is absolutely inconsistent with the day of the Lord judgments of God, then the cause of that seal cannot be assigned to God. This, of course, is where the fifth-seal martyrs contribute to the understanding of these verses. Since the fifth seal martyrdom cannot be the judgment of God, the Lord has not begun His end-time judgments. That conclusion would also mean that seals 1–4 cannot be God's end-time judgments.

In addition to the fifth seal, we will discover that in the sixth seal, the Lord will seal the 144,000 Jews and gather the great multitude out of the great tribulation. The purpose of these two actions will be to protect and rescue His people from the Antichrist. These actions show that God is preparing to *begin* His end-time judgments rather than being the actual day of the Lord judgments.

The distinction of whether breaking the seals means the Lord is or is not the author and agent of the events revealed has been clouded by the pretribulationists' assumption for so many decades that Christ must personally be responsible for the events displayed when each seal is broken. To show how it has been clouded, I would like to illustrate the seals in a modern way. This will help us better understand that the process of breaking the seals does not in any way require the Lamb of God to be the cause of the events displayed. For the benefit of pretribulationists, I will even present the illustration from their perspective, since they believe each broken seal displays the contents of the scroll under that seal. I will still be able to demonstrate how

Jesus can break the seals without being the cause of the events He reveals.

Picture us in my neighbor Josh's bonus room, where we find seven locked doors on one wall (conveniently numbered 1–7). Josh has hired Bungalow Construction Company (BCC) to remodel rooms 1–5. Josh has the only key for unlocking these seven doors, and he sequentially unlocks and opens each one. Josh's opening of door 1 shows BCC employees watching TV, door 2 shows BCC employees playing cards, door 3 shows BCC employees wrestling on the floor, door 4 shows BCC employees sleeping, door 5 shows BCC employees breaking through the wall between rooms 5 and 6, and door 6 shows Josh's family who are waiting to help him move the furniture into the rooms once the renovation is completed. When door 7 is opened, we see all the furniture Josh has bought and stored for the seven rooms.

Since you have no pre-learned expectations, it is easy to see that, although Josh is the only one qualified to unlock the doors and reveal what is happening in the rooms, he is not responsible for whether the BCC employees are carrying out the tasks they have been hired to do. Josh is personally involved in the activities behind doors 6 and 7, since he has gathered his family in preparation for moving the furniture.

Now let's apply that to the seven seals. Although the Lord is the only one qualified to break the seals and reveal the events when seals 1–7 are broken, Revelation 6 will show that Christ cannot be the author and agent of the first through fifth seals. Context must determine who provides the power for the events displayed when the seals are broken. Although seals 1–4 could be consistent with the active work of God, they can also be consistent with the active work of Satan, the Antichrist, and his followers independent of God. However, since God cannot have caused the death of the fifth-seal martyrs, His end-time judgments have not begun. Therefore, the events of seals 1–4 are not caused by God either.

The Breaking of Seals One through Four

[1] And I saw when the Lamb broke one of the seven seals, and I heard one of the four living creatures saying as with a voice of thunder, "Come."

² And I looked, and behold, a white horse, and he who sat on it had a bow; and a crown was given to him; and he went out conquering, and to conquer.

³ And when He broke the second seal, I heard the second living creature saying, "Come."

⁴ And another, a red horse, went out; and to him who sat on it, it was granted to take peace from the earth, and that men should slay one another; and a great sword was given to him.

⁵ And when He broke the third seal, I heard the third living creature saying, "Come." And I looked, and behold, a black horse; and he who sat on it had a pair of scales in his hand.

⁶ And I heard as it were a voice in the center of the four living creatures saying, "A quart of wheat for a denarius, and three quarts of barley for a denarius; and do not harm the oil and the wine."

⁷ And when He broke the fourth seal, I heard the voice of the fourth living creature saying, "Come."

⁸ And I looked, and behold, an ashen horse; and he who sat on it had the name Death; and Hades was following with him. And authority was given to them over a fourth of the earth, to kill with sword and with famine and with pestilence and by the wild beasts of the earth.

(Revelation 6:1–8)

Revelation 6:1–8 covers the events displayed when Christ breaks the first four seals. Most proponents of the pretrib and Pre-Wrath rapture positions teach the following:

➢ When Christ breaks the first seal, we are shown the rise of the Antichrist to worldwide power *without* war (a white horse whose rider has a bow but no arrows).

➢ When Christ breaks the second seal, we are shown the worldwide wars that the Antichrist wages (a red horse and its rider).

➢ When Christ breaks the third seal, we are shown worldwide famine (a black horse and its rider).

➢ When Christ breaks the fourth seal, we are shown worldwide death (a pale horse and its rider).

The most common teaching regarding the relationship between seals 1–4 of Revelation 6 is that after the Antichrist comes to power (first seal), he secures his kingdom with worldwide war (second seal). As a result of worldwide war, famine spreads throughout the world (third seal), and then famine brings death to 25 percent of the population (fourth seal). However, since the fourth seal is not claimed to merely be the consequence of the third seal, it is likely that, after the abomination of desolation, the Antichrist will use any means necessary to kill all of his enemies. This conclusion would be consistent with the fourth seal being the beginning of hard labor within the great tribulation.

> [7] And when He broke the fourth seal, I heard the voice of the fourth living creature saying, "Come."
> [8] And I looked, and behold, an ashen horse; and he who sat on it had the name Death; and Hades was following with him. And authority was given to them over a fourth of the earth, to kill with sword and with famine and with pestilence and by the wild beasts of the earth.
> (Revelation 6:7–8)

Notice that verse 8 speaks of killing by "wild beasts." This Greek word for beasts is *theerion*. Henry M. Morris points out that all thirty-seven other times that *theerion* is used in Revelation; the word is used to depict a leader who is ungodly, powerful, and evil.[87] Revelation 6:7–8 is consistent with Matthew 24:23–26, which shows that demonic activity will be prominent within the great tribulation. Therefore, demons empowering evil people would be the likely meaning of the "wild beasts" in Revelation 6. Also consistent with this, many holding to the pretrib and Pre-Wrath rapture positions teach that the Antichrist is inhabited by Satan around the time of the abomination of desolation.

Conclusion

The fact that the Lamb of God is the only one who can break the seals and open the scroll does not automatically make Him the cause of the future events revealed. If breaking even one of the seals displays an event that is absolutely inconsistent with the day of the Lord activities of God, then the cause of that seal cannot be assigned to God. In the next chapter we will discover the fifth seal proves that God's judgments have not yet begun.

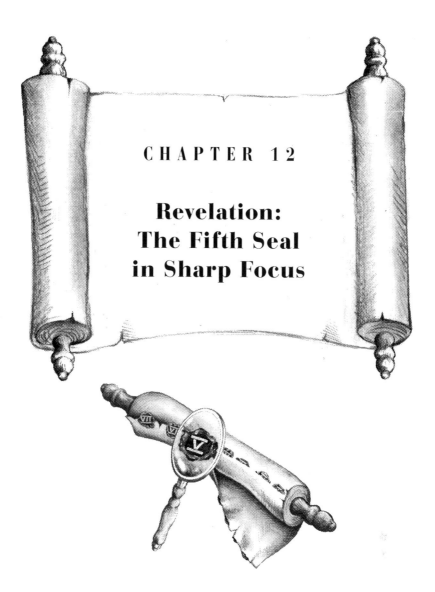

CHAPTER 12

Revelation:
The Fifth Seal
in Sharp Focus

Is the Fifth Seal the Judgment of God?

[9] "Then they will deliver you to tribulation, and will kill you, and you will be hated by all nations *on account of My name.*
[10] "And at that time many will fall away and will deliver up one another and hate one another.
(Matthew 24:9–10, emphasis added)

[9] And when He broke the fifth seal, I saw underneath the altar the souls of those who had been slain because of the word of God, and because of the testimony which they had maintained;

> ¹⁰ and they cried out with a loud voice, saying, "How long, O Lord, holy and true, wilt Thou refrain from judging and avenging our blood on those who dwell on the earth?"
> ¹¹ And there was given to each of them a white robe; and they were told that they should rest for a little while longer, until the number of their fellow servants and their brethren who were to be killed even as they had been, should be completed also.
> (Revelation 6:9–11)

➤ The martyrs will be hated and killed on account of Christ's name (Matthew 24:9).

➤ The martyrs appear under the altar in heaven—a place that is only open to the redeemed in Christ (Revelation 6:9).

➤ The martyrs were slain because of the Word of God and the testimony that they maintained; this reason can only apply to the redeemed in Christ (Revelation 6:9).

➤ The martyrs were given white robes—garments of the redeemed in Christ (Revelation 6:11).

Not one word is said about the fifth-seal martyrs that would qualify them for God's end-time judgments. The pretribulationist's position that the fifth seal is a judgment of God is without any biblical merit. Revelation 20 also speaks of the martyrs who were slain because of their testimony and because of the word of God. This helps us identify who these martyrs are.

> ⁴ And I saw thrones, and they sat upon them, and judgment was given to them. And I saw the souls of those who had been beheaded because of the testimony of Jesus and because of the word of God, and those who had not worshiped the beast or his image, and had not received the mark upon their forehead and upon their hand; and they came to life and reigned with Christ for a thousand years.
> ⁵ The rest of the dead did not come to life until the thousand years were completed. This is the first resurrection.
> ⁶ Blessed and holy is the one who has a part in the first resurrection; over these the second death has no power, but they will be priests of God and of Christ and will reign with Him for a thousand years.
> (Revelation 20:4–6)

Notice that because of their faithfulness—even unto death—the martyrs will reign with Christ in the millennial kingdom. It is only believers in Christ who will reign with Him. Included in verse five is the testimony that the martyrs came to life in the first resurrection; therefore, they will be included in the rapture. Notice that this also means the rapture has not yet happened.

These martyrs did not worship the beast or his image, and they did not receive his mark. Since the pretribulationist agrees with the Pre-Wrath rapture that the mark is administered *after* the abomination of desolation, this rejects the pretribulationist's claim that all seven seals occur in the first half the tribulation period! The fifth-seal martyrdom must occur within the great tribulation.

It is noteworthy that in Revelation 6:10, these martyrs plead to God for divine retribution against their persecutors. The martyrs' own plea also proves that God is not their persecutor and not the author of their martyrdom. If God did cause their martyrdom, the martyrs would not plead to Him!

Pretribulationists claim that, since seals 1–4 are consistent with what could be God's behavior; God's judgments must have already begun right after the peace treaty. However, pretribulationists rarely suggest that the actions described in the first four seals can also be consistent with the behavior of despotic men, independent of God. They also rarely attempt to prove the fifth seal

> **Is it consistent with God's behavior to make martyrs of those who are faithful believers in Christ and testify of Him?**

is consistent with what can be God's behavior. In fact, many completely ignore the fifth seal! If seals 1–5 *are* judgments of God, then the pretribulationist should be able to show with biblical evidence that it is consistent with God's behavior to make martyrs of those who are believers in Christ and faithfully testify of Him. Of course, this cannot be shown. Tim LaHaye also rejects Marvin Rosenthal's teaching on seals 1–5.

> Rosenthal does not seem to realize that surrendering the church to five-and-one-half years of Tribulation—which includes the

four horsemen, a world war, famine, the death of a quarter of the world, and the martyrdom of millions of Christians—is a betrayal of our Lord's promise to "keep [us] from the hour of trial which shall come upon the whole world, to test those who dwell on the earth (Revelation 3:10)[88] [Comment in bracket was added by LaHaye.]

Suggesting as he does that these first six seals of prophetic judgment are not Tribulation events is to reject the words of Scripture at their primary, literal meaning, even though he claims he does not do that.[89]

LaHaye's claim that Rosenthal suggests the "first six seals of prophetic judgment are not Tribulation events" [90] is not correct. Rosenthal agrees that through the fifth seal there are events of tribulation. However, Rosenthal has never called them "the first six seals prophetic judgments," since the Pre-Wrath rapture claims God's judgments do not begin until the first trumpet judgment. This distinction is extremely important! The fact that there is tribulation within Daniel's seventieth week does not automatically mean the tribulation is caused by God any more than saying the tribulation in World War II was caused by God. That the Lord allows people to go their evil ways does not make God the author and agent of the evil they commit!

You may have been surprised to find that LaHaye specifically includes "the martyrdom of millions of Christians"[91] in his list as part of God's "first six seals of prophetic judgment."[92] This is in spite of the fact that he correctly identifies these martyrs as Christians! Even more surprising, LaHaye uses this to prove that the rapture happens before the tribulation period because of the Lord's promise to "keep [us] from the hour of trial which shall come upon the whole world!"[93] Apparently, LaHaye does not believe that Revelation 3:10 applies to those he clearly identified as the Christian martyrs of the fifth seal. If the fifth seal is a judgment from God, then the fifth-seal martyrs would not be kept from that hour of trial, even though they maintained a faithful testimony!

Many other pretribulationists agree with LaHaye's claim that Rosenthal dates the rapture at five-and-one-half years after the start of Daniel's seventieth week. However, you will not be able to find any words claiming this in his book, *The Pre-Wrath Rapture of the Church*. Rosenthal is very clear in repeatedly stating that one cannot determine the date of the rapture.[94] Let's revisit LaHaye's first quote from above.

> Rosenthal does not seem to realize that surrendering the church to five-and-one-half years of Tribulation—which includes the four horsemen, a world war, famine, the death of a quarter of the world, and the martyrdom of millions of Christians—is a betrayal of our Lord's promise to "keep [us] from the hour of trial which shall come upon the whole world, to test those who dwell on the earth (Revelation 3:10)[95] [Comment in bracket was added by LaHaye.]

Rosenthal and all others who teach the Pre-Wrath rapture are clear in stating that we cannot determine the date of the rapture. It should also be pointed out that the midpoint of the second half would actually be five-and-a-quarter years after the start of Daniel's seventieth week, not five-and-a-half years, as LaHaye and many other pretribulationists have claimed.

There is only one possible way that one can come to the (false) conclusion that Rosenthal places the rapture at three fourths of the way through Daniels Seventieth Week.[96] The end-time charts in Rosenthal's book show that the rapture happens *after* the great tribulation is cut short and *before* the day of the Lord begins. It just so happens that the space needed for the phrases "the great tribulation" and "the day of the Lord" in these charts requires the same size block. The following chart is found on page 112 of *The Pre-Wrath Rapture of the Church:*

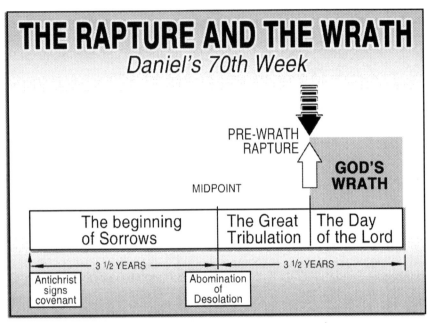

THE RAPTURE AND THE WRATH
Daniel's 70th Week

PRE-WRATH
RAPTURE

GOD'S
WRATH

MIDPOINT

The beginning of Sorrows	The Great Tribulation	The Day of the Lord

— 3 1/2 YEARS — — 3 1/2 YEARS —

Antichrist signs covenant	Abomination of Desolation

Permission for the use of the photographic image above is
specifically granted by Thomas Nelson, Inc.[97]

Keep in mind that the Pre-Wrath rapture claims we cannot date the rapture, just as the pretribulationist claims. In light of that, notice that Rosenthal's chart cannot be drawn any other way. If the division between the great tribulation and the day of the Lord was in any other position relative to the abomination of desolation and the end of Daniel's seventieth week, the reader would assume that Marvin would have purposely made a statement regarding when the rapture happens!

Some pretribulationists recognize the difficulty of assigning God's end-time judgments to the fifth seal. They solve this problem by claiming that these martyrs were killed before the fifth seal is broken, explaining that we are merely shown the martyrs in heaven at this point. Renald E. Showers is one who takes this position by appealing to the perfect tense of "had been slain."

⁹ And when He broke the fifth seal, I saw underneath the altar the souls of those who had been slain because of the word of God, and because of the testimony which they had maintained;

¹⁰ and they cried out with a loud voice, saying, "How long, O Lord, holy and true, wilt Thou refrain from judging and avenging our blood on those who dwell on the earth?"

¹¹ And there was given to each of them a white robe; and they were told that they should rest for a little while longer, until the number of their fellow servants and their brethren who were to be killed even as they had been, should be completed also. (Revelation 6:9–11)

First, note what John saw—and what he did not see—when Christ broke the fifth seal. Revelation 6:9–11 indicates that John did *not* see believers being martyred when the fifth seal was broken. Instead, he saw the disembodied souls of believers who had been slain already. The verb form translated "were slain" (v. 9) is in the Greek perfect tense.[98]

The fact that John did not see believers being slain, but instead saw the disembodied souls of saints who had been slain before he saw them, forces the conclusion that these believers were killed before the fifth seal was broken. Thus, the breaking of the fifth seal does not instigate or cause the martyrdom of believers. In addition, this fact means that the fifth seal can involve the wrath of God without making God responsible for the killing of His own people.[99]

In response to the Pre-Wrath rapture claim that God would not judge the fifth-seal martyrs for being faithful, Showers points out that these believers were martyred prior to the breaking of the fifth seal. The Pre-Wrath rapture agrees with this. However, Showers' *conclusion* from this truth does not match the biblical record nor does it disprove the Pre-Wrath rapture.

➤ All Showers has done is said that the martyrs were killed before the fifth seal was broken. Even if they were killed earlier in Daniel's seventieth week, that possibility would still place them within the time period the pretribulationist calls the judgment of God! Regardless of when the martyrs are killed within Daniel's seventieth week, their martyrdom still proves that the events leading up to and including their martyrdom cannot be God's judgment.

➤ The only solution consistent with the pretrib rapture is if the fifth-seal martyrs are killed before the peace treaty. That would avoid the obvious pretribulationist problem of Christians supposedly receiving the judgments of God. However, it would then become absolutely meaningless for them to be mentioned here, since they would have nothing to do with Daniel's seventieth week. They would also have nothing to do with the Antichrist, since he does not rise to power until the time of the peace treaty.

➤ It is true that the use of the perfect tense means that the action against these martyrs is complete. At the moment of the fifth seal being broken, they have already been slain. However, that only applies to these martyrs. Showers' conclusion is that at the breaking of the fifth seal, the martyrdom of believers in Christ has been halted. If there are more martyrs to come after the fifth seal is broken, then the martyrdom is not complete; it would still be ongoing beyond the moment the fifth seal is broken. This would, of course, defeat Showers' argument. According to Revelation 6:11, there are still more martyrs to be slain!

> And there was given to each of them a white robe; and they were told that they should rest for a little while longer, *until the number of their fellow servants and their brethren who were to be killed even as they had been, should be completed also.*
> (Revelation 6:11, emphasis added)

➤ Related to the previous two items, since God says their martyrdom is not complete (Revelation 6:11), the present number seen in heaven clearly counts martyrs right up to this very moment when John sees the fifth seal broken. The fifth seal is merely a snapshot at this moment. Since their martyrdom is not complete, God's day of the Lord wrath has not begun. The martyrdom will be completed when God cuts short the great tribulation for the sake of the elect (Matthew 24:21–22, 29–31).

➤ Since the martyrdom is not complete at this point, why are the martyrs even mentioned at the time the fifth seal is broken if they are not related to the fifth seal? They would either be mentioned when their martyrdom began, when it is complete, or both. That they are mentioned while the martyrdom is ongoing can only be explained by the fact that the fifth seal is about them.

> Since the fifth seal only presents the martyrs, the fifth seal is either about the martyrs or (as Showers claims[100]) it is an event that God has chosen not to disclose. If God discloses what the events are of seals 1–4, seals 6–7, the seven trumpet judgments, and the seven bowl judgments, why would He choose not to disclose the fifth seal if it is His judgment? The claim that the prophecy is concealed here is an unreasonable and arbitrary conclusion that allows the pretribulationist to escape a serious problem in defending the pretrib rapture: if the breaking of the fifth seal only displays an event which cannot be the end-time judgment of God, then pretribulationists must explain the fifth-seal martyrs. They cannot hide or discard these martyrs as if they are not related to the fifth seal.

> The martyrs cry, "How long, O Lord, holy and true, wilt Thou refrain from judging and avenging our blood on those who dwell on the earth?" (Revelation 6:10). If God is already judging the world (and of course, slaying the wicked in those judgments), why do these martyrs conclude after five seals are broken that God is still not doing anything to avenge their blood? This fact makes it impossible to discount the martyrs' testimony. The fifth seal is about the martyrs. Since God has not avenged their blood, this is another proof that God has not begun His end-time judgments.

> Finally, if the fifth-seal martyrdom was caused by God's judgment, the martyrs would not plead to God to avenge their blood!

The Pre-Wrath rapture has a clear explanation for the fifth-seal martyrs: they are killed within the great tribulation by the Antichrist and his followers "because of the word of God, and because of the testimony which they had maintained" (Revelation 6:9). Their martyrdom will be halted (completed) when God cuts short the great tribulation for the sake of the elect (Matthew 24:22). This happens just before the sixth seal is broken.

Conclusion

It is inconceivable that God would slay the fifth-seal martyrs "because of the word of God, and because of the testimony which they had maintained" (Revelation 6:9). Therefore, the fifth seal cannot be the wrath of God. The pretribulationist's position that the fifth seal is a judgment of God is without any biblical merit, since the martyrs are not said to have committed any crimes that qualify them to be recipients God's end-time judgments. Therefore, seals 1–4 are also not God's end-time judgments, since God has not begun His day of the Lord judgments yet.

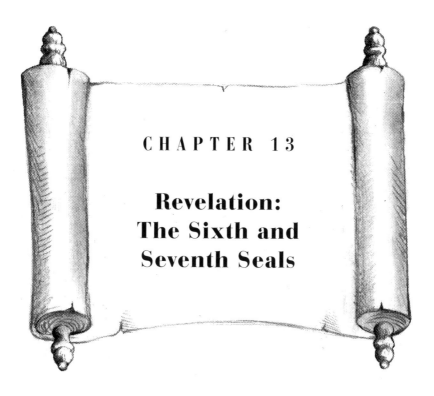

CHAPTER 13

Revelation: The Sixth and Seventh Seals

A Clear Dividing Line

We have concluded that, since God would never judge the faithful fifth seal martyrs, He cannot be the cause of the events displayed when the first five seals of the seven-sealed scroll are broken. We now turn to the sixth seal. Yes, the sixth seal is caused by God; however, we will discover that His end-time judgments still have not begun!

> [12] And I looked when He broke the sixth seal, and there was a great earthquake; and the sun became black as sackcloth made of hair, and the whole moon became like blood;
>
> [13] and the stars of the sky fell to the earth, as a fig tree casts its unripe figs when shaken by a great wind.
>
> [14] And the sky was split apart like a scroll when it is rolled up; and every mountain and island were moved out of their places.
>
> [15] And the kings of the earth and the great men and the commanders and the rich and the strong and every slave and free man, hid themselves in the caves and among the rocks of the mountains;

> [16] and they said to the mountains and to the rocks, "Fall on us and hide us from the presence of Him who sits on the throne, and from the wrath of the Lamb;
> [17] for the great day of their wrath has come; and who is able to stand?"
> (Revelation 6:12–17)

Notice that it is not until the sixth seal that the people realize God's wrath has come. John MacArthur leans away from concluding that the seals are the full force of the day of the Lord until the sixth seal is broken.

> **[Revelation] 6:12 sixth seal.** The force described in this seal is overpowering fear (cf. Lk 21:26). While the first 5 seals will result from human activity God used to accomplish His purposes, at this point He begins direct intervention (cf. Mt 24:29; Lk 21:25). The previous 5 seals will be precursors to the full fury of the Day of the Lord which will begin with the sixth seal (v. 17).[101]

I agree that there is a specific change in action at the sixth seal. In the sixth seal, as a result of the cosmic disturbances (including the darkening of the sun and moon), the people know that the great day of God's wrath is about to begin. We have already discovered in chapter 2 that according to Matthew 24:29 and Acts 2:20, the sun and moon darken *after* the great tribulation is cut short for the sake of the elect and *before* the day of the Lord. MacArthur agrees that, for the first time, the people of the world recognize the source of their trouble.

> **[Revelation] 6:16 wrath of the Lamb.** Earth's inhabitants will recognize for the first time the source of their trouble *(see note on 5:6).* Incredibly, prior to this they will be living life as usual (Mt 24:37–39)."[102]

From the Pre-Wrath rapture perspective, there is nothing incredible about this at all. The people of this world have lived life as usual, because there was no sign that the events of seals 1–5 were caused by God. In fact, the primary targets during the great tribulation are not the unsaved people of the world who have sealed their fate by taking the Antichrist's mark. The Antichrist's targets are the Jews, Christians, and unsaved who have refused the mark. Tim LaHaye also recognizes a clear dividing line between the fifth and sixth seals. This separation at the sixth seal is consistent with the Pre-Wrath rapture.

> Up to this point, the judgments that have come upon the earth during the Tribulation are largely the consequences of man's actions. But from here onward, however, the judgments are clearly supernatural. Revelation 6:12–15 describes a massive earthquake so large that "every mountain and island was moved out of its place." Massive volcanic eruptions seem to occur as well, causing the sky to turn black and the moon to appear red. The apostle John also writes of objects like meteorites crashing to the earth. The people of earth will be fully aware that they are witnessing the hand of God at work.[103] [LaHaye *does* write that the *sky* turns black instead of saying the *sun* turns black.]

I agree that the events *before* Revelation 6:12 "are largely the consequences of man's actions,"[104] since these events are the work of the Antichrist and his followers, independent of God. I also agree with LaHaye that the cosmic disturbances of Revelation 6:12–14 "are clearly supernatural."[105] It is here at the breaking of the sixth seal that God announces and prepares for His coming judgments. LaHaye sees the same dividing line as the Pre-Wrath rapture position teaches; however, he (so far) is not able to see its impact. The difference, of course, is that LaHaye claims God works through the Antichrist for seals 1–5; the Pre-Wrath rapture teaches that the Antichrist works independent of God during these five seals.

J. Dwight Pentecost presents a large number of verses claiming that they uniquely display God's wrath and not the wrath of Satan or humanity. Surprisingly, these actually support the Pre-Wrath rapture:

> Scripture abounds in assertions that this period is not the wrath of men, nor even the wrath of Satan, but the time of the wrath of God.[106]

Between these two paragraphs, Pentecost quotes Isaiah 24:1, 26:21; Joel 1:15; Zephaniah 1:18; and Revelation 6:16–17, 11:18, 14:7, 14:10, 14:19, 15:4, 15:7, 16:1, 16:7, 16:19 and 19:1–2.[107]

From these Scriptures it cannot be denied that this period is peculiarly the time when God's wrath and judgment fall upon the earth. This is not wrath from men, nor from Satan, except as God may use these agencies as channels for the execution of His will; it is tribulation from God. This period differs from all preceding tribulation, not only in intensity but also in the kind of tribulation, since it comes from God Himself.[108]

Once again, I agree with the pretribulationist! These passages uniquely display God's actions. However, the Old Testament passages that Pentecost has quoted offer no timing that would allow us to differentiate between the pretrib and Pre-Wrath rapture positions, and every one of the Revelation passages covers events that chronologically occur *after* the sixth seal is broken. That is consistent with the Pre-Wrath rapture, not the pretrib rapture. Notice that Pentecost does not even mention the events of seals 1–5 (Revelation 6:1–11) in his list of proof texts!

Although it is possible that many will die as a result of the cosmic disturbances presented after the sixth seal is broken, notice that there is no mention of any life lost. Revelation does speak about people dying *before* the sixth seal (the fourth and fifth seals) and *after* the seventh seal (the trumpet and bowl judgments). Therefore, it is likely that all of the sixth-seal events are non-lethal signs that God causes to show to everyone that His end-time judgments are about to begin.

It is noteworthy that the wrath of God is not mentioned in seals one through five. If all of the seals are the judgments of God and the sixth seal is merely a more direct action on the part of God, why did the people not understand the events to be the wrath of God in any of the preceding seals? The lack of mention previous to this point is consistent with the Pre-Wrath rapture's claim that the Lord's end-time judgments have not yet begun. The argument from silence is appropriate here, since Acts 2:20 says that the sun and moon of the sixth seal darkens before the day of the Lord. God's wrath is not mentioned in seals one through five because God's wrath has not begun.

One of the passages on the day of the Lord that Pentecost did not mention is Isaiah 13:6–9. This passage parallels the sixth seal of Revelation, showing, once again that God's judgments have not begun. The relative positioning of the sun and moon darkening provides the dividing line that separates the Antichrist's work from God's judgments.

> [6] Wail, for the day of the Lord is near! It will come as destruction from the Almighty.
> [7] Therefore all hands will fall limp, and every man's heart will melt.
> [8] And they will be terrified, pains and anguish will take hold of them; they will writhe like a woman in labor, they will look at one another in astonishment, their faces aflame.
> [9] Behold, the day of the Lord is coming, cruel, with fury and burning anger, to make the land a desolation; and He will exterminate its sinners from it.
> [10] For the stars of heaven and their constellations will not flash forth their light; the sun will be dark when it rises and the moon will not shed its light.
> [11] Thus I will punish the world for its evil and the wicked for their iniquity; I will also put an end to the arrogance of the proud and abase the haughtiness of the ruthless.
> (Isaiah 13:6–11)

The People Know!

> [15] And the kings of the earth and the great men and the commanders and the rich and the strong and every slave and free man, hid themselves in the caves and among the rocks of the mountains;
> [16] and they said to the mountains and to the rocks, "Fall on us and hide us from the presence of Him who sits on the throne, and from the wrath of the Lamb;
> [17] for the great day of their wrath has come; and who is able to stand?"
> (Revelation 6:15–17)

The pretribulationist claims that the wrath of God begins right after the peace treaty and continues far beyond the present moment of Revelation 6:17. If the wrath of God began with the first seal, why is Revelation 6:15–17 placed where it is, and why do the people of this world now (for the first time) conclude that the wrath of the Lamb has finally come? If God's wrath begins at the first seal, this passage would be placed after the first seal is broken. The only reasonable purpose for "has come" to be placed here is if God's end-time judgments are very near.

The people of the world have witnessed war, famine, desolation, death, martyrdom, a worldwide earthquake, and the sun and moon darkening, and they have seen another earthquake so great that "every island and mountain is moved out of its place" (Revelation 6:14). In Revelation 6:16–17, the people

The unsaved know it is time for the day of the Lord!

want to be hidden, because they know that the wrath of God is upon them. They plead—even demand—that the mountains and rocks fall on them *before* God can judge them with His wrath.

Why do they wait until this moment to try to hide for the first time from God's wrath if His judgments have already begun before the sixth seal? Clearly, they know what is about to happen is far more terrifying than even being crushed and buried by mountains and rocks. That forces "for the great day of their wrath has come" (Revelation 6:17) to be an event that they expect to begin very shortly *after* their plea. Matthew 24 adds two events to the darkening of the sun and moon, which also announce that the end has come.

> [29] "But immediately after the tribulation of those days the sun will be darkened, and the moon will not give its light, and the stars will fall from the sky, and the powers of the heavens will be shaken,
> [30] and then the sign of the Son of Man will appear in the sky, and then all the tribes of the earth will mourn, and they will see the Son of Man coming on the clouds of the sky with power and great glory.
> [31] "And He will send forth His angels with a great trumpet and they will gather together His elect from the four winds, from one end of the sky to the other.
> (Matthew 24:29–31)

After the whole world sees the darkening of the sun and moon, they will see the sign of the Son of Man appear in the sky, and then they will see Christ coming on clouds with power and great glory. That is why there is no doubt in the mind of anyone on earth that the wrath of the Lamb is about to begin! Notice one more thing: the people of the world specifically know that it is the Lamb of God who does the judging. This is consistent our Lord being the Creator and Judge.

> [15] And He is the image of the invisible God, the first-born of all creation.
> [16] "For by Him all things were created, both in the heavens and on earth, visible and invisible, whether thrones or dominions or rulers or authorities—all things have been created by Him and for Him.
> (Colossians 1:15-16)

> "For not even the Father judges anyone, but He has given all judgment to the Son,
> (John 5:22)

> [23] But each in his own order: Christ the first fruits, after that those who are Christ's at His coming,
> [24] then comes the end, when He delivers up the kingdom to the God and Father, when He has abolished all rule and all authority and power.
> [25] For He must reign until He has put all His enemies under His feet.
> (1 Corinthians 15:23–28)

The Gap between Revelation 6:17 and Revelation 8:1

There is a question that may be raised at this point. If, as the Pre-Wrath rapture teaches, the day of the Lord judgments begin right after the rapture, how can God's wrath begin with the trumpet judgments when there appears to be a huge gap between Revelation 6:17 and the first trumpet judgment (Revelation 8:1)? The key to understanding this gap is found in the answer to Revelation 6:15–17.

> [15] And the kings of the earth and the great men and the commanders and the rich and the strong and every slave and free man, hid themselves in the caves and among the rocks of the mountains;

¹⁶ and they said to the mountains and to the rocks, "Fall on us and hide us from the presence of Him who sits on the throne, and from the wrath of the Lamb;

¹⁷ for the great day of their wrath has come; and who is able to stand?"

(Revelation 6:15–17)

This passage is followed by Revelation 7, which shows the sealing of the 144,000 Jews and the appearance of a great uncountable multitude in heaven. The 144,000 sealed Jews and the great multitude are those who are able to stand. We will discover in a few pages that the great multitude that appears in heaven is the just raptured church (the great multitude is a focus on those raptured out of the great tribulation alive). If this is so, then it would take only a moment for God to seal the 144,000 Jews and only a "twinkling of an eye" (1 Corinthians 15:51–52) to rapture His church. Therefore, there are many events and many verses between Revelation 6:17 and the first trumpet judgment but almost no time. The sealing of the 144,000 and the rapture of the church may even be God's visible confirmation to the people of the world that they are correct in claiming that His wrath has arrived!

Provisions for the 144,000 Sons of Israel

¹ After this I saw four angels standing at the four corners of the earth, holding back the four winds of the earth, so that no wind should blow on the earth or on the sea or on any tree.

² And I saw another angel ascending from the rising of the sun, having the seal of the living God; and he cried out with a loud voice to the four angels to whom it was granted to harm the earth and the sea,

³ saying, "Do not harm the earth or the sea or the trees, until we have sealed the bond-servants of our God on their foreheads."

⁴ And I heard the number of those who were sealed, one hundred and forty-four thousand sealed from every tribe of the sons of Israel:

⁵ from the tribe of Judah, twelve thousand were sealed, from the tribe of Reuben twelve thousand, from the tribe of Gad twelve thousand,

⁶ from the tribe of Asher twelve thousand, from the tribe of Naphtali twelve thousand, from the tribe of Manasseh twelve thousand,

[7] from the tribe of Simeon twelve thousand, from the tribe of Levi twelve thousand, from the tribe of Issachar twelve thousand,
[8] from the tribe of Zebulun twelve thousand, from the tribe of Joseph twelve thousand, from the tribe of Benjamin, twelve thousand were sealed.
(Revelation 7:1–8)

The Lord will set apart and seal a remnant from the twelve tribes of Israel. Although tribal distinctions have been ignored for centuries, God quietly prepares twelve thousand from each tribe! Notice that this includes tribes from the Northern Kingdom, the supposed "lost tribes of Israel." Since they will remain on earth after the rapture, surely the seal protects the 144,000 from experiencing the Lord's judgments.

Revelation 7:1 places this event *after* seals 1–6 are broken. This positioning is very hard to explain from the pretrib rapture perspective. If seals 1–6 are God's wrath, it would be reasonable to expect that God would seal and protect the 144,000 from His wrath at or near the peace treaty. That God would wait until now (after six seals have been broken) shows once again that God's judgments are still being held back. His judgments will not begin until sometime after He seals His 144,000 (Revelation 7:1–3), precisely what the Pre-Wrath rapture claims.

According to Revelation 14:1, the seal on the forehead of the 144,000 is the name of the Father and the name of the Lamb of God. Therefore, the 144,000 are Jewish believers in Christ.

And I looked, and behold, the Lamb was standing on Mount Zion, and with Him one hundred and forty-four thousand, having His name and the name of His Father written on their foreheads. (Revelation 14:1)

One of the likely features of this seal is that the 144,000 will be able to proclaim the Father and the Son without fear of reprisal from the Antichrist or his people. Most pretribulationists agree. In fact, since they believe the church has already been raptured, they teach that the witnessing ministry of the 144,000 accounts for the salvation of the great multitude. Here is an example from Pentecost.

> After these things I looked, and behold, a great multitude, which no one could count, from every nation and all tribes and peoples and tongues, standing before the throne and before the Lamb, clothed in white robes, and palm branches were in their hands; (Revelation 7:9)

> In chapter seven the 144,000 are sealed by God, set apart to a special ministry, before the great tribulation begins. They seem to be sealed at the very outset of the tribulation period. In all probability the multitude of Gentiles, described in the passage that follows (Rev. 7:9–17), has come to a knowledge of salvation through the ministry of this group.[109]

Notice that Pentecost concludes the 144,000 are sealed at the beginning of the tribulation period. This conclusion is necessary for the pretribulationist to explain how they are protected after the peace treaty. It also provides the time necessary for the great multitude to be saved. However, Pentecost's conclusion is not consistent with the Bible.

> [2] And I saw another angel ascending from the rising of the sun, having the seal of the living God; and he cried out with a loud voice to the four angels to whom it was granted to harm the earth and the sea,
> [3] saying, "Do not harm the earth or the sea or the trees, *until we have sealed the bond-servants of our God on their foreheads.*"
> [4] And I heard the number of those who were sealed, one hundred and forty-four thousand sealed from every tribe of the sons of Israel:
> (Revelation 7:2–4, emphasis added)

As of verse 3, the 144,000 have not been sealed yet! Consider the implication of this. Pretribulationists abhor the very idea that the church could "enter into the Tribulation Period."[110] Yet the 144,000 are on earth (*before* they are sealed) at a time that the pretribulationist claims "the first five seal judgments" are happening![111] If the 144,000 can safely live during the first five seals (without God's protection), why does the pretribulationist find it impossible for Jewish and Gentile Christians to be on earth after the peace treaty? If God's wrath began at the peace treaty, it is inconceivable that the Lord would wait until the sixth seal to protect His 144,000 bondservants! Revelation 7:3 is another proof that God's judgments have not begun yet.

The only explanation possible for the 144,000 not being sealed until after the sixth seal is that God has not begun His judgments. Once that is realized, it is also very hard to apply the 144,000's witnessing effort to the salvation of the great multitude. The 144,000 are not sealed by God until *after* the sixth seal is broken; yet the great multitude appears in heaven shortly after the 144,000 are sealed. Unless one claims that the span from the sixth seal to the seventh seal encompasses many years, there would not even begin to be enough time for the 144,000 to travel all over the world (to every people group) in order to evangelize this uncountable multitude! The claim would be doubly hard for pretribulationists, since they teach that all seven seals are broken *before* the abomination of desolation. This leaves even less time between the sixth and seventh seals!

Secondly, if the 144,000's witnessing ministry is specifically to evangelize the great multitude, why are they left on earth *after* the great multitude appears in heaven? The great multitude appears in heaven *before* the seventh seal is broken. Clearly, the purpose of sealing the 144,000 is not merely to evangelize the great multitude, or they would appear in heaven at the same time as the great multitude! Instead, they remain on earth. The 144,000 and the two witnesses appear to be the only ones protected from the judgments of God; therefore, the 144,000 are likely a proof and constant reminder to the people of the world that *after* the seventh seal is broken, it is God who now judges them.

Who Is this Great Multitude?

[9] After these things I looked, and behold, a great multitude, which no one could count, from every nation and all tribes and peoples and tongues, standing before the throne and before the Lamb, clothed in white robes, and palm branches were in their hands;
[10] and they cry out with a loud voice, saying, "Salvation to our God who sits on the throne, and to the Lamb."
[11] And all the angels were standing around the throne and around the elders and the four living creatures; and they fell on their faces before the throne and worshiped God,
[12] saying, "Amen, blessing and glory and wisdom and thanksgiving and honor and power and might, be to our God forever and ever. Amen."

¹³ And one of the elders answered, saying to me, "These who are clothed in the white robes, who are they, and from where have they come?"

¹⁴ And I said to him, "My Lord, you know." And he said to me, "These are the ones who come out of the great tribulation, and they have washed their robes and made them white in the blood of the Lamb.

¹⁵ "For this reason, they are before the throne of God; and they serve Him day and night in His temple; and He who sits on the throne shall spread His tabernacle over them.

¹⁶ "They shall hunger no more, neither thirst anymore; neither shall the sun beat down on them, nor any heat;

¹⁷ for the Lamb in the center of the throne shall be their shepherd, and shall guide them to springs of the water of life; and God shall wipe every tear from their eyes."

(Revelation 7:9–17)

Notice that verse nine states "After these things"—the events of Revelation 7:9–17 occur *after* the sun and moon darken (Revelation 6:12), *after* the sealing of the 144,000 Jews (Revelation 7:2–8), and *before* the breaking of the seventh seal (Revelation 8:1). God is still not finished preparing for the day of the Lord.

Pretribulationists, of course, have concluded that the church is raptured before the peace treaty. That assumption keeps them from even considering that the great multitude could be included in the rapture. What you may find surprising is that some deny that this great multitude is even part of the church. Here is an example from Tim LaHaye.

Also, keep in mind that the saints who are martyred during the Tribulation are *not part of the church*. They are defined in Revelation 7:14 as "the ones who come out of the Great Tribulation, and [have] washed their robes and made them white in the blood of the Lamb."¹¹² (Emphasis added.)

According to the pretrib rapture, no true Christians (indwelled by the Holy Spirit) exist on earth after the peace treaty. However, who except members of the church have the testimony that their robes were made white in the blood of the Lamb (Revelation 7:14)? If they are not true Christians, why do they even appear in heaven? No tricks of interpretation are necessary if we simply recognize this great multitude as Christians.

In the above quote, LaHaye also claims that the great multitude is made up of the martyred saints, a condition never stated in Revelation 7:9–17. Am I saying that the gathering at the rapture does not include the fifth-seal martyrs? Of course not; the rapture includes those taken out of the great tribulation alive (the great multitude), those who have been martyred within the great tribulation (the fifth-seal martyrs), and believers who have died in Christ throughout church history. Although it is not stated in the Bible, it is possible that the rapture even includes faithful Jews who have died before Christ came, such as those who have placed their faith in the coming Messiah. This can be inferred by the existence of the twenty-four elders and the testimony of Daniel 12.

> [1] "Now at that time Michael, the great prince who stands guard over the sons of your people, will arise. And there will be a time of distress such as never occurred since there was a nation until that time; and at that time your people, everyone who is found written in the book, will be rescued.
> [2] "And many of those who sleep in the dust of the ground will awake, these to everlasting life, but the others to disgrace and everlasting contempt.
> (Daniel 12:1-2)

In Revelation 7:9–17, the focus is on the portion of the raptured church that faithfully persevered to the end and came out of the great tribulation alive, just as the focus of Revelation 6:9–11 is on the portion of the church that faithfully persevered (even unto death) within the great tribulation. In a similar quote to the one above, LaHaye explains why it is impossible for him to see this great multitude as the church.

> The Pretribulation view is the only one that resolves the contrasting difficulties of Revelation 3:10 and 7:14. For if Christians are among the martyrs of 7:14 who are killed during the Tribulation, then the Lord has not kept His promise in 3:10. And that is unthinkable! Pre-Tribulationists explain that there are no Christians on the earth during the Tribulation to be martyred. They are raptured before it began–fulfilling the Lord's promise.[113]

> Because you have kept the word of My perseverance, I also will keep you from the hour of testing, that hour which is about to come upon the whole world, to test those who dwell upon the earth.
> (Revelation 3:10)

Notice that Revelation 3:10 does not say God promised to keep Christians from the tribulation or the tribulation period—instead, God promised to keep them "from the hour of testing, that hour which is about to come upon the whole world." Here is where my attempt to show deference to the language of the pretrib rapture breaks down. Although people will experience tribulation, the seven-year period is never called "the tribulation" or "the tribulation period" in the Bible.

I have to step away from using the pretribulationist's "tribulation period" at this moment and call it a more appropriate term—Daniel's seventieth week. Pretribulationists call this time "the tribulation," because they believe that the whole of Daniel's seventieth week is God's wrath on the world. Therefore, they conclude that Christians cannot be on earth after the peace treaty. LaHaye claims that if the church is still here, "the Lord has not kept His promise in 3:10."[114] If God's end-time judgments begin sometime after the great multitude appear in heaven, then Revelation 3:10 can still be a promise that would apply to the great multitude.

Pretribulationists have it backwards; they assume that God begins His wrath at the peace treaty and then are forced to conclude that the great multitude (which is clearly made up of believers in Christ) cannot be like Christians today. Who could these people be if they are not the raptured church? Is this great multitude merely the completion of the martyrs of Revelation 6:9–11, as LaHaye claims? If they are, why are there no answers to the following questions?

➢ Why does Revelation 7:9–14 not call them martyrs?

➢ Why are these people not under the altar with the martyrs of the fifth seal? If they are the completion of the martyrs, they would also appear under the altar.

➢ Why did John not recognize them as martyrs if he recognized the martyrs of Revelation 6:9 without having to be told that they were martyrs?

➤ Why did the elder ask John who this great multitude was if this is merely the completed gathering of martyrs already identified in Revelation 6:9? By this point, if the great multitude only consists of martyrs, the numbers would merely have increased.

➤ Why did the elder not explain that they were martyrs after asking John who they were? John responded, "My Lord, you know" (Revelation 7:14).

These questions are made even more appropriate when we look at Revelation 20:4.

> [4] And I saw thrones, and they sat upon them, and judgment was given to them. And I saw the souls of those who had been beheaded because of the testimony of Jesus and because of the word of God, and those who had not worshiped the beast or his image, and had not received the mark upon their forehead and upon their hand; and they came to life and reigned with Christ for a thousand years.
> [5] The rest of the dead did not come to life until the thousand years were completed. This is the first resurrection.
> [6] Blessed and holy is the one who has a part in the first resurrection; over these the second death has no power, but they will be priests of God and of Christ and will reign with Him for a thousand years.
> (Revelation 20:4–6)

Many claim that the martyrs of Revelation 20:4 are a different group than those of Revelation 6:9, since Revelation 20:4 states that they "came to life and reigned with Christ for a thousand years." The claim is that this supposedly places their resurrection after the end of Daniel's seventieth week. However, Revelation 20:5 says, "This is the first resurrection," rejecting such a conclusion.

Both the pretrib and Pre-Wrath rapture positions recognize that the first resurrection (when the dead in Christ are raised) happens at the rapture, not after the end of Daniel's seventieth week. However, some pretribulationists do teach that the faithful Jews will be resurrected after the end of Daniel's seventieth week—especially the pretribulationists who claim the fifth-seal martyrs are Jews. The fifth-seal martyrs are slain because of the Word of God and because of the testimony that they have maintained; therefore, they are Christians.

Notice that Revelation 20:4 claims the fifth-seal martyrs were martyred because they refused the mark of the beast. Since the martyrs of Revelation 20:4–6 are resurrected at the rapture (the first resurrection), they are the fifth-seal martyrs who were slain within the great tribulation. This passage looks at a time after the completion of the fifth-seal martyrdom, explaining that they will reign with Christ in the millennial kingdom.

John knew that this group consists of martyrs, even clarifying how they died! Therefore, if without being told, John recognized martyrs as "martyrs" in the fifth seal (Revelation 6:9–11), and without being told, John recognized martyrs as "martyrs" at a time after their resurrection (Revelation 20:4), why is the great multitude never specifically called or identified as being the completion of the martyrs? The only reasonable explanation is that John did not know who this great multitude was until it was explained to him. The claim that they are the completion of the fifth-seal martyrdom is without merit.

Now let's gather the evidence about this great multitude. The following compilation of facts points to the great multitude that came out of the great tribulation as being the most likely candidates for the raptured church.

➤ They did not die in the great tribulation; they came out of it.

And I said to him, "My Lord, you know." And he said to me, "These are the ones who come *out of* the great tribulation, and they have washed their robes and made them white in the blood of the Lamb.
(Revelation 7:14, emphasis added)

➤ If the great tribulation ends at the pretribulationist's second coming, this great multitude would greet the Lord Jesus at His return to earth. Instead, the great multitude appears in heaven! Therefore, the great tribulation is cut short to rescue this very group of people.

➤ They have come "from every nation, tribe, people and language" (Revelation 7:9); therefore, the Great Commission has been fulfilled.

"And this gospel of the kingdom shall be preached in the whole world for a witness to all the nations, and then the end shall come. (Matthew 24:14)

> According to Matthew 24, the elect are gathered *after* the abomination of desolation (Matthew 24:15), *after* the great tribulation begins (Matthew 24:21), *after* the great tribulation is cut short (Matthew 24:22), and *after* the sun and moon are darkened (Matthew 24:29–30). When this is compared to the timing of the sun and moon darkening in Revelation 6:12–14, the great multitude appears in heaven (Revelation 7:9–17) at the same time as the gathering of the elect in Matthew 24:31. This is *after* the sixth seal is broken and *before* the seventh seal is broken! The gathering of Matthew 24:31 does not match the timing or conditions of the pretribulationist's second coming at all, but it does match the timing of the rapture according to the Pre-Wrath rapture position.

At this point, the pretribulationist will object to the claim that this great multitude is the raptured church, since the verses do not make that claim. However, the pretrib and Pre-Wrath rapture positions agree that the rapture occurs just before the day of the Lord. As shown repeatedly, Matthew 24, Revelation 6, and Acts 2 show that the day of the Lord begins after the great tribulation is cut short and after the sixth seal is broken.

But immediately after the tribulation of those days the sun will be darkened, and the moon will not give its light, and the stars will fall from the sky, and the powers of the heavens will be shaken, (Matthew 24:29)

And I looked when He broke the sixth seal, and there was a great earthquake; and the sun became black as sackcloth made of hair, and the whole moon became like blood; (Revelation 6:12)

'THE SUN SHALL BE TURNED INTO DARKNESS, AND THE MOON INTO BLOOD, BEFORE THE GREAT AND GLORIOUS DAY OF THE LORD SHALL COME. (Acts 2:20)

God has cut short the great tribulation to save the lives of His elect. He intervenes to bring the great multitude home before the completion of the Antichrist's planned genocide against the Lord's people (Matthew 24:21–22). Mighty is their deliverance! This is why the rapture is so dramatic and sudden. When the world sees Christ coming with power and great glory to take His children home, there will be no doubt that God is preparing to judge the world. Therefore, even the rapture will be one of the visible signs to all the inhabitants of the earth that God's judgments are very near. This is consistent with Revelation 1:7.

> Behold, He is coming with the clouds, and *every* eye will see Him, even those who pierced Him; and all the tribes of the earth will mourn over Him. Even so. Amen.
> (Revelation 1:7, emphasis added)

> [29] "But immediately after the tribulation of those days the sun will be darkened, and the moon will not give its light, and the stars will fall from the sky, and the powers of the heavens will be shaken,
> [30] and then the sign of the Son of Man will appear in the sky, and then all the tribes of the earth will mourn, and they will see the Son of Man coming on the clouds of the sky with power and great glory.
> [31] And He will send forth His angels with a great trumpet and they will gather together His elect from the four winds, from one end of the sky to the other.
> (Matthew 24:29–31)

> [12] And I looked when He broke the sixth seal, and there was a great earthquake; and the sun became black as sackcloth made of hair, and the whole moon became like blood;
> [13] and the stars of the sky fell to the earth, as a fig tree casts its unripe figs when shaken by a great wind.
> [14] And the sky was split apart like a scroll when it is rolled up; and every mountain and island were moved out of their places.
> [15] And the kings of the earth and the great men and the commanders and the rich and the strong and every slave and free man, hid themselves in the caves and among the rocks of the mountains;
> [16] and they said to the mountains and to the rocks, "Fall on us and hide us from the presence of Him who sits on the throne, and from the wrath of the Lamb;

[17] for the great day of their wrath has come; and who is able to stand?"
(Revelation 6:12–17)

It should be noted that once God cuts short the great tribulation for the sake of the elect, He will not delay His rapture. Therefore, in very short order, God will cut short the great tribulation, seal His 144,000, rapture His church, and then begin his end-time judgments. We have studied the following sequence of events.

➢ In Revelation 6:9–11, the fifth seal is broken, and John sees under the altar the fifth-seal martyrs "who had been slain because of the word of God, and because of the testimony which they had maintained" (Revelation 6:9). After their martyrdom is complete, they will be part of the first resurrection (Revelation 20:4–5).

➢ In Revelation 6:12–17, the sixth seal is broken, showing the darkening of the sun and moon as well as other universal cosmic disturbances, such as the sky splitting apart (Revelation 6:14) and the sign of the Son of Man appearing in the sky (Matthew 24:30). The followers of the Antichrist are terrified when they see these events, since they know God's wrath is about to begin.

➢ In Revelation 7:1–8, 144,000 men of Israel are sealed by the Lord to remain on earth. They are fully protected from the Antichrist and his followers as well as being fully protected from God's wrath upon the rest of the world.

➢ Revelation 7:9–17: the great multitude is taken out of the great tribulation, and they appear before the throne of God. This great multitude is the living church raptured from earth. The dead in Christ (including the fifth-seal martyrs) will rise, and those who are alive will rise with them meet the Lord in the air.

The Seventh Seal: Silence, then the Day of the Lord

[1] And when He broke the seventh seal, there was silence in heaven for about half an hour.
[2] And I saw the seven angels who stand before God; and seven trumpets were given to them.

³ And another angel came and stood at the altar, holding a golden censer; and much incense was given to him, that he might add it to the prayers of all the saints upon the golden altar which was before the throne.
⁴ And the smoke of the incense, with the prayers of the saints, went up before God out of the angel's hand.
⁵ And the angel took the censer; and he filled it with the fire of the altar and threw it to the earth; and there followed peals of thunder and sounds and flashes of lightning and an earthquake.
⁶ And the seven angels who had the seven trumpets prepared themselves to sound them.
(Revelation 8:1–6)

As God is now about to begin His day of the Lord judgments, Revelation 8 opens with silence in heaven. For those who believe that God's end-time judgments began shortly after the peace treaty, it would be hard to understand why this silence is being recorded for the first time in Revelation. However, if God has not begun His wrath yet, the silence is quite understandable. There are at least two reasons for this silence in heaven.

➢ I have already mentioned the first reason: the contents of the scroll cannot be seen or read until after all seven seals of the scroll are broken. The silence now in heaven is in anticipation of finally discovering what will be presented after the scroll is opened.

➢ The second reason for this silence is a consequence of the first. It is the realization of what is about to happen. All worldly events leading up to God's wrath are now complete. There are no events left that must happen before the day of the Lord begins. All of those in heaven join together and pause for thirty minutes, to reflect on all of history leading up to this moment. If you would allow some speculation here about why there is this silence, I would like to present a reasonable illustration. Imagine we are members of a jury. In this trial, a man is being accused of an act of vicious murder, and we are about to be polled for our verdict. We pause and take a deep breath before the monumental task that surely will lead to this man being found guilty and worthy of the highest level of judgment. In the same sense, all of heaven pauses for about thirty minutes. The time has finally come for

God to begin His day of the Lord judgments. After the thirty minutes of silence, the seven trumpet judgments and seven bowl judgments come. According to the Pre-Wrath rapture, the first trumpet judgment occurs very shortly after the great tribulation is cut short for the sake of the elect; this is much later in Daniel's seventieth week than the pretribulationist places it.

Conclusion

God is clearly responsible for the events of the sixth seal; however, since there is no mention of death, it is quite possible that no death occurs. This is substantiated by the fact that people die during the events before the sixth seal is broken and after the seventh seal.

The events presented in the sixth seal (Revelation 6:12–7:17) parallel those found in Matthew 24:29–31. In rapid sequence, the people witness a worldwide earthquake, then the darkening of the sun and moon, then a second worldwide earthquake, then the sealing of the 144,000, and then the rapture of the church. The events shown when the sixth seal is broken are the Lord's signs that His judgments are very near. The first trumpet judgment would begin the day of the Lord.

CHAPTER 14

Closing Comments

I close with one final encouragement that matches how I started this study. Although I disagree with the end-time conclusions of those who adhere to the pretrib rapture position, if they are saved by the blood of Christ, they are my Christian brothers and sisters. Please do not let the body of believers in Christ be divided over an issue that should not have anything to do with our walk before the throne of God and our service in His name while still here on earth. Regardless of when God may choose to rapture us, let's work together for His glory, since we are guaranteed that we will be raptured before God begins His end-time judgments.

If the timing of the rapture is not a doctrine even remotely on par with salvation in Christ, why have I put such an intensive effort into this study? The answer is found in my concern for the church. It is clear that many Christians will enter into Daniel's seventieth week and then be raptured very soon after the Lord cuts short the great tribulation for the sake of the elect. We should not teach that the blessed hope is our guarantee of being raptured before the peace treaty.

Matthew 24:29–31, Revelation 6:12–17, and Acts 2:20–21 make it clear that the day of the Lord (and the rapture before it) will not happen until *after* the sixth seal of the seven-sealed scroll is broken. Depending on escaping the tribulation period will leave a multitude of believers in Christ discouraged and defeated if they are still here when Daniel's seventieth week begins. Some who trust in the pretrib rapture and are isolated from other believers may even conclude that they are not saved and have missed the rapture. Either result would be a great victory for Satan!

Although Daniel's seventieth week has not arrived, it is possible that we are very close to that day. We will need to be ready, since God will have a great work for us to do! For some of us, that will even include assisting Jews in Israel as they flee the Antichrist immediately after he commits the abomination of desolation.

As we approach the end times, this world will cry out for a great leader rather than trusting God. Even Israel will trust Satan's Antichrist for peace and security. The Antichrist will likely be swept into power because of a great international crisis that all others have failed to resolve. The world will fall for his beguiling offer. However, Christians on earth at this time must not be caught off guard. Although we cannot date the rapture, the Scriptures have given us the necessary events to look for so that we know if and when we are within Daniel's seventieth week. We need not fear God's wrath while we are still here on earth, since our Lord has promised that *before* He begins His end-time judgments against the Antichrist and his followers, we will be taken home by our Savior, Jesus Christ!

We must accept the possibility that some of us will witness events within Daniel's seventieth week; yet this will be *before* God's end-time judgments begin. Our attitude should not be fear. Instead, we should be excited that our Lord has counted us worthy to carry His gospel to the whole world during this terrible time. We will have the unbelievable privilege of being involved in God's calling of the last of His elect across the threshold into everlasting life! The church must be prepared to serve the Lord faithfully within this time, and we must be ready to encourage each other with boldness for the gospel's sake.

In light of the signs that Daniel's seventieth week could be near, please consider one final study before closing this book. The Appendix provides a compilation of the end-time events surrounding the darkening of the sun and moon. While chapter 2 covered parts of Matthew 24, Acts 2, and Revelation 6–8, the Appendix will look at these chapters more extensively as well as adding Isaiah, Joel, Mark, and Luke. Near the end of the Appendix, the events will be charted chronologically. Included in the result are more than forty events that must happen before the rapture and more than fifty events that must happen before the beginning of God's end-time judgments! If you are still here when these events begin, knowing what is coming and the order of these events will contribute to your being a good and faithful servant of the Lord regardless of what happens in this world. However, keep in mind that we are guaranteed that we will be raptured *before* God's end-time judgments begin.

APPENDIX

Charting the Darkening of the Sun and Moon

As stated in chapter 2, I discovered passages within Isaiah, Joel, Matthew, Mark, Luke, Acts, and Revelation that speak about "the darkening of the sun and moon" in which the events of Daniel's seventieth week are said to occur before, around the same time as, or after this darkening event. In this appendix, we will examine all of these passages, and then near the end of this chapter, the events will be charted in chronological order. As we study these events, please keep the following points in mind.

➤ All of the primary passages included in this study specifically speak about the darkening of the sun and moon. Some passages include the darkening of the stars and stars falling from the sky. Falling stars would be non-stellar objects, such as meteorites.

➤ Through the examination of these passages, we will see that this darkening of the sun and moon becomes the centering pillar around which the other key end-time events are placed in the chronology. This darkening event, along with volcanic activity and the heavens and earth quaking, are commonly called "cosmic disturbances."

➤ Although the order may not be clear in the earlier passages we will look at, I will list the events after each passage in the sequence consistent with how the order will unfold as we progress through the Scriptures. I will also indicate the chart's line item for each event. The resulting chronological order will become increasingly clear as we accumulate these related verses.

➤ We will see in the book of Revelation that there is a worldwide earthquake before and after the sun and moon darken. Although some believe that Revelation 6:14 ("every mountain and island were moved out of their places") is merely the consequence of the Revelation 6:12 earthquake, since Joel 3:16 presents the earthquake after the sun, moon, and stars darken, I will list the two Revelation events as separate entries.

➤ There is no mention of any death during either earthquake or during the darkening of the sun, moon, and stars. Therefore, these events are non-lethal announcements that God's wrath is near!

Isaiah 13:6–13

⁶ Wail, for the day of the Lord is near! It will come as destruction from the Almighty.
⁷ Therefore all hands will fall limp, and every man's heart will melt.
⁸ They will be terrified, pains and anguish will take hold of them; they will writhe like a woman in labor, they will look at one another in astonishment, their faces aflame.
⁹ Behold, the day of the Lord is coming, cruel, with fury and burning anger, to make the land a desolation; and He will exterminate its sinners from it.
¹⁰ For the stars of heaven and their constellations will not flash forth their light; the sun will be dark when it rises and the moon will not shed its light.
¹¹ Thus I will punish the world for its evil and the wicked for their iniquity; I will also put an end to the arrogance of the proud and abase the haughtiness of the ruthless.
¹² I will make mortal man scarcer than pure gold and mankind than the gold of Ophir.

[13] Therefore I will make the heavens tremble, and the earth will be shaken from its place at the fury of the Lord of hosts in the day of His burning anger.
(Isaiah 13:6–13)

Notice that about the time that the sun, moon, and stars are darkened, the day of the Lord is near. The events presented in Isaiah 13:6–13 are:

➤ The sun, moon, and stars are darkened (Isaiah 13:10). See item 28 of the chronological chart near the end of this appendix.

➤ The heavens tremble (Isaiah 13:13). See item 30.

➤ The whole earth is shaken (Isaiah 13:13). See item 32.

➤ The people of the earth are terrified (Isaiah 13:6–8). See item 37.

➤ The day of the Lord judgments are near (Isaiah 13:6, 9). See item 54.

➤ The day of the Lord (Isaiah 13:11–13). See item 59.

Joel 2:10–11

[10] Before them the earth quakes, the heavens tremble, the sun and the moon grow dark, and the stars lose their brightness.
[11] And the Lord utters His voice before His army; surely His camp is very great, for strong is he who carries out His word. The day of the Lord is indeed great and very awesome, and who can endure it?
(Joel 2:10–11)

The events presented in Joel 2:10–11 are:

➤ The sun, moon, and stars are darkened (Joel 2:10). See item 28.

➤ The heavens tremble (Joel 2:10). See item 30.

➤ Earthquakes (Joel 2:10). See item 32.

➤ The Lord utters His voice before His army (Joel 2:11). See item 55.

➤ The day of the Lord (Joel 2:11). See item 59.

It is likely that "the Lord utters His voice before His army" (Joel 2:11) is a call to battle. This would occur shortly before God begins His day of the Lord judgments. Notice also that Joel said the sun and moon grow dark and the stars lose their brightness around the time of the day of the Lord. It appears to be an action that is directly applied to the sun and moon. This condition of darkening will become even clearer as we study other passages.

Joel 3:14–16

[14] Multitudes, multitudes in the valley of decision! For the day of the Lord is near in the valley of decision.
[15] The sun and moon grow dark, and the stars lose their brightness.
[16] And the Lord roars from Zion and utters His voice from Jerusalem, and the heavens and the earth tremble. But the Lord is a refuge for His people and a stronghold to the sons of Israel. (Joel 3:14–16)

Here we see that "the Lord is a refuge for His people" and He is "a stronghold to the sons of Israel." The first may be a promise of the rapture and the second may be the sealing of the 144,000 just before the rapture. The events presented in Joel 3:14–16 are:

➢ The sun, moon, and stars darken (Joel 3:15). See item 28.

➢ The heavens tremble (Joel 3:16). See item 30.

➢ The earth trembles (Joel 3:16). See item 32.

➢ The Lord is a stronghold to the Sons of Israel (Joel 3:16). See item 44.

➢ The Lord is a refuge for His people (Joel 3:16). See item 48.

➢ The day of the Lord is near (Joel 3:14). See item 54.

➢ The Lord roars from Zion and utters His voice from Jerusalem (Joel 3:16). This is likely the same call to battle as Joel 2:11. See item 55.

Let's now turn to Matthew 24. It is from this Gospel that much chronology is added.

Matthew 24:5–14

5 "For many will come in My name, saying, 'I am the Christ,' and will mislead many.

6 "And you will be hearing of wars and rumors of wars; see that you are not frightened, for those things must take place, but that is not yet the end.

7 For nation will rise against nation, and kingdom against kingdom, and in various places there will be famines and earthquakes.

8 But all these things are merely the beginning of birth pangs.

9 "Then they will deliver you to tribulation, and will kill you, and you will be hated by all nations on account of My name.

10 And at that time many will fall away and will deliver up one another and hate one another.

11 And many false prophets will arise, and will mislead many.

12 And because lawlessness is increased, most people's love will grow cold.

13 But the one who endures to the end, he shall be saved.

14 And this gospel of the kingdom shall be preached in the whole world for a witness to all the nations, and then the end shall come. (Matthew 24:5–14)

Notice that the focus is on Jewish and Gentile Christians, since they are hated on account of Christ's name (Matthew 24:9). The events presented in Matthew 24:5–14 are:

➤ The beginning of birth pangs (Matthew 24:6–8). See item 5.

➤ Wars and rumors of wars (Matthew 24:6–7). See item 6.

➤ Famine (Matthew 24:7). See item 7.

➤ Earthquakes in various places (Matthew 24:7). See item 8.

➤ The beginning of hard labor: the coming events of the great tribulation (Matthew 24:9–11). See item 13.

➤ False Christs and false prophets arise (Matthew 24:5, 11). See item 15.

➤ Christ's elect are hated by all the nations (Matthew 24:9). See item 16.

➤ Apostasy arises within the church (Matthew 24:9–10). See item 17.

➢ Christ's elect are betrayed (Matthew 24:10). See item 18.

➢ Christ's elect are martyred (Matthew 24:9). See item 21.

➢ Those who endure to the end will be saved (Matthew 24:13). See item 23.

➢ The gospel will be preached to the whole world (Matthew 24:14). See item 51.

➢ Then the end will come (Matthew 24:14). See item 56.

Matthew 24:15–22

¹⁵ "Therefore when you see the abomination of desolation which was spoken of through Daniel the prophet, standing in the holy place (let the reader understand),
¹⁶ then let those who are in Judea flee to the mountains;
¹⁷ let him who is on the housetop not go down to get the things out that are in his house;
¹⁸ and let him who is in the field not turn back to get his cloak.
¹⁹ But woe to those who are with child and to those who nurse babes in those days!
²⁰ But pray that your flight may not be in the winter, or on a Sabbath;
²¹ for then there will be a great tribulation, such as has not occurred since the beginning of the world until now, nor ever shall.
²² And unless those days had been cut short, no life would have been saved; but for the sake of the elect those days shall be cut short.
(Matthew 24:15–22)

Prior to the abomination of desolation, the temple must already have been built (or a tabernacle, since it also would be consistent with the prophecy). This will be added to the chart.

Notice also that Matthew 24:15 says, "When you see the abomination of desolation which was spoken of through Daniel the prophet, standing in the holy place...." Usually this is expressed as the Antichrist committing the abomination of desolation. Although he will desecrate the temple and have his image set up, it is possible the Antichrist even becomes the abomination of desolation in the temple! This is consistent with 2 Thessalonians 2:4, which explains that the

Antichrist displays himself as being God. The events presented in Matthew 24:15–22 are:

➢ The temple is built (assumed from Matthew 24:15). See item 9.

➢ The abomination of desolation (Matthew 24:15). See item 10.

➢ Jews (and Christians) in Judea must flee to the mountains (Matthew 24:16–20). See item 12.

➢ Then the great tribulation begins (Matthew 24:21). See item 13.

➢ Christ's elect are martyred (Matthew 24:21–22). See item 21.

➢ The great tribulation is cut short for the sake of Christ's elect (Matthew 24:22). See item 24.

Matthew 24:23–28

[23] Then if anyone says to you, 'Behold, here is the Christ,' or 'There He is,' do not believe him.
[24] For false Christs and false prophets will arise and will show great signs and wonders, so as to mislead, if possible, even the elect.
[25] Behold, I have told you in advance.
[26] If therefore they say to you, 'Behold, He is in the wilderness,' do not go forth, or, 'Behold, He is in the inner rooms,' do not believe them.
[27] For just as the lightning comes from the east, and flashes even to the west, so shall the coming of the Son of Man be.
[28] Wherever the corpse is, there the vultures will gather.
(Matthew 24:23–28)

The events presented in Matthew 24:23–28 are:

➢ False Christs and false prophets arise, performing signs and wonders so great that they may even mislead the elect (Matthew 24:23–26). See item 15.

➢ The Son of Man will come, visible to all (Matthew 24:27). See item 43.

Matthew 24:29–31

²⁹ "But immediately *after* the tribulation of those days the sun will be darkened, and the moon will not give its light, and the stars will fall from the sky, and the powers of the heavens will be shaken,
³⁰ and *then* the sign of the Son of Man will appear in the sky, and *then* all the tribes of the earth will mourn, and they will see the Son of Man coming on the clouds of the sky with power and great glory.
³¹ And He will send forth His angels with a great trumpet and they will gather together His elect from the four winds, from one end of the sky to the other.
(Matthew 24:29–31, emphasis added)

I will place "The powers of the heavens will be shaken" (verse 29) after "the heavens and the earth tremble" (Joel 3:16). Verse 29 could refer to the trembling heavens of Joel 3:16 or it could even refer to the demons shaking, since they know their judgment is near. The events presented in Matthew 24:29–31 are:

- ➢ The great tribulation is cut short (Matthew 24:29). See item 24.

- ➢ The sun and moon are darkened (Matthew 24:29). See item 28.

- ➢ Stars fall from the sky (Matthew 24:29). See item 29.

- ➢ The powers of the heavens are shaken (Matthew 24:29). See item 31.

- ➢ The sign of the Son of Man appears in the sky (Matthew 24:30). See item 35.

- ➢ All the tribes of the earth mourn (Matthew 24:30). See item 37.

- ➢ The Son of Man comes on clouds, visible to all (Matthew 24:30). See item 43.

- ➢ The Son of Man sends forth His angels to gather the elect (Matthew 24:31). See item 49.

- ➢ A great trumpet sounds (Matthew 24:31). See item 50.

- ➢ Angels gather Christ's elect. This is the rapture (Matthew 24:31). See item 52.

Let's now look at Mark and Luke, two books that provide parallel passages to Matthew 24. In the gospel of Mark, we find the same sequence, plus some clarity is added regarding the identity of the elect.

Mark 13:6–13

[6] "Many will come in My name, saying, 'I am He!' and will mislead many.

[7] "And when you hear of wars and rumors of wars, do not be frightened; those things must take place; but that is not yet the end.

[8] "For nation will arise against nation, and kingdom against kingdom; there will be earthquakes in various places; there will also be famines. These things are merely the beginning of birth pangs.

[9] "But be on your guard; for they will deliver you to the courts, and you will be flogged in the synagogues, and you will stand before governors and kings for My sake, as a testimony to them.

[10] "And the gospel must first be preached to all the nations.

[11] 'And when they arrest you and deliver you up, do not be anxious beforehand about what you are to say, but say whatever is given you in that hour; for it is not you who speak, but it is the Holy Spirit.

[12] "And brother will deliver brother to death, and a father his child; and children will rise up against parents and have them put to death.

[13] 'And you will be hated by all on account of My name, but the one who endures to the end, he shall be saved.
(Mark 13:6–13)

The events presented in Mark 13:6–13 are:

➢ The beginning of birth pangs (Mark 13:7–8). See item 5.

➢ Wars and rumors of wars (Mark 13:7–8). See item 6.

➢ Famine (Mark 13:8). See item 7.

➢ Earthquakes in various places (Mark 13:8). See item 8.

➢ The beginning of hard labor: the coming events of the great tribulation (Mark 13:9, 11–13). See item 13.

- False Christs and false prophets arise (Mark 13:6). See item 15.

- Christ's elect are hated by all the nations because of His name (Mark 13:13). See item 16.

- Christ's elect are betrayed, even by members of their own families (Mark 13:9, 11–12). See items 17 and 18.

- Christ's elect are arrested (Mark 13:9, 11). See item 19.

- Christ's elect testify of Him before the world's leaders (Mark 13:9, 11). See item 20.

- Christians who endure to the end will be saved (Mark 13:13). See item 23.

- The gospel is preached to all the nations (Mark 13:10). See item 51.

Mark 13:14–23

¹⁴ "But when you see the abomination of desolation standing where it should not be (let the reader understand), then let those who are in Judea flee to the mountains.
¹⁵ "And let him who is on the housetop not go down, or enter in, to get anything out of his house;
¹⁶ and let him who is in the field not turn back to get his cloak.
¹⁷ "But woe to those who are with child and to those who nurse babes in those days!
¹⁸ "But pray that it may not happen in the winter.
¹⁹ "For those days will be a time of tribulation such as has not occurred since the beginning of the creation which God created, until now, and never shall.
²⁰ "And unless the Lord had shortened those days, no life would have been saved; but for the sake of the elect whom He chose, He shortened the days.
²¹ "And then if anyone says to you, 'Behold, here is the Christ'; or, 'Behold, He is there'; do not believe him;
²² for false Christs and false prophets will arise, and will show signs and wonders, in order, if possible, to lead the elect astray.
²³ "But take heed; behold, I have told you everything in advance. (Mark 13:14–23)

Notice that, consistent with Matthew, in Mark 13:20, we are shown that the elect in the great tribulation are Christians. This is substantiated by the fact that even many pretribulationists agree the elect who are gathered in Mark 13:27 (below) are believers in Christ. The elect of Mark 13:20 and the elect of Mark 13:27 must be interpreted the same. The events presented in Mark 13:14–23 are:

➤ The abomination of desolation (Mark 13:14). See item 10.

➤ Jews (and Christians) in Judea must flee to the mountains (Mark 13:14–18). See item 12.

➤ The great tribulation begins (Mark 13:19). See item 13.

➤ False Christs and false prophets arise, performing great signs and wonders (Mark 13:21–22). See item 15.

➤ Christ's elect are martyred (Mark 13:20). See item 21.

➤ The great tribulation is cut short for the sake of Christ's elect (Mark 13:20). See item 24.

Mark 13:24–27

[24] "But in those days, after that tribulation, the sun will be darkened, and the moon will not give its light,
[25] and the stars will be falling from heaven, and the powers that are in the heavens will be shaken.
[26] "And then they will see the Son of Man coming in clouds with great power and glory.
[27] "And then He will send forth the angels, and will gather together His elect from the four winds, from the farthest end of the earth, to the farthest end of heaven.
(Mark 13:24–27)

We are shown in verse 27 that Christ's elect are gathered from the farthest ends of the earth to the farthest ends of heaven. This fits the rapture; it does not fit the pretribulationist's second coming. The events presented in Mark 13:24–27 are:

➤ After the great tribulation, the sun and moon are darkened (Mark 13:24). See items 24 and 28.

➤ Stars fall from the sky (Mark 13:25). See item 29.

➤ The powers of the heavens are shaken (Mark 13:25). See item 31.

➤ The Son of Man comes, visible to all (Mark 13:26). See item 43.

➤ The Son of Man sends forth His angels to gather His elect. This is the rapture (Mark 13:27). See items 49 and 52.

Luke 21:25–28

²⁵ "And there will be signs in sun and moon and stars, and upon the earth dismay among nations, in perplexity at the roaring of the sea and the waves,
²⁶ men fainting from fear and the expectation of the things which are coming upon the world; for the powers of the heavens will be shaken.
²⁷ "And then they will see the Son of Man coming in a cloud with power and great glory.
²⁸ "But when these things begin to take place, straighten up and lift up your heads, because your redemption is drawing near.
(Luke 21:25–28)

It is noteworthy that Luke 21:25 uses the phrase "there will be signs in sun and moon and stars." Although it does not say here that the sun, moon, and stars darken, this occurs at the same time as the darkening event occurs in other passages. Therefore, it is very likely that Luke wrote about the darkening of the sun, moon, and stars.

Luke 21:25 mentions "the roaring of the sea and the waves." These are probably worldwide tsunamis caused by the earthquakes, so I will place this event after the earthquakes. As soon as Christians see the signs in the sun, moon, and stars and then see the Son of Man coming in a cloud, they are to look up, because their redemption is near! The events presented in Luke 21:25–28 are:

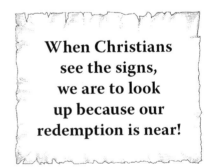

When Christians see the signs, we are to look up because our redemption is near!

➤ The sun, moon, and stars darken (Luke 21:25). See item 28.

➤ The powers of the heavens are shaken (Luke 21:26). See item 31.

➤ The roaring of the seas and the waves (Luke 21:25). See item 33.

- ➢ The people of the earth are terrified and mourn (Luke 21:25–26). See item 37.

- ➢ The Son of Man comes in a cloud, visible to all (Luke 21:27). See item 43.

- ➢ Christians are to look up, because our redemption draws near (Luke 21:28). See item 46.

Revelation 6:1–6

[1] And I saw when the Lamb broke one of the seven seals, and I heard one of the four living creatures saying as with a voice of thunder, "Come."
[2] And I looked, and behold, a white horse, and he who sat on it had a bow; and a crown was given to him; and he went out conquering, and to conquer.
[3] And when He broke the second seal, I heard the second living creature saying, "Come."
[4] And another, a red horse, went out; and to him who sat on it, it was granted to take peace from the earth, and that men should slay one another; and a great sword was given to him.
[5] And when He broke the third seal, I heard the third living creature saying, "Come." And I looked, and behold, a black horse; and he who sat on it had a pair of scales in his hand.
[6] And I heard as it were a voice in the center of the four living creatures saying, "A quart of wheat for a denarius, and three quarts of barley for a denarius; and do not harm the oil and the wine."
(Revelation 6:1–6)

Futurists agree that these events will begin after the peace treaty is signed between the Antichrist and Israel. The events presented in Revelation 6:1–6 are:

- ➢ The first seal is broken: the Antichrist rises to power and prepares to conquer (Revelation 6:1–2). See item 4.

- ➢ The second seal is broken: war is waged everywhere in the world except Israel, since the Antichrist is still guaranteeing peace within Israel (Revelation 6:3–4). See item 6.

- ➢ The third seal is broken: worldwide famine (Revelation 6:5–6). See item 7.

Revelation 6:7–11

⁷ And when He broke the fourth seal, I heard the voice of the fourth living creature saying, "Come."

⁸ And I looked, and behold, an ashen horse; and he who sat on it had the name Death; and Hades was following with him. And authority was given to them over a fourth of the earth, to kill with sword and with famine and with pestilence and by the wild beasts of the earth.

⁹ And when He broke the fifth seal, I saw underneath the altar the souls of those who had been slain because of the word of God, and because of the testimony which they had maintained;

¹⁰ and they cried out with a loud voice, saying, "How long, O Lord, holy and true, wilt Thou refrain from judging and avenging our blood on those who dwell on the earth?"

¹¹ And there was given to each of them a white robe; and they were told that they should rest for a little while longer, until the number of their fellow servants and their brethren who were to be killed even as they had been, should be completed also.
(Revelation 6:7–11)

The Pre-Wrath rapture teaches that the deaths of the fourth and fifth seals occur within the great tribulation. Although it is possible that the fourth seal is the event which causes the fifth seal martyrdom, I lean toward the fourth seal being the killing of the lost within the great tribulation, since only the lost are associated with Hades. They are killed by the sword, famine, and pestilence.

The fifth-seal martyrs are killed because of the word of God and their faithful testimony. These Christians are singled out because they have faithfully refused to take the Antichrist's mark and worship him, even though it meant being martyred for their faith. The events presented in Revelation 6:7–11 are:

➢ The fourth seal is broken: 25 percent of the world's population dies; they are likely headed for Hades (Revelation 6:7–8). See item 14.

➢ The fifth seal is broken; martyrs appear under the altar in heaven (Revelation 6:9). See item 21.

- ➤ The martyrs are slain because of the Word of God and because of the testimony they maintained (Revelation 6:9). See item 21.

- ➤ The martyrs are given white robes (Revelation 6:11). See item 21.

- ➤ The martyrs cry out to God to avenge their blood on those who slew them (Revelation 6:10). See item 22.

- ➤ The martyrs are told to rest a little while longer until the martyrdom is complete (Revelation 6:11). See item 22.

Revelation 6:12–17

[12] And I looked when He broke the sixth seal, and there was a great earthquake; and the sun became black as sackcloth made of hair, and the whole moon became like blood;
[13] and the stars of the sky fell to the earth, as a fig tree casts its unripe figs when shaken by a great wind.
[14] And the sky was split apart like a scroll when it is rolled up; and every mountain and island were moved out of their places.
[15] And the kings of the earth and the great men and the commanders and the rich and the strong and every slave and free man, hid themselves in the caves and among the rocks of the mountains;
[16] and they said to the mountains and to the rocks, "Fall on us and hide us from the presence of Him who sits on the throne, and from the wrath of the Lamb;
[17] for the great day of their wrath has come; and who is able to stand?
(Revelation 6:12–17)

Now it is clear why the great men of the earth are terrified! In what appears to be a very short span of time, there is a great worldwide earthquake, the sun and moon darken, and "every mountain and island were moved out of their places" (Revelation 6:14). As terrible as the quakeing events of verses 12 and 14 are, they are not the most terrifying events. As we saw in Matthew 24, when these events happen, the sign of the Son of Man also appears in the sky. Revelation 6:16–17 offers another event that happens at the same time. Apparently, when the sky is split apart like a scroll, they also see God on His throne![115] There will be no question that the wrath of the Lamb is about to begin.

Notice also in Revelation 6:12, that at the same time the sun became black as sackcloth, the moon merely became like blood! There have been times in the past during which the whole world was at least marginally covered by clouds that caused the darkening of the sun, moon, and stars. For instance, in 1815–1816, there was an eruption of four volcanoes followed by a monstrous eruption of Mount Tambora. The climate of the whole world was so severely affected that 1816 was known as "the year without a summer." Applying this to the darkening of the sun, moon, and stars, one could claim that the sun would be so thickly covered that the sky turns black, and the moon turns red because the volcanic clouds are thinner where the moon is visible. However, there is also a sense of suddenness to the sun and moon darkening. This is not a condition that would match the progressively thickening of the clouds if it was caused by volcanic activity.

Secondly, for the darkening of the sun, moon, and stars to be a sign of the end of the age, it must be an absolutely unique event, not merely another worldwide cloud or ash covering. To be a sign, its uniqueness must be on par with the sign of the Son of Man appearing in the sky. Otherwise it is merely a recurrence of a past event.

Are the Four Blood Moons of 2014–2015 a Fulfillment of the Sun and Moon Darkening?

Some pretribulationists recognize the problem with attributing the darkening of the sun and moon to clouds and have concluded that this appears to be a total eclipse of the sun (which would make it appear black) and a total eclipse of the moon (which would make it appear to be the color of blood). Many have written extensively over the past few years about the coming of four blood moons during 2014 and 2015, since they occur during Israel's feasts. The last two times they occurred during Israel's feasts were shortly after Israel became a nation again in 1948 and surrounding the 1967 war.

This has been intriguing speculation; however, based on the moon turning to blood *after* the great tribulation is cut short (Matthew 24:29), there is insufficient time between now and the third blood moon of April 4, 2015 (the blood moon nearest the March 20, 2015 eclipse of the sun). This is a critical point since there will not be another set of four blood moons at the time of Israel's feasts for the rest of this century!

It is noteworthy that even the two examples which are the basis of the pretribulationist's claim are not consistent. Israel became a nation in 1948, *before* the four blood moons. The 1967 war was *between* the first and second blood moons. If God designed these darkening events in order to point us to the 2014–2015 blood moons as a testimony that the end of the age has arrived, they would surely perfectly match! Of course, it is possible for the 2014–2015 blood moons to announce another great event concerning Israel at this time, but it cannot be the Matthew 24:29 darkening event. However, there are many far more concrete reasons why the eclipse of the sun and moon is not a reasonable explanation for the biblical darkening of the sun and moon.

➢ The most obvious reason is that sun and moon cannot be eclipsed at the same time, since it is the moon that eclipses the sun.

➢ An eclipse of the sun and the eclipse of the moon are only visible to a small portion of the world at any time. Most of the world will not even know an eclipse is happening.

➢ It cannot be a sequence of events, since even if the sun, earth, and moon are aligned so that the moon eclipses the sun and then, at the very next opportunity, the earth fully eclipses the moon, the darkening of the moon would be separated from the darkening of the sun by about two weeks. In fact, the third blood moon of 2014–2015 will occur 15 days after the sun's eclipse on March 20, 2015. Matthew 24:29 (a parallel event to Revelation 6:12) explains that "Immediately after the tribulation of those days the sun will be darkened, and the moon will not give its light, and the stars will fall from the sky." *Immediately* has absolutely no meaning if there is a two-week gap between the sun and moon darkening. This is truly a miraculous one-time event that is impossible with a sequence of solar and lunar eclipses.

➤ It is possible, with the right atmospheric circumstances during a total eclipse of the sun, for the moon to appear reddish-brown (from sunlight reflected from the earth). However, Joel 2:10 says, "The sun and moon grow dark and the stars lose their brightness." In a total solar eclipse, the stars become *more* visible, since they no longer have to compete with the much stronger light of the sun. Clearly, the sun and stars turning to black and the moon turning to red (all at the same time) is naturally impossible.

➤ Finally, as already stated, the darkening of the sun and moon must be such a unique event that it has never happened before; otherwise it cannot demonstrate that the end of the age has come (Matthew 24:3, 29). That uniqueness is not the case for an eclipse of the sun, eclipse of the moon, or volcanic activity. All naturally explained events are rejected because they have happened before. This event can only be one which is miraculously and concurrently applied to the sun, moon, and stars by God.

The events presented in Revelation 6:12–17 are:

➤ The sixth seal is broken (Revelation 6:12). See item 25.

➤ A great earthquake (Revelation 6:12). See item 27.

➤ The sun turns black, and the moon becomes like blood (Revelation 6:12). See item 28.

➤ The "stars" fall to the earth (Revelation 6:13). See item 29.

➤ Every mountain and island is moved out of its place (Revelation 6:14). See item 32.

➤ The sky is split apart like a scroll when it is rolled up (Revelation 6:14). See item 34.

➤ The people see God on His throne. (Revelation 6:16). See item 36.

➤ All the unsaved people of the earth are terrified (Revelation 6:15–16). See item 37.

➤ The unsaved people of the earth hide in caves and among the rocks of the mountains (Revelation 6:15). See item 38.

- The unsaved people of the earth cry for the mountains to fall on them to hide them from the wrath of the Lamb (Revelation 6:16). See item 39.

- The unsaved people of the earth know that what is about to happen is the wrath of the Lamb (Revelation 6:16–17). See items 40 and 54.

Revelation 7:1–8

¹ After this I saw four angels standing at the four corners of the earth, holding back the four winds of the earth, so that no wind should blow on the earth or on the sea or on any tree.
² And I saw another angel ascending from the rising of the sun, having the seal of the living God; and he cried out with a loud voice to the four angels to whom it was granted to harm the earth and the sea,
³ saying, "Do not harm the earth or the sea or the trees, until we have sealed the bond-servants of our God on their foreheads."
⁴ And I heard the number of those who were sealed, one hundred and forty-four thousand sealed from every tribe of the sons of Israel:
⁵ from the tribe of Judah, twelve thousand were sealed, from the tribe of Reuben twelve thousand, from the tribe of Gad twelve thousand,
⁶ from the tribe of Asher twelve thousand, from the tribe of Naphtali twelve thousand, from the tribe of Manasseh twelve thousand,
⁷ from the tribe of Simeon twelve thousand, from the tribe of Levi twelve thousand, from the tribe of Issachar twelve thousand,
⁸ from the tribe of Zebulun twelve thousand, from the tribe of Joseph twelve thousand, from the tribe of Benjamin, twelve thousand were sealed.
(Revelation 7:1–8)

I am adding Revelation 14:1 to Revelation 7:1–8, since it provides commentary of the seal applied to the 144,000 sons of Israel.

And I looked, and behold, the Lamb was standing on Mount Zion, and with Him one hundred and forty-four thousand, having His name and the name of His Father written on their foreheads. (Revelation 14:1)

Four angels hold back the wind, and they are instructed to not harm the earth until the 144,000 sons of Israel are sealed. Because the 144,000 are called "sons of Israel" (Revelation 7:4), this is likely the fulfillment of the second half of Joel 3:16: "But the Lord is a refuge for His people and a stronghold to the sons of Israel." It does happen at the same time, so I will place them together. The events presented in Revelation 7:1–8 are:

➢ Four angels hold back the four winds of the earth (Revelation 7:1). See item 41.

➢ Another angel instructs the four angels to not harm any of the earth until the bondservants of God are sealed on their foreheads (Revelation 7:2–3). See item 42.

➢ One hundred and forty-four thousand—12,000 from each tribe of Israel—are sealed on their foreheads with the name of the Father and the name of the Lamb of God (Revelation 7:3–8 and Revelation 14:1). See item 45.

Revelation 7:9–14

⁹ After these things I looked, and behold, a great multitude, which no one could count, from every nation and all tribes and peoples and tongues, standing before the throne and before the Lamb, clothed in white robes, and palm branches were in their hands;
¹⁰ and they cry out with a loud voice, saying, "Salvation to our God who sits on the throne, and to the Lamb."
¹¹ And all the angels were standing around the throne and around the elders and the four living creatures; and they fell on their faces before the throne and worshiped God,
¹² saying, "Amen, blessing and glory and wisdom and thanksgiving and honor and power and might, be to our God forever and ever. Amen."
¹³ And one of the elders answered, saying to me, "These who are clothed in the white robes, who are they, and from where have they come?"
¹⁴ And I said to him, "My Lord, you know." And he said to me, "These are the ones who come out of the great tribulation, and they have washed their robes and made them white in the blood of the Lamb.
(Revelation 7:9–14)

After the 144,000 are sealed, a great uncountable multitude from every people group in the world appears in heaven. Based on the darkening of the sun and moon in Matthew 24:29 and Revelation 6:12, this great multitude is the raptured church gathered alive out of the great tribulation when it is cut short for their sake (Matthew 24:31). Included in the rapture, of course, are those who have died in Christ (including the fifth-seal martyrs). The events presented in Revelation 7:9–14 related to the rapture are:

➢ A great uncountable multitude arrives in heaven, having come out of the great tribulation (Revelation 7:9). See items 52 and 53.

➢ This great multitude comes from every nation and all tribes, peoples, and tongues; therefore, the great commission has been completed (Revelation 7:9). See item 52.

➢ This great multitude stands before God's throne and the Lamb of God (Revelation 7:9). See item 53.

➢ The people of this great multitude are clothed in white robes washed in the blood of the Lamb (Revelation 7:13–14). See item 53.

Revelation 8:1–7

[1] And when He broke the seventh seal, there was silence in heaven for about half an hour.
[2] And I saw the seven angels who stand before God; and seven trumpets were given to them.
[3] And another angel came and stood at the altar, holding a golden censer; and much incense was given to him, that he might add it to the prayers of all the saints upon the golden altar which was before the throne.
[4] And the smoke of the incense, with the prayers of the saints, went up before God out of the angel's hand.
[5] And the angel took the censer; and he filled it with the fire of the altar and threw it to the earth; and there followed peals of thunder and sounds and flashes of lightning and an earthquake.
[6] And the seven angels who had the seven trumpets prepared themselves to sound them.

⁷ And the first sounded, and there came hail and fire, mixed with blood, and they were thrown to the earth; and a third of the earth was burned up, and a third of the trees were burned up, and all the green grass was burned up.
(Revelation 8:1–7)

The events presented in Revelation 8:1–7 are:

➢ The seventh seal is broken, and there is silence in heaven for half an hour (Revelation 8:1). See item 57.

➢ Preparations are made for the first trumpet judgment (Revelation 8:5–6). See item 58.

➢ The first trumpet judgment begins the day of the Lord (Revelation 8:7). See item 59.

Other Sun and Moon Darkening Events

Some may have noticed that I did not comment on eight passages that appear to also speak of the darkening of the sun and moon. Before I finalize the chronological charting of the end-time events surrounding the darkening of the sun and moon, I will add Acts 2:14–21 and Joel 2:28–32. These Scripture passages greatly impact the understanding of the sequence of events within Daniel's seventieth week. Delaying the examination of these critical passages until now substantiates everything presented up to this point, since on their own they show that the pretrib rapture is impossible. In addition to these two passages, I will also add to the chronological chart Isaiah 28:15–19, Daniel 9:27, Daniel 12:1–2, 1 Corinthians 15:51–52, 1 Thessalonians 4:16–17, 2 Thessalonians 2:1–4, and Revelation 1:7. These passages do not speak about the sun and moon darkening; however, they offer valuable insight to the events that transpire through the seven seals.

Finally, after the chronological end-times chart is completed, I will explain why Ecclesiastes 12:1–4, Isaiah 24:18–23, Ezekiel 32:7, Revelation 8:12, Revelation 9:1–11, and Revelation 16:10–11 are not equivalent events. Let's now look at one of the most monumental end time prophecies in all of the Bible.

Acts 2:14–21

¹⁴ But Peter, taking his stand with the eleven, raised his voice and declared to them: "Men of Judea, and all you who live in Jerusalem, let this be known to you, and give heed to my words.

¹⁵ "For these men are not drunk, as you suppose, for it is only the third hour of the day;

¹⁶ but this is what was spoken of through the prophet Joel:

¹⁷ 'AND IT SHALL BE IN THE LAST DAYS,' God says, 'THAT I WILL POUR FORTH OF MY SPIRIT UPON ALL MANKIND; AND YOUR SONS AND YOUR DAUGHTERS SHALL PROPHESY, AND YOUR YOUNG MEN SHALL SEE VISIONS, AND YOUR OLD MEN SHALL DREAM DREAMS;

¹⁸ EVEN UPON MY BONDSLAVES, BOTH MEN AND WOMEN, I WILL IN THOSE DAYS POUR FORTH OF MY SPIRIT.'

And they shall prophesy.

¹⁹ 'AND I WILL GRANT WONDERS IN THE SKY ABOVE, AND SIGNS ON THE EARTH BENEATH, BLOOD, AND FIRE, AND VAPOR OF SMOKE.

²⁰ 'THE SUN SHALL BE TURNED INTO DARKNESS, AND THE MOON INTO BLOOD, *BEFORE* THE GREAT AND GLORIOUS DAY OF THE LORD SHALL COME.

²¹ 'AND IT SHALL BE, THAT EVERYONE WHO CALLS ON THE NAME OF THE LORD SHALL BE SAVED.'

(Acts 2:14–21, emphasis added).

At Pentecost, Peter stood up and proclaimed to the people in Jerusalem that what they witnessed among the disciples had been prophesied in Joel 2:29–32. Peter then added the phrase "And they shall prophesy" (between verses 18 and 19). Notice that it is not capitalized. This phrase does not exist in the Hebrew or the Septuagint LXX Greek texts of the Joel 2 passage.[116] Taken in that context, Peter only claimed in verse 18b that these men *shall prophecy* about Acts 2:19–21. Therefore, Acts 2:17–18 would be Pentecost events that have just happened and Acts 2:19–21 would be

The sun darkens and the moon turns to blood *before* the day of the Lord (Acts 2:20)!

events that, as of Peter's proclamation, have not yet happened. Let's now look at Joel 2:28–32.

Joel 2:28-32

[28] "And it will come about after this that I will pour out My Spirit on all mankind; and your sons and daughters will prophesy, your old men will dream dreams, your young men will see visions.
[29] "And even on the male and female servants I will pour out My Spirit in those days.
[30] "And I will display wonders in the sky and on the earth, blood, fire, and columns of smoke.
[31] "The sun will be turned into darkness, and the moon into blood, *before* the great and awesome day of the Lord comes.
[32] "And it will come about that whoever calls on the name of the Lord will be delivered; for on Mount Zion and in Jerusalem there will be those who escape, as the Lord has said, even among the survivors whom the Lord calls.
(Joel 2:28–32, emphasis added)

The blood, fire, and columns of smoke are probably caused by the worldwide volcanic activity. However, just as we found in Revelation, the sun is still said to be turned to darkness and the moon is merely turned to blood. The Greek and Hebrew words for the sun's darkening in the previous passages could be interpreted as either the sun being hidden or it became dark on its own. However, in Acts 2:20, the Greek *metastrepho* and in Joel 2:31, the Hebrew *haphak* mean to change or be changed.[117] This is a unique event applied directly to the sun and moon; as would be expected for it to be matched with the sign of Christ's coming and the end of the age.

We also see in Acts 2:21 and Joel 2:32 that there is deliverance for those who call on the name of the Lord. When we match the sun and moon darkening of Joel 2:28–32 with Matthew 24:21–31 and Revelation 7:9–14, it is clear that this deliverance fits perfectly in time and sequence with the rapture occurring very soon after the great tribulation is cut short for the sake of the elect. At the same time, the great multitude appears in heaven (Revelation 7). Therefore, the deliverance of Joel 2:32 would be an Old Testament reference to the rapture.

The darkening of the sun and moon is the centering pillar of this study. This darkening event will happen *before* the day of the Lord. Since this darkening event and the day of the Lord which follows it happen after the sixth seal is broken (Revelation 6:12), the day of the Lord cannot begin near the peace treaty. Therefore, since the rapture happens shortly before the day of the Lord, the rapture also cannot happen before the peace treaty. Acts 2:20 and Joel 2:31 make this irrefutable! The events presented in Acts 2:14–21 and Joel 2:28–32 related to the end times are:

➢ Blood, fire, and columns of smoke appear, likely from worldwide volcanic activity (Joel 2:30 and Acts 2:19). See item 26.

➢ The sun is turned to darkness, and the moon is turned to blood *before* the day of the Lord (Joel 2:31 and Acts 2:20). See item 28.

➢ Whoever calls on the name of the Lord will be delivered (Joel 2:32 and Acts 2:21). This deliverance at the time of the sun and moon darkening fits the timing of the Pre-Wrath rapture position. See items 47 and 52.

Contextual Additions

In the composite chronology that will be charted in about three pages, I have added the following passages. Although they do not speak about the darkening of the sun and moon, they do instruct us on the other events of this time.

Isaiah 28:15–19

[15] Because you have said, "We have made a covenant with death, and with Sheol we have made a pact. The overwhelming scourge will not reach us when it passes by, for we have made falsehood our refuge and we have concealed ourselves with deception."
[16] Therefore thus says the Lord God, "Behold, I am laying in Zion a stone, a tested stone, a costly cornerstone for the foundation, firmly placed. He who believes in it will not be disturbed.
[17] "And I will make justice the measuring line, and righteousness the level; then hail shall sweep away the refuge of lies, and the waters shall overflow the secret place.
[18] "And your covenant with death shall be canceled, and your pact with Sheol shall not stand; when the overwhelming scourge passes through, then you become its trampling place.

[19] "As often as it passes through, it will seize you. For morning after morning it will pass through, anytime during the day or night. And it will be sheer terror to understand what it means." (Isaiah 28:15–19)

➢ Israel signs the covenant with death. This is Israel's apostasy for trusting God's enemy for peace (Isaiah 28:15–19). In horror, they will discover what they have done at the abomination of desolation. See items 2 and 11.

Daniel 9:27

"And he will make a firm covenant with the many for one week, but in the middle of the week he will put a stop to sacrifice and grain offering; and on the wing of abominations will come one who makes desolate, even until a complete destruction, one that is decreed, is poured out on the one who makes desolate." (Daniel 9:27)

➢ The seven-year peace treaty; Israel's apostasy (Daniel 9:27). See items 1 and 2.

➢ The beginning of Daniel's seventieth week (Daniel 9:27). See item 3.

➢ The abomination of desolation, which requires the building of the temple beforehand (Daniel 9:27). See items 9 and 10.

Daniel 12:1–2

[1] "Now at that time Michael, the great prince who stands guard over the sons of your people, will arise. And there will be a time of distress such as never occurred since there was a nation until that time; and at that time your people, everyone who is found written in the book, will be rescued.
[2] "And many of those who sleep in the dust of the ground will awake, these to everlasting life, but the others to disgrace and everlasting contempt.
(Daniel 12:1–2)

➢ The beginning of Daniel's time of distress and the great tribulation (Daniel 12:1). See item 13.

> Rescue for those written in the book (Daniel 12:1). This is the rapture of believers who are alive on earth. See item 52.

> Resurrection unto everlasting life (Daniel 12:2). This is the rapture of believers who have already died. See item 52.

1 Corinthians 15:51–52

[51] Behold, I tell you a mystery; we shall not all sleep, but we shall all be changed,
[52] in a moment, in the twinkling of an eye, at the last trumpet; for the trumpet will sound, and the dead will be raised imperishable, and we shall be changed.
(1 Corinthians 15:51–52)

> The last trumpet will sound (1 Corinthians 15:52). See item 50.

> The dead in Christ will be raised (1 Corinthians 15:52). See item 52.

> Those who are alive will be changed (1 Corinthians 15:51–52). See item 52.

1 Thessalonians 4:16–17

[16] For the Lord Himself will descend from heaven with a shout, with the voice of the archangel, and with the trumpet of God; and the dead in Christ shall rise first.
[17] Then we who are alive and remain shall be caught up together with them in the clouds to meet the Lord in the air, and thus we shall always be with the Lord.
(1 Thessalonians 4:16–17)

> The Lord will descend with a shout (1 Thessalonians 4:16). See item 43.

> The trumpet of God will sound (1 Thessalonians 4:16). See item 50.

> The dead in Christ will be raised (1 Thessalonians 4:16). See item 52.

> Those alive in Christ will rise with the resurrected to meet the Lord in the air (1 Thessalonians 4:17). See item 52.

2 Thessalonians 2:1–4

¹ Now we request you, brethren, with regard to the coming of our Lord Jesus Christ, and our gathering together to Him,
² that you may not be quickly shaken from your composure or be disturbed either by a spirit or a message or a letter as if from us, to the effect that the day of the Lord has come.
³ Let no one in any way deceive you, for it will not come unless the apostasy comes first, and the man of lawlessness is revealed, the son of destruction,
⁴ who opposes and exalts himself above every so-called god or object of worship, so that he takes his seat in the temple of God, displaying himself as being God.
(2 Thessalonians 2:1–4)

➤ Israel's apostasy: the covenant with death
(2 Thessalonians 2:3-4). See items 1 and 2.

➤ The revealing of the Antichrist at the abomination of desolation
(2 Thessalonians 2:3–4). See items 10 and 11.

➤ Christ's coming (2 Thessalonians 2:1). See item 43.

➤ We are gathered together to Christ (2 Thessalonians 2:1).
See item 52.

➤ The day of the Lord (2 Thessalonians 2:1–3). See item 59.

Revelation 1:7

Behold, He is coming with the clouds, and every eye will see Him, even those who pierced Him; and all the tribes of the earth will mourn over Him. Even so. Amen.
(Revelation 1:7)

➤ The Lord's return, visible to all (Revelation 1:7). See item 43.

Chronological Chart of the Sun and Moon Darkening

Adding these five passages above to Isaiah 13, Joel 2–3, Matthew 24, Mark 13, Luke 21, Acts 2, and Revelation 6–8 and then charting the events produces this final composite chronology:

	SUN, MOON, AND STARS DARKENING
	Event & Supporting Scriptures
1	The seven year peace treaty _Daniel 9:27; 2 Thessalonians 2:3–4_
2	Israel's apostasy, signing the covenant with death; trusting the Antichrist for peace instead of God: _Daniel 9:27; Isaiah 28:15–19; 2 Thessalonians 2:3–4_
3	The beginning of Daniel's seventieth week: _Daniel 9:27_
4	The first seal is broken: The Antichrist rises to power: _Revelation 6:1–2_
5	The beginning of birth pangs: _Matthew 24:6–8, Mark 13:7–8_
6	The second seal is broken: Wars and rumors of wars everywhere except Israel: _Matthew 24:6–7; Mark 13:7–8; Revelation 6:3–4_
7	The third seal is broken: Worldwide famine: _Matthew 24:7; Mark 13:8; Revelation 6:5–6_
8	Earthquakes in various places: _Matthew 24:7; Mark 13:8_
9	The new temple is completed: [Assumed from _Daniel 9:27; Matthew 24:15_]
10	The revealing of the Antichrist: The abomination of desolation: _Daniel 9:27;_ _Matthew 24:15; Mark 13:14; 2 Thessalonians 2:3–4_
11	Israel discovers her apostasy in trustitng the Antichrist for peace: _Isaiah 28:15-19; 2 Thessalonains 2:3–4_
12	Jews (and Christians) in Judea must flee to the mountains: _Matthew 24:16–20; Mark 13:14–18_
13	Hard Labor: The beginning of Daniel's time of distress and the great tribulation: _Daniel 12:1; Matthew 24:9–11, 21; Mark 13:9, 11–13, 19_
	Chart continues on next page

221

		Event & Supporting Scriptures
14		The fourth seal is broken: 25% of the world's unsaved are killed and headed for Hades: Revelation 6:7–8
15		False Christs and False Prophets will arise, performing great signs and wonders: *Matthew 24:5, 11, 23–26; Mark 13:6, 21–22*
16		Christ's elect are hated by all the nations because of His Name: *Matthew 24:9; Mark 13:13*
17		Great apostasy from within the church: *Matthew 24:10; Mark 13:9, 11–12*
18		Christ's elect are betrayed, even by members of their own family: *Matthew 24:10; Mark 13:9, 11–12*
19		Christ's elect are arrested: *Mark 13:9, 11*
20		Christ's elect testify of Him before the world leaders: *Mark 13:9, 11*
21		The fifth seal is broken: Christ's elect are martyred in the great tribulation, appear under the altar in heaven, and are given white robes: Matthew 24:9, 21–22; *Mark 13:20; Revelation 6:9, 11*
22		The fifth seal martyrs cry out for justice and are told that more will die before God would judge their killers: *Revelation 6:10–11*
23		Those who endure to the end will be saved: *Matthew 24:13; Mark 13:13*
24		The great tribulation is cut short for Christ's elect: *Matthew 24:22, 29; Mark 13:20, 24*
25		[Items 26–56 happen in very rapid succession]: The sixth seal is broken: *Revelation 6:12*
26		Worldwide volcanic activity with blood, fire, and columns of smoke: *Joel 2:30; Acts 2:19*
		Chart continues on next page

	Event & Supporting Scriptures
27	A great earthquake: *Revelation 6:12*
28	The sun and stars turn black and the moon turns to the color of blood *before* the day of the Lord: *Isaiah 13:10; Joel 2:10, 2:31, 3:15; Matthew 24:29;* *Mark 13:24; Luke 21:25; Acts 2:20; Revelation 6:12*
29	"Stars" fall from the sky: *Matthew 24:29; Mark 13:25; Revelation 6:13*
30	The heavens tremble: *Isaiah 13:13; Joel 2:10, 3:16*
31	The powers of the heavens are shaken: *Matthew 24:29; Mark 13:25; Luke 21:26*
32	Every mountain and island is moved out of its place: *Isaiah 13:13; Joel 2:10, 3:16; Revelation 6:14*
33	The roaring of the sea and the waves: *Luke 21:25*
34	The sky is split apart like a scroll when it is rolled up: *Revelation 6:14*
35	The *sign* of the Son of Man appears in the sky: *Matthew 24:30*
36	The people of the world see God on His throne: *Revelation 6:16*
35	The *sign* of the Son of Man appears in the sky: *Matthew 24:30*
36	The people of earth see God on His throne: *Revelation 6:16*
37	All the unsaved people of earth are terrified and mourn: *Isaiah 13:6–8; Matthew 24:30;* *Luke 21:25–26; Revelation 6:15–16*
	Chart continues on next page

		Event & Supporting Scriptures
38		The unsaved people of earth hide in caves and among the rocks of the mountains: *Revelation 6:15*
39		The unsaved people of earth cry for the mountains and the rocks to fall on them: *Revelation 6:16*
40		The unsaved people of earth know the day of the Lord is coming: *Revelation 6:16–17*
41		Four angels hold back all wind on earth: *Revelation 7:1*
42		Four angels are told to not harm the earth until the 144,000 Jews are sealed: *Revelation 7:2–3*
43		The Son of Man comes on clouds with a shout, visible to all: *Matthew 24:27, 30; Mark 13:26; Luke 21:27; 1 Thessalonians 4:16; 2 Thessalonians 2:1; Revelation 1:7*
44		The Lord is a stronghold for the sons of Israel: *Joel 3:16*
45		144,000 Sons of Israel, 12,000 from each tribe are sealed with the name of the Father and the Lamb of God: *Revelation 7:3–8; 14:1*
46		Christians are to look up because our redemption is near: *Luke 21:28*
47		Whoever calls on the Name of the Lord will be delivered: *Joel 2:32; Acts 2:21*
48		The Lord is a refuge for His people: *Joel 3:16*
49		The Son of Man sends forth the angels to gather the elect: *Matthew 24:31; Mark 13:27*
50		The last trumpet will sound: *Matthew 24:31; 1 Corinthians 15:52; 1 Thessalonians 4:16*
51		The gospel of the kingdom has been preached to the whole world: *Matthew 24:14; Mark 13:10*
		Chart continues on next page

	Event & Supporting Scriptures
52	**THE RAPTURE:** The dead in Christ are raised and a great uncountable multitude are gathered out of the great tribulation to join them to meet the Lord in the air: *Joel 2:32; Daniel 12:1–2; Matthew 24:31; Mark 13:27; Acts 2:21; 1 Corinthians 15:51–52; 1 Thessalonians 4:16–17; 2 Thessalonians 2:1; Revelation 7:9*
53	The great uncountable multitude from all tribes, peoples, and tongues (the raptured church) stands before God's throne and the Lamb of God clothed in white robes washed in the blood of the Lamb: *Revelation 7:9, 13–14*
54	The day of the Lord judgments are near: *Isaiah 13:6, 9; Joel 3:14; Revelation 6:16–17*
55	Call to battle: The Lord utters His voice before His army from Jerusalem: *Joel 2:11, 3:16*
56	… and then the end will come: *Matthew 24:14*
57	The seventh seal is broken: Silence in heaven: *Revelation 8:1*
58	Preparations for the day of the Lord judgments: *Revelation 8:5–6*
59	**THE DAY OF THE LORD** The first trumpet judgment begins: *Isaiah 13:11–13; Joel 2:11; Joel 2:31; Acts 2:20; 2 Thessalonians 2:1–3; Revelation 8:7*

Clearly, there are many events that must happen *before* the rapture! This rejects the pretrib rapture concept of imminency (the claim that there are no end-time events that must precede the rapture). Imminency was addressed in chapter 4.

Darkening Events that Do Not Apply

Ecclesiastes 12:1–4, Isaiah 24:18–23, and Ezekiel 32 will not be included in this study. Even if they speak about the end-time darkening events, they do not contribute anything to the chronology regarding the rapture and the day of the Lord. Finally, let's examine the three remaining Revelation darkening events to determine if they should be included with the others:

Revelation 8:12

> And the fourth angel sounded, and a third of the sun and a third of the moon and a third of the stars were smitten, so that a third of them might be darkened and the day might not shine for a third of it, and the night in the same way.
> (Revelation 8:12)

Why have I not included this passage with the others? Notice that the event presented in Revelation 8:12 is very different from the other passages we have looked at. The darkening of the sun, moon, and stars is a specific percentage of darkening (one third of the sun, moon, and stars are darkened), while the darkening of the sun, moon, and stars we have just studied are a full measure of darkening (with the moon miraculously turned into the color of blood). The Revelation 8:12 event is also for a specific amount of time (third of the day and third of the night). If one is inclined to think that this merely gives more information on the Revelation 6:12--13 darkening event, this is countered by the fact that it is the fourth trumpet judgment, not the sixth seal.

What is the purpose of this Revelation 8 darkening event? When one examines the first four trumpet judgments together, we will see that they are judgments against the very creation we depend on for life.

> [7] The first sounded, and there came hail and fire, mixed with blood, and they were thrown to the earth; and a third of the earth was burned up, and a third of the trees were burned up, and all the green grass was burned up.

[8] The second angel sounded, and something like a great mountain burning with fire was thrown into the sea; and a third of the sea became blood,
[9] and a third of the creatures which were in the sea and had life, died; and a third of the ships were destroyed.
[10] The third angel sounded, and a great star fell from heaven, burning like a torch, and it fell on a third of the rivers and on the springs of waters.
[11] The name of the star is called Wormwood; and a third of the waters became wormwood, and many men died from the waters, because they were made bitter.
[12] The fourth angel sounded, and a third of the sun and a third of the moon and a third of the stars were struck, so that a third of them would be darkened and the day would not shine for a third of it, and the night in the same way.
(Revelation 8:7–12)

➤ First trumpet judgment (Revelation 8:7): a third of the earth's vegetation is burned up. This is a judgment on land-dependent life.

➤ Second trumpet judgment (Revelation 8:8–9): a third of the sea is turned to blood, and a third of the sea life dies. This is a judgment on saltwater-dependent life.

➤ Third trumpet judgment (Revelation 8:10–11): a third of the rivers and springs are turned bitter, and many men die from this bitter water. This is a judgment on freshwater-dependent life.

➤ Fourth trumpet judgment (Revelation 8:12): a third of the sun, moon, and stars are darkened. Daytime will also be a third shorter. Even a third of the stars will darken for a third of the night! This is a judgment on all light-dependent life.

Revelation 9:1–11

[1] And the fifth angel sounded, and I saw a star from heaven which had fallen to the earth; and the key of the bottomless pit was given to him.
[2] And he opened the bottomless pit; and smoke went up out of the pit, like the smoke of a great furnace; and the sun and the air were darkened by the smoke of the pit.

³ And out of the smoke came forth locusts upon the earth; and power was given them, as the scorpions of the earth have power.
⁴ And they were told that they should not hurt the grass of the earth, nor any green thing, nor any tree, but only the men who do not have the seal of God on their foreheads.
⁵ And they were not permitted to kill anyone, but to torment for five months; and their torment was like the torment of a scorpion when it stings a man.
⁶ And in those days men will seek death and will not find it; and they will long to die and death flees from them.
⁷ And the appearance of the locusts was like horses prepared for battle; and on their heads, as it were, crowns like gold, and their faces were like the faces of men.
⁸ And they had hair like the hair of women, and their teeth were like the teeth of lions.
⁹ And they had breastplates like breastplates of iron; and the sound of their wings was like the sound of chariots, of many horses rushing to battle.
¹⁰ And they have tails like scorpions, and stings; and in their tails is their power to hurt men for five months.
¹¹ They have as king over them, the angel of the abyss; his name in Hebrew is Abaddon, and in the Greek he has the name Apollyon.
(Revelation 9:1–11)

This passage presents a covering of the sun by a dense cloud full of locusts. The events surrounding the fifth trumpet judgment are dissimilar to all of the other darkening events we have covered.

Revelation 16:10–11

¹⁰ And the fifth angel poured out his bowl upon the throne of the beast; and his kingdom became darkened; and they gnawed their tongues because of pain,
¹¹ and they blasphemed the God of heaven because of their pains and their sores; and they did not repent of their deeds.
(Revelation 16:10–11)

In this passage, the darkness actually causes pain and sores, a condition never stated regarding the darkening of the sun, moon, and stars. The judgment is also specifically on the Antichrist's kingdom; therefore it may not even be worldwide.

Conclusion

When one compiles the verses throughout the Bible that present events happening before and after the darkening of the sun and moon, it becomes clear that the sequence of events as taught by the pretribulationist cannot stand the test of the Scriptures. The Pre-Wrath rapture agrees with the pretribulationist that we will be raptured *before* God begins His end-time judgments; however, the Scriptures show that the rapture occurs *after* the sixth seal of Revelation is broken, not before the first seal is broken. Consistent with that, the day of the Lord does not begin until a short time after the seventh seal is broken.

Until our Lord comes for us, we must be faithful in proclaiming Him. Praise God that He has promised to remove us before He begins His end-time judgment of this evil world!

> [20] He who testifies to these things says, "Yes, I am coming quickly." Amen. Come, Lord Jesus.
> [21] The grace of the Lord Jesus be with all. Amen.
> (Revelation 22:20–21)

Index of
Bible Quotes

Except as noted, Scripture taken from the NEW AMERICAN STANDARD BIBLE®, © Copyright 1960, 1962, 1963, 1968, 1971, 1972, 1973, 1975, 1977 by The Lockman Foundation. Used by permission.

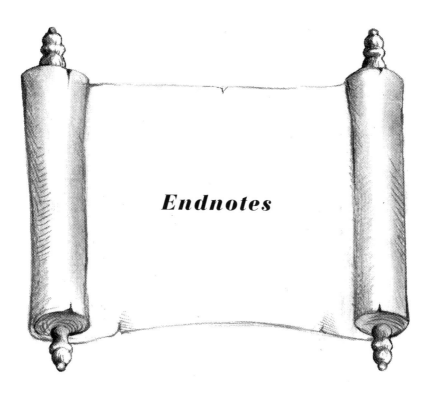

Endnotes

1   H. L. Nigro, *Before God's Wrath: The Bible's Answer to the Timing of the Rapture* (Bellefonte, Pennsylvania: Strong Tower Publishing, 2004), 198–209.

2   Ibid., 198–199.

3   Marvin Rosenthal, *The Pre-Wrath Rapture of the Church* (Nashville: Thomas Nelson, 1990), 221–222, paraphrased.

4   Tim LaHaye, *The Rapture: Who Will Face the Tribulation?* (Eugene, Oregon: Harvest House Publishers, 2002), 71.

5   Trent C. Butler, Marsha A. Ellis Smith, Forrest W. Jackson, Phil Logan, Chris church, eds., Holman Bible Dictionary, (Nashville: Holman Bible Publishers, 1991), s.v. "Millennium."

6   Ibid. s.v. "Amillennialism."

7   Ibid. s.v. "Postmillennialism."

8   Ibid. s.v. "Premillennialism."

9   M. R. DeHaan, *Coming Events in Prophecy* (Grand Rapids: Zondervan Publishing House, 1962), 127.

10   John F. Walvoord, *The Rapture Question* (Grand Rapids: Zondervan Publishing House, 1979), 230.

[11] Ibid., 243.

[12] DeHaan, *Coming Events in Prophecy*, 131–132.

[13] Rosenthal, *The Pre-Wrath Rapture of the Church*, 116–117.

[14] Wayne A. Brindle, "Imminence," *The Popular Encyclopedia of Bible Prophecy*, Tim LaHaye and Ed Hindson, eds., (Eugene, Oregon: Harvest House Publishers, 2004), 144.

[15] J. Dwight Pentecost, *Things to Come: A Study in Biblical Eschatology* (Grand Rapids, Michigan: Zondervan, 1958), 204.

[16] Ibid, 204.

[17] John F. Walvoord, *Prophecy In The New Millennium: A Fresh Look At the Future Events* (Grand Rapids, Michigan: Kregel Publications, 2001), 124.

[18] LaHaye, *The Rapture: Who Will Face the Tribulation?* 200.

[19] Walvoord, *Prophecy In The New Millennium: A Fresh Look At the Future Events*, 38–39.

[20] Ibid., 38.

[21] DeHaan, *Coming Events in Prophecy*, 125–126.

[22] LaHaye, *The Rapture: Who Will Face the Tribulation?* 71.

[23] David Hunt, "'Pre–Wrath' or 'Pre–Trib' Rapture?" *The Omega–Letter*, January 1991, 17–18, paraphrased.

[24] Walvoord, *The Rapture Question*, 41.

[25] Ibid., 41.

[26] Ibid., 79.

[27] Ibid., 79.

[28] Ibid., 80.

[29] Ibid., 79–80.

[30] Ibid., 80.

[31] Ibid., 242.

[32] Ibid., 243.

[33] Pentecost, *Things to Come: A Study in Biblical Eschatology*, 296.

[34] Ibid., 296.

[35] John MacArthur, *The MacArthur Study Bible*, (Nashville: Thomas Nelson, 2006), 1824, n1.

[36] Mal Couch, "Restrainer," *The Popular Encyclopedia of Bible Prophecy* (Eugene, Oregon: Harvest House Publishers, 2004), 326.

[37] Ibid., 325.

[38] DeHaan, *Coming Events in Prophecy*, 134–135.

[39] Walvoord, *The Rapture Question*, 244.

[40] MacArthur, *The MacArthur Study Bible*, 1823, n4.

[41] Ibid., 1823.

[42] Ibid., 1823.

[43] Couch, "Apostasy," *The Popular Encyclopedia of Bible Prophecy*, 32.

[44] Ibid., 32.

[45] John F. Walvoord, *Major Bible Prophecies* (Grand Rapids, Michigan: Zondervan Publishing House, 1991), 300.

[46] Ibid., 351–352.

[47] Grant R. Jeffrey, *Armageddon—Appointment With Destiny* (Toronto: Frontier Research Publications, 1990), 137.

[48] Randall Price, "Abomination of Desolation," *The Popular Encyclopedia of Bible Prophecy* (Eugene, Oregon: Harvest House Publishers, 2004), 6.

[49] Gerhard Kittel and Gerhard Friedrich, eds., *Theological Dictionary of the New Testament*, vol. I, (Grand Rapids, Michigan: Eerdmans, 1977), s.v. "ἀφίστημι."

[50] H. Wayne House, "Apostasia in 2 Thessalonians 2:3: Apostasy or Rapture," *When the Trumpet Sounds*, Thomas Ice and Timothy Demy, eds., (Eugene, Oregon: Harvest House Publishers, 1995), 267–268, paraphrased.

[51] Robert Gundry, *The Church and the Tribulation* (Grand Rapids, Michigan: Zondervan, 1976), 116, paraphrased.

[52] *Theological Dictionary of the New Testament*, vol. I, s.v. "ἀποστασία."

[53] Ibid., 513.

[54] Paul D. Feinberg, "2 Thessalonians 2 and the rapture," *When the Trumpet Sounds*, 310, paraphrased.

[55] *Theological Dictionary of the New Testament*, Vol. I, s.v. "ἀποστασία."

[56] Walvoord, *The Rapture Question*, 41.

[57] Price, "Abomination of Desolation," *The Popular Encyclopedia of Bible Prophecy*, 6.

[58] Renald E. Showers, *The Pre-Wrath Rapture View: An Examination and Critique* (Grand Rapids, Michigan: Kregel Publications, 2001), 34.

[59] Walvoord, *The Rapture Question*, 228.

[60] Arnold G. Fruchtenbaum, "Is There a Pre-Wrath Rapture?" *When the Trumpet Sounds* (Eugene, Oregon: Harvest House Publishers, 1995), 387–388.

[61] Showers, *The Pre-Wrath Rapture View: An Examination and Critique*, 30.

62   Stanley D. Toussaint, "Are the Church and the Rapture in Matthew 24?" *When the Trumpet Sounds* (Eugene, Oregon: Harvest House Publishers, 1995), 249.

63   MacArthur, *The MacArthur Study Bible*, 1407, n6.

64   Walvoord, *The Rapture Question*, 165.

65   Ibid., 37.

66   Ibid., 37, paraphrased.

67   Ibid., 165.

68   Walvoord, *Major Bible Prophecies*, 263.

69   MacArthur, *The MacArthur Study Bible*, 1525, n3.

70   Walvoord, *The Rapture Question*, 100–101.

71   Ibid., 104.

72   Ibid., 104.

73   Ibid., 162.

74   Tim LaHaye and Richard Mayhue, "Rapture," *The Popular Encyclopedia of Bible Prophecy*, 315.

75   Walvoord, *The Rapture Question*, 231.

76   Ibid., 231.

77   Ibid., 231.

78   Ibid., 231.

79   Rosenthal, *The Pre-Wrath Rapture of the Church*, 287, paraphrased.

80   Ibid., 288, paraphrased.

81   MacArthur, *The MacArthur Study Bible*, 1968, n3.

82   Pentecost, *Things to Come: A Study in Biblical Eschatology*, 209.

83   Ibid., 209.

84   MacArthur, *The MacArthur Study Bible*, 1515, n5, paraphrased.

85   Marvin J. Rosenthal, "The Question of Chronology," *Zion's Fire*, January–February 2011, 11, paraphrased.

86   Ibid.

87   Henry M. Morris, *The Revelation Record* (Wheaton, Illinois: Tyndale House Publishers, 1983), 117–118, paraphrased.

88   LaHaye, *The Rapture: Who Will Face the Tribulation?* 200–201.

89   Ibid., 201.

90   Ibid., 201.

91   Ibid., 200.

[92] Ibid., 201.

[93] Ibid., 201.

[94] Rosenthal, *The Pre-Wrath Rapture of the Church*, 110, 112, 117, 137, 139–140, 150–153, 181, 185, 189–190, 219–222, 228, 240–241, 248, paraphrased.

[95] LaHaye, *The Rapture: Who Will Face the Tribulation?* 200–201.

[96] Ibid., 200.

[97] Rosenthal, *The Pre-Wrath Rapture of the Church*, 112.

[98] Showers, *The Pre-Wrath Rapture View: An Examination and Critique*, 73.

[99] Ibid., 74.

[100] Ibid., 74.

[101] MacArthur, *The MacArthur Study Bible*, 1971, n3.

[102] MacArthur, *The MacArthur Study Bible*, 1971, n6.

[103] Tim LaHaye, "Great Tribulation," *The Popular Encyclopedia of Bible Prophecy* (Eugene, Oregon: Harvest House Publishers, 2004), 124.

[104] Ibid., 124.

[105] Ibid., 124.

[106] Pentecost, *Things to Come: A Study in Biblical Eschatology*, 235–236.

[107] Ibid., 236, paraphrased.

[108] Ibid., 236–237.

[109] Ibid., 300.

[110] LaHaye, *The Rapture: Who Will Face the Tribulation?* 139, paraphrased.

[111] Ibid., 139, paraphrased.

[112] Ibid., 63.

[113] Ibid., 139.

[114] Ibid., 139.

[115] Alan Kurschner, Eschatos Ministries, Pompton Lakes, NJ; personal comments on Greek word usage, January 2013.

[116] *The Pulpit Commentary* (Seattle: BibleSoft, 2006), CD-ROM, paraphrased.

[117] *Biblesoft's New Exhaustive Strong's Numbers and Concordance With Expanded Greek-Hebrew Dictionary*, (Des Moines, Washington, 2006), paraphrased.

Printed in the United States
By Bookmasters